SOUTHERN LITERARY STUDIES

SOUTHERN LITERARY STUDIES

edited by
Louis D. Rubin, Jr.

A SEASON OF DREAMS: *The Fiction of Eudora Welty*
ALFRED APPEL, JR.

THE HERO WITH THE PRIVATE PARTS
ANDREW LYTLE

HUNTING IN THE OLD SOUTH: *Original Narratives of the Hunters*
CLARENCE GOHDES, EDITOR

Joel
Chandler Harris

Joel
Chandler Harris

a biography

by

PAUL M. COUSINS

LOUISIANA STATE UNIVERSITY PRESS
BATON ROUGE

To my wife Marjorie and Paul, Jr.

FOREWORD

SOME THREE YEARS AGO, after plans for the Southern Literary Studies series were first announced, I was invited to consider for inclusion in the series a biographical study of Joel Chandler Harris. I asked to be allowed to examine the manuscript, and was interested to discover that not only did it contain much hitherto unpublished material about Harris and his times, but also that some of the citations were to actual interviews which the author had had with some of Harris' schoolmates and other friends. Since Harris had died in 1908, or more than a half-century before, this seemed very odd. Upon inquiry, I discovered that the author, Professor Paul M. Cousins of Mercer University, had first begun work on his study of Harris some four decades ago, for a doctoral dissertation at Columbia University. In 1933 he had been named president of Shorter College, where he had been teaching since 1915, and had put aside further work on his dissertation, four chapters of which were then complete, to undertake his presidential duties. He had served as president of Shorter College until 1948. Thereupon, at an age when most men would have been content to wind up a lifetime's work and enjoy the pleasures of well-earned leisure, he had returned to full-time teaching at his alma mater, Mercer University, and had resumed work on his doctoral dissertation. In 1966 he presented the completed manuscript to the Department of English and Comparative Literature at Columbia University, was examined upon it, and, at the age of seventy-six, was awarded the degree of Doctor of Philosophy! Meanwhile his manuscript had been read and accepted for book publication. Now, in its author's seventy-eighth year (1968), it is being published.

It has been fifty years since anyone has produced a full-scale biography of Joel Chandler Harris. In 1918 two were published: his daughter-in-law Julia Collier Harris' *The Life and Letters of Joel Chandler Harris*, and Robert Lemuel Wiggins' *The Life of Joel Chandler Harris from Obscurity in Boyhood to Fame in Early Manhood*. Since that day three book-length works on Harris have appeared: a popular biography which added little new information, a study of Harris as folklorist, and a second book by his daughter-in-law on Harris as editor and essayist. Thus a new biography, making use of scholarly research techniques, has been long overdue.

Most modern-day readers who are not closely familiar with Southern literature are probably unaware that the Uncle Remus stories represented only part of Joel Chandler Harris' published output and that he also spent considerable time and effort in writing about the middle-class whites of rural antebellum Georgia. Harris' work in this field has long been out of print, and Cousins performs a distinct historical service in describing it at length and relating it to Harris' own life. Harris was uniquely qualified to write about this relatively unchronicled segment of Southern society, having been born in humble circumstances, and raised in a small middle Georgia town. Professor Cousins draws attention to various elements in the stories which doubtless bear a close relationship to Harris' own circumstance.

At the age of thirteen, Harris became apprentice printer at Turnwold, the plantation of Joseph Addison Turner, who throughout the Civil War published there *The Countryman*, a literary journal of some significance. Harris' first literary efforts were published in this journal, and he had access to Turner's extensive library. This remarkable man, Joseph Addison Turner, is not only of considerable importance to Joel Chandler Harris' career but is also an interesting Southern literary and cultural phenomenon in his own right. Quite properly, Professor Cousins has felt that Turner merits extensive attention, and in the third and fourth chapters of this book he places all students of nineteenth-century Southern literature and life in his debt by providing the first authoritative and detailed account of Joseph Addison Turner and his work.

In 1876 Harris went to work for the Atlanta *Constitution*, one of whose editors was another unusual Georgian, Henry W. Grady. Until Grady's premature death in 1889 the two were friends and associates. Thus, writing editorials across the same desk from each other were the man who, most of all, was apostle to the coming of industrialization to the South and the man whose Uncle Remus stories played a leading role in casting a golden aura over the earlier, agrarian South. Cousins provides much information concerning the two men's association with each other; he shows, too, that Harris was thoroughly in accord with Grady's program for a forward-looking New South, and yet that, especially later in his life, Harris grew increasingly distrustful of the growing emphasis upon business and money-getting that was the logical outcome of Grady's enterprise.

It is upon the life of Harris himself, in his own right, that Professor Cousins' book is properly focused, however, and it seems safe to say that future scholars who may wish to cast additional psychological light on the personality of the shy, deeply-introverted author of Uncle Remus will be greatly indebted to Professor Cousins for having given in such abundant detail the salient facts of Harris' life and the definitive history of his literary career. This is the literary biographer's chief task, and Cousins, out of his knowledge of Harris' milieu and his research into his literary and journalistic career, has done that task well.

One of the most attractive features of this book, I think, is the way in which, through its very thoroughness and scrupulous attention to detail, it suggests new approaches to Harris and his work, and possible topics for fruitful literary inquiry. One would like, for example, to learn more about that novel entitled *Sister Jane*, the autobiographical possibilities of which Cousins convincingly establishes. It is indeed interesting that Harris has the father of the illegitimate child in that novel turn out to be a nearby plantation owner—especially in light of the fact that Harris' own father was apparently an Irish day laborer who disappeared soon after the birth of the child and about whom nothing whatever is known, not even his name, since Harris was given his mother's name.

Indeed, in presenting the facts and the main outlines of Harris' career in such detail as he does, Professor Cousins causes his reader to become very curious about Harris—about his obscure origins, his inordinate shyness, his stammering, his frequent references to his life as having been sad and unfortunate, the fact that shortly before his death he was received into the Roman Catholic Church. Many fascinating hints are suggested about the personality of Harris, and the

relationship of his art to his life, that future students will doubtless
want to follow up.

Professor Cousins demonstrates that in his portrayal of the Negro
during Reconstruction, Harris exhibited an understanding of why the
freedman might want to explore the full opportunities of his new freedom, an understanding which contrasts sharply with the way in which
most Southern writers of the time wrote about Reconstruction. He
points out, too, that in Harris' early story, "Free Joe," he was quite
severe in his depiction of the treatment that a free Negro could expect
in the Old South; and he also notes that late in his life Harris invented
a new Negro character, Aunt Minervy Ann, who held very strong
opinions about the positive virtues of being a Negro. All this, from the
man who created Uncle Remus and thus did more than any other
writer of his or any other time to fix the image of the Gentle Old-
Time Darky squarely in the American consciousness, makes one want
to see some of the implications of Harris' portrayal of the Negro
followed up, in the light of the work done in recent years about the
Negro in the post-Reconstruction South.

All of which is to suggest that Professor Cousins' biography is not
only a valuable account of the life and work of an important Southern
author, but also that through its biographical thoroughness it supplies
many leads that future scholars may wish to investigate. Scholars in
the field of Southern studies, therefore, as well as of American life
and particularly of Negro history, have every reason to be grateful
that Professor Cousins has persevered in his task these many years. One
may say simply that the information he has given us about the career
of Joel Chandler Harris is irreplaceable.

Louis D. Rubin, Jr.

University of North Carolina
Chapel Hill

INTRODUCTION

Time has confirmed the critical judgment of Joel Chandler Harris' contemporaries that he created in Uncle Remus an original and permanent character in American fiction. In the literature of the Southern plantation this venerable Negro storyteller stands pre-eminent, but his monumental figure has overshadowed the many other significant characters both Negro and white whom Harris created and dimmed the importance of his other contributions to America's literature.

Harris' non-folklore writings included a wide range of themes that were indigenous to Southern life. He had attained a national reputation as a humorist through his newspaper column of paragraph comments on current affairs before he had published any of the folklore tales as told by Uncle Remus. He knew the Southern plantation from end to end, and he dealt with both its pleasant and its harsh features. He portrayed the fortunes of the planters and their former slaves after the Civil War and also the problems of economic and racial readjustments which confronted the South during the years of Reconstruction. In doing so, however, he kept clear of sentimental propaganda in defense of a lost cause. His stories threw a revealing light on the status of the aristocratic planters, the democratic middle class, and the poor whites as well as that of the Southern Negro, whether slave or free. In his literary criticism he boldly condemned the old-style Southern writers for the inclusion of politics in their literature, for their sectional prejudices, their lack of national vision, their resentment of just criticism, and their excessive romanticism. In his own writings he was a pioneer in a movement to reconstruct literature in the South on a foundation of literary artistry and wholesome realism. Moreover, writing at a time when the fires of sectional bitterness were still smoldering, he was the South's ambassador of moderation and reconciliation to a nation which had been divided by a civil war.

My overall objective, therefore, has been to bring into clear focus all of the various segments of Joel Chandler Harris' contributions as a regional writer to America's literature without in any wise diminishing the stature of Uncle Remus.

No previous study of Harris has included either an accurate or an adequate account of his indebtedness to Joseph Addison Turner. To conclude that if it had not been for the cultural advantages which Turner gave the boy during his literary apprenticeship on his Turnwold plantation Joe Harris might not have become Joel Chandler Harris is conjectural, but it is also within the range of probability.

I have endeavored to keep Harris in character both as a man and as an author. When I first began this study a number of years ago, many of Harris' personal friends and newspaper associates were still living and it was from them that I gained an insight into his personality traits. As a boy he was extremely shy and as he grew older and became acutely aware of his unfortunate history, he developed a morbid sensitivity which he later overcame through a happy marriage and a growing confidence in himself which his success in journalism gave him. Harris was a plain man of the people, and he was content to live quietly and simply in the midst of a developing complex society. He never actively engaged in politics, never made a public address, never thought of himself as a literary person, never read from any of his stories, never even remotely sought to capitalize on his popularity as an author to promote the sale of his books, and yet what he wrote carried his name and fame to all parts of the United States and into many foreign countries.

Since Harris' death in 1908 the South which he depicted in his writings has undergone swiftly moving changes, but the problems which then confronted his section and the nation have not yet been finally solved. Section is still arrayed against section, old loyalties against new ideas, race against race, and the agrarian against the industrialist. His advocacy of moderation, his spirit of tolerance and conciliation, his respect for minority groups, his temperate and balanced presentation of the South's problems and prospects, and his concern for the unity and welfare of the nation as a whole have relevance for the South and

America today in an even more swiftly changing society than the one of which he wrote.

Harris was a voluminous writer over a period of forty-six years. The attempt to read and evaluate his work as a literary historian has required patient industry. The undertaking, however, was a pleasant and rewarding experience because of the generous assistance which I received from numerous individuals. I am under particular obligation to Professor Thomas H. English of Emory University for giving me full access to Harris' manuscripts, letters, and other pertinent material which Harris' family placed in the Joel Chandler Harris Memorial Collection at Emory University. Professor English also gave me helpful suggestions in regard to my treatment of Harris' indebtedness to Joseph Addison Turner at the beginning of his literary career. The late John DeJarnette Turner, a grandson of Joseph Addison Turner, permitted me to read and make use of his grandfather's manuscript journals which were then in his possession, and my references to the journals are from this source. Turner's granddaughter-in-law, Mrs. Dennis Turner of Milledgeville, Georgia, furnished me biographical data on the Joseph Addison Turner family. One of Turner's granddaughters, Mrs. E. F. Griffith of Eatonton, Georgia, gave me duplicate copies of *The Countryman;* allowed me to have a photograph made of her daguerrotype of her grandfather and grandmother, Louisa Dennis Turner; and she was gracious in the information which she gave me about the early history of Eatonton. Personal interviews are acknowledged in the notes.

I also express my appreciation to the officials of the following libraries for their courtesies to me during my research: Washington Memorial Library, Macon; Hardman (now Eugene W. Stetson Memorial) Library, Mercer University, Macon; Woman's College of Georgia, Milledgeville; Atlanta Historical Society; Atlanta Public Library; State of Georgia Library, Atlanta; Asa Griggs Candler Library, Emory University; Georgia Historical Society, Savannah; Howard-Tilton Memorial Library, Tulane University; New Orleans Public Library; Low Library, Columbia University; New York Public Library. Houghton Mifflin Company, Boston, permitted me to read its correspondence file on Harris. Grants made by the Shell Oil Company to Mercer University enabled me to continue my research from time to time.

Since this book is an outgrowth of the dissertation which I submitted to the Department of English and Comparative Literature, Columbia University, in partial fulfillment of the requirements for the doctor of philosophy degree, I gratefully acknowledge my indebtedness to Professor Lewis Leary, chairman of the department, who read my manuscript and offered invaluable criticism and beneficial counsel. I express my appreciation to President Rufus Carrollton Harris of Mercer University for his friendly personal interest in the progress of my manuscript toward its publication. Beyond all others, I am indebted to my wife Marjorie for the constant encouragement which she gave me to complete this biography of Joel Chandler Harris after its preparation had been interrupted by a long tenure of administrative duties at Shorter College, Rome, Georgia.

PAUL M. COUSINS

Mercer University
Macon, Georgia

CONTENTS

ILLUSTRATIONS

*Joel
Chandler Harris*

Arthur Burdett Frost's pen and ink drawing of Free Joe, a character in the title story in Harris' volume *Free Joe and Other Georgian Sketches*

1

A GEORGIA HERITAGE

Joel Chandler Harris was born in Eatonton, the county seat of Putnam County, Georgia, on December 9, 1848. During his boyhood he lived in an environment of antebellum plantation culture which had had its origin in the crude but vigorous era of the American Revolution. The mores of this plantation culture became the dominant influence in the formation of his character and the source of inspiration for his most enduring stories of the Southern region. After he had attained international fame through the first and second volumes of his Uncle Remus folklore legends of the old plantation, he declared that the inherent qualities of life which characterized the people of his native county had been a force sufficiently strong to regulate men's lives. "I know," he confessed, "it was so in my own case. I have never attempted or accomplished anything that I did not ask myself, 'What will the people of Putnam think of this.' " [1]

Before Harris settled permanently in Atlanta in 1876 he had followed a journalistic career in Macon, Georgia, in New Orleans, and in Forsyth and Savannah, Georgia, but Putnam County was the brier-patch in which he had been born and bred and in whose cultural climate he was most at home. In spirit he never left it and the qualities of its civilization pervaded his writings. When, therefore, he wrote about its people and their way of life he could say as did Uncle Remus to his Miss Sally, "Dey ain't no hear-tell 'bout dis, Miss Sally, kaze I seed it wid my own eyes."

By the time of Harris' birth, the many diverse cultural elements of the region had been merged into a stable, homogeneous society which was unique in Georgia's history. According to one historian, this middle Georgia plantation society had its beginning when "one George Matthews bought a disputed title to a tract of land on the Broad River in the County of Wilkes just above its conjunction

[1] Atlanta *Constitution*, October 14, 1888.

3

with the Savannah, and in 1784 he and a great number of his friends and relations moved to Georgia with their families." Later, other families from Virginia and the Carolinas followed these pioneers and settled in the Piedmont counties of Wilkes, Burke, and Richmond. They, too, were small farmers, but as time passed they increased their holdings and added their contributions to the development of this incipient planter society.

These early migrants from the older, more settled states were doubtless motivated by a desire to improve their economic and social status. Attracted, therefore, by the prospect of acquiring extensive acreages at a low cost in this sparsely settled region with its favorable climate and fertile soil, they moved their families and possessions into the new territory. Those from Virginia brought with them the traditional concept of a planter aristocracy which they knew about but which they had not been able to attain for themselves, since the owners of large plantations were holding their estates intact. At first, the hard necessity of building modest homes and clearing land for cultivation prevented them from establishing a country-gentleman society. The concept, however, remained with them and the better educated and more prosperous among them eventually would realize their objectives, but in a far more democratic form than had existed among the landed gentry in Virginia and South Carolina.

Some of these pioneers remained in the older counties which had already been established on the eastern boundary of the state near the Savannah River. Others moved westward across the state into the newer counties of Baldwin, Hancock, Morgan, Greene, Madison, Jasper, and Putnam which had not yet been firmly settled.

The pioneers from Virginia at first began to cultivate tobacco as they had formerly done, but they soon discovered by experimentation that both the soil and the climate were better for growing cotton. The amount which they could produce, however, was limited because it was necessary to separate the lint from the seed by hand, a process which was slow and time consuming.

The cultivation of cotton instead of tobacco found a new incentive in 1793 when Eli Whitney, a Yale graduate who had come to Georgia to teach school, invented the cotton gin and thereby revolutionized farming not only in that area of Georgia but throughout the South. Henceforth, cotton was on its way toward becoming the king of agricultural products. The middle Georgia pioneer farmers turned from tobacco to cotton as their principal crop, and it became the source of their material prosperity. A cycle then began to be repeated from year to year: more land was cleared, a more extensive acreage was planted in cotton, and more slaves, of necessity, were acquired to cultivate it.

This procedure was not without its disadvantages, for it frequently served to create an economic problem for the planters. Slave labor was essential, but the price of Negroes who were physically fit to work in the fields was high, and their owners were obligated to house, feed and clothe them, and to provide medical care when they were sick. Moreover, competent overseers had to be employed to supervise the work of the field hands in order to produce maximum yields of cotton, corn, and necessities for maintaining the plantations. The planters themselves had to exercise careful business management so as not to go into debt. Neither the size of a plantation nor the number of slaves which a planter owned was always a true index of his actual wealth. Then, too, since there was no centrally located cotton market of importance in Putnam or adjacent counties, it was necessary for the planters to make the long haul by wagon to Augusta to deliver cotton in quantity and to bring back such needed supplies as could not be raised or made on their plantations.

As the social order became increasingly stable in the rural communities and as the population of the county-seat towns increased, the wealthier planters built more pretentious homes on their plantations or in the small towns, and they began to live more in keeping with their concept of the life of country gentlemen. They took pride in their spirited horses and in the superior breed of their highly trained hunting dogs. They not only engaged in field sports, but also became more active in the political, educational, and religious affairs of their respective communities. Some of them spent a part of their leisure time reading favorite classical and English authors, but they looked askance upon authorship as a profession which they would deliberately choose. If perchance there happened to be one among them willing to incur the adverse effect which a reputation as a serious writer might have upon his standing in his community, he could send his manuscripts to *De Bow's Review* in New Orleans, or to the *Southern Quarterly Review* or *Russell's Magazine* in Charleston or to the *Southern Literary Messenger* in Richmond. But an amateur and unknown writer of belles-lettres in Georgia before the Civil War stood little chance of getting his pieces accepted for publication even in these Southern periodicals. More sensitive to current political issues than to literary creativity, the planters read books for the pleasure which they derived from them and kept informed about state and national affairs through the Milledgeville and Augusta newspapers.

During the 1840's and 1850's when the plantation regime in middle Georgia was in its most flourishing state, the country-gentlemen planters were influential in setting the pattern of the social amenities in their respective localities and in giving direction to political ideas. They were far outnumbered, however, by the small farmers. The United States census of 1860 listed 41,084 of 118,000 white families in Georgia as slaveholders. Of these slaveholding families 66 percent owned less than ten slaves each, only 5 percent held more than a hundred, and the majority owned less than twenty each.[2] Only 408 of the 2,956 white families in Putnam County were listed as slaveowners, and of these 408 there were 50 families which owned only one and only 5 which owned as many as a hundred but less than two hundred.[3]

Most of Georgia's white population before the Civil War were hardy and respected citizens who, as we have seen, owned comparatively few slaves or none at all. Frank Lawrence Owsley pointed out in his study of the organization of social life in the Old South that "the core of the social structure was a massive body of plain folk who were neither rich nor very poor. . . . The group included the small slaveholding farmers; the nonslaveholders who owned the land which they cultivated; the numerous herdsmen on the frontier, pine barrens, and mountains; and those tenant farmers whose agricultural production, as recorded in the census, indicated thrift, energy, and self-respect." [4]

These plain folk constituted the majority of the people who lived in Putnam County both before and during Harris' boyhood. Most of them lived on their own land, worked hard, dressed plainly,

[2]Ralph Betts Flanders, *Plantation Slavery in Georgia* (Chapel Hill: University of North Carolina Press, 1933), 127.
[3]U. S. Census Office, *Eighth Census of the United States: 1860.*
[4]Frank Lawrence Owsley, *Plain Folk of the Old South* (Baton Rouge: Louisiana State University Press, 1949), 7, 8.

fared heartily but not sumptuously, and relished humor of a broad, earthy nature as a relief from their labor in the fields. Having acquired very little formal education, they spoke a language which bore little resemblance to orthodox grammar. Highly individualistic, they were independent in their thinking and forthright in the expression of their opinions on any subject in which their interests were involved. After they had laid by their crops, they attended the summer camp meetings with somewhat the same degree of fervor they manifested at political stump speakings and barbecues. By the time of Harris' birth in 1848 the frontier era of inhumane fighting, barbarous pranks, and excessive drinking had been restrained by the refining influence of church and school. But there were many among the upper and the middle classes who were not at all averse to the stimulating and enlivening effect which a good, stiff dram or a generous toddy could produce. In their social contacts they mixed freely with those who were better educated and more wealthy, and if they ever gave a thought to their lack of even a semi-aristocratic background, they more than likely took pride in its absence. Clement Eaton has written that on the eve of the Civil War this "middle class of landowning farmers were perhaps the most self-respecting group in the world." [5]

In addition to the planters and small farmers who composed the two largest groups in old plantation society, there were lawyers (many of whom were also planters and politicians), physicians, teachers, ministers, merchants, and blacksmiths. They were not directly involved in the plantation system, but they played an important role in community affairs in the rural settlements as well as in the more populous towns. Finally, there was a lower economic group who possessed no professional nor business skills but who earned a livelihood through such employment as might be available for them as seamstresses, employees in taverns, or in the few factories in or near the towns.

The very lowest class in the economic and social scale was made up of poor whites, of whom there were two levels. In the upper level were those who owned small plots of ground but no slaves, who lived in very humble dwellings and yet managed to maintain

---

[5] Clement Eaton, "Class Differences in the Old South," *Virginia Quarterly Review*, XXXIII (Summer, 1957), 370.

their economic independence, but whose uncouth speech revealed their illiteracy. Although they were poor and uneducated, many of them were proud and highly sensitive to any attitude of condescension which they felt the gentry manifested toward them. In the lower level there were those scorned even by the slaves as "poor white trash" because of their indolence, addiction to drink, and hand-to-mouth existence. "These listless, uncouth, shambling refugees from the world of competition," as the historian Ulrich B. Phillips described them, were never enumerated, but apparently they comprised only a small portion of the non-slaveholding population.[6] However few they may have been in number, they were an integral part of the total cultural heritage which Harris received from Georgia's antebellum society. Georgia writers before Harris who made mention of them did so as a source of comic effect and therefore failed to take note of their pathetic condition.

Although the population of Georgia was composed of many different classes, from the topmost planters to the poor whites, society was organized on the basis of the simplest democracy. In his reminiscences of life in middle Georgia before the Civil War, Richard Malcolm Johnston, the writer whom Harris regarded as the best chronicler of old times in Georgia, recalled the democratic relationship that existed among its people. "In general," he wrote, "every neighbor used to sit at every other neighbor's board, neither feeling that he was receiving or imparting favors other than such as flow from the needs of social existence."[7] In his study of antebellum society in Georgia as a whole, Ralph Betts Flanders states that the easy and congenial relationship which existed between the planter and the middle-class groups was one of its most pronounced features. Flanders found that although the large planter dominated the political and social life of the state, the lot of the small landowner with only a few slaves was not a poor one. "There was," he affirmed, "no rigid social system in ante-bellum Georgia. It was by no means unusual for the average slaveholder to labor with his Negroes in the field, and the dignity of labor was appreciated. Too many of the planters

[6]Ulrich B. Phillips, *Life and Labor in the Old South* (Boston: Little, Brown, and Company, 1937), 348.

[7]Richard Malcolm Johnston, "Middle Georgia Rural Life," *Century Magazine*, XLIII (March, 1892), 738.

had risen to prominence and power through their own ability to assume a haughty attitude toward others." [8]

Equally important in Harris' background was the uninhibited fondness of people for humor which took the form of practical jokes, amusing pranks, and comical situations. Any gathering in the backwoods settlements was likely to be enlivened by hilarious antics and capers which never failed to produce loud guffaws of laughter but which a more effete culture would have frowned upon as crude and indecorous, for these pranks sometimes involved cruelty to man and beast.

Clement Eaton, in his *The Mind of the Old South,* asserts that Georgia was the cradle of Southern humor.[9] It would be more specific to say that humor flourished to a greater extent in the Putnam County area of middle Georgia than in any other locality of the old South. "By-the-by," Harris wrote to William M. Baskervill in 1895, "if you will take a map of Georgia, pick out Putnam County, and then put your finger on the counties surrounding it—Morgan, Greene, Hancock, Baldwin, Jones, and Jasper—you will have under your thumb the seat of Southern humor." [10] Harris once described the character and individuality of the area as astonishing even to those who were familiar with the strange shapes in which these intangibles might appear. "Every settlement," he said, "had its peculiarities, and every neighborhood boasted of its humorists—its clowns, whose pranks and jests were limited by no license. Out of this has grown a literature which, in some of its characteristics, is not matched elsewhere on the globe." [11]

Harris went on to express his regret that the all too few illustrations of this peculiar middle Georgia humor which had been preserved in print were not comparable to the great body of it which had perished for lack of someone industrious enough to chronicle it. Even though only a portion of this humor was ever committed

---

[8]Flanders, *Plantation Slavery in Georgia,* 128.

[9]Clement Eaton, *The Mind of the Old South* (Baton Rouge: Louisiana State University Press, 1964), 105.

[10]Quoted in Jay B. Hubbell, "Two Letters of Uncle Remus," *Southwest Review,* XXIII (January, 1938), 216.

[11]Joel Chandler Harris, *Stories of Georgia* (New York: American Book Company, 1896), 241.

to the printed page, posterity is indebted to four of its chroniclers—
Augustus Baldwin Longstreet, William Tappan Thompson, Richard Malcolm Johnston, and Bill Arp (Charles Henry Smith)—for
recording some of its peculiar features. Their contributions to
Harris' cultural heritage covered the period from the crude and
raw manners of the frontier settlements to the more refined social
customs which civilizing agencies had effected by the time of his
childhood in Eatonton.

Longstreet was born in Augusta, Richmond County, in 1790, only
thirteen years after the county had been created in what was then
frontier territory. After his graduation from Yale he practiced law
in Augusta, edited the *States Rights Sentinel,* and became judge of
the superior court of the Ocmulgee circuit. In his travels through
the counties of Baldwin, Greene, Jasper, Jones, Morgan, Putnam,
and Wilkinson in his judicial capacity, he observed the practices and
the speech of the backwoodsmen and villagers at a time when their
culture was unrefined, but vigorous and picturesque. He later turned
his observations into racy, realistic sketches which he contributed to
the Milledgeville *Southern Recorder* and the Augusta *States Rights
Sentinel.* His humorous accounts of rural dances, horse-swaps, fights,
gander pullings, fox hunts, shooting matches, and other masculine
forms of entertainment which the frontiersmen devised met with
such a cordial response from the humor-loving middle Georgia readers of these newspapers that he issued them in book form in 1835
under the title *Georgia Scenes.*

Writing in an era of Southern literary culture when an elegant
and orthodox style was expected of its writers, and being himself a
man of culture, Longstreet in his preface to the book explained for
the benefit of those readers who had "taken exception to the coarse,
inelegant, and sometimes ungrammatical language" which he occasionally used that it was language *"accommodated to the capacity of
the person to whom he represents himself as speaking."* In other
words, he emphasized that in writing *Georgia Scenes* he had not
attempted to compose polite literature but to show that both the
characters he described and the language he attributed to them
were true to the life portrayed. Although the stories did not conform to accepted literary standards, they did possess the virtue of
honest reporting by a competent writer. *Georgia Scenes* is what the

author intended it to be, as John Donald Wade pointed out in his biography of Longstreet, "a very valuable source book of the social status of Georgia in the first fifty years of the Republic—and incidentally not of Georgia only." [12]

Georgia Scenes was widely read and favorably received. Edgar Allan Poe praised its humor and realism in a review in the *Southern Literary Messenger,* and other Southern writers followed the Longstreet pattern in their characterization of the pioneer backwoodsmen in their respective states. Among them were Johnson Jones Hooper of Alabama in his *Some Adventures of Captain Simon Suggs* (1845); Joseph Glover Baldwin, also of Alabama, in his *The Flush Times of Alabama and Mississippi* (1853); and George Washington Harris of Tennessee in his *Sut Lovingood: Yarns Spun by a Nat'ral Born Fool* (1867). These writers, however, were more nearly the predecessors of Mark Twain than they were of Joel Chandler Harris. Like Longstreet, their purpose was to elicit hearty laughter from their readers, not to write polite literature.

Notable progress toward a more improved status of society in middle Georgia than that portrayed by Longstreet was chronicled by William Tappan Thompson in his *Major Jones's Courtship.* Thompson was born in Ohio in 1812 but settled in middle Georgia in his early manhood. In 1835 he became associated with Longstreet on the *State Rights Sentinel* and afterwards acquired the *Southern Miscellany,* a weekly newspaper published in Madison, Morgan County, to which he contributed his amusing letters of Major Joseph Jones of Pineville. His primary purpose in the letters was merely to entertain the readers of his newspaper from week to week, but they proved to be so popular that he republished a collection of them as a book in 1843 entitled *Major Jones's Courtship.* The book took its place alongside *Georgia Scenes,* but the absence of shrewd horsetraders, loudmouth boasters, ferocious fighters, and the inhumane treatment of man and beast indicated a more civilized Georgia culture than Longstreet had described and one that approached the qualities which prevailed during Harris' boyhood.

As portrayed by Thompson, Major Jones was a respected middle Georgia small farmer who owned his home and a few slaves. He

[12]John Donald Wade, *Augustus Baldwin Longstreet* (New York: Macmillan Company, 1924), 164.

had no formal education but he was intuitively intelligent and a keen observer of the foibles of his rural Pineville neighbors and, indeed, of human nature in general. His observations were often mildly satirical but were characterized by genial good humor and down-to-earth common sense.

The humorous comments and comical experiences of Major Jones caught on with readers both in and beyond Georgia, and Thompson subsequently produced two additional volumes, *Chronicles of Pineville* (1845) and *Major Jones's Sketches of Travel* (1848).

Like Longstreet and Thompson, Richard Malcolm Johnston also set forth the humorous aspects of rural life in middle Georgia as he had observed them as a young man. He was born in 1822 in Hancock County, to which his grandfather had migrated from Virginia in 1779. He first attended the old field schools in his native county in which the rod was an effective instrument in the teaching process. In 1841 he graduated from Mercer University at Penfield, Morgan County. Reduced to poverty by the fall of the Confederacy, he moved to Baltimore in 1867 and established a school for boys.

Johnston was a man of personal attractiveness, refined tastes, and religious sensitivity and he was well versed in both classical and English literature. Like Longstreet and Thompson, he had an aptitude for observing the humorous aspects of middle Georgia pioneer society. Before his removal to Baltimore he had published in various magazines some sketches of rural life as he had observed it during his boyhood at Powellton, a village near his birthplace, but he did not publish *Dukesborough Tales*, a collection of his reminiscences, until 1871.

In these sketches, Johnston told of the old, log cabin Goosepond school and its strict disciplinarian Israel Meadows, of a rural wedding and its bountiful supper of "pig, lamb, turkey, chicken, duck, pea-fowl, goose, partridge, pigeon, cake, syllabub" with fiddling and dancing lasting until nearly midnight, and of the excitement created in the village by the coming of the circus. All of these were incidents which he had actually seen, but his reminiscent rendering of the rustic manners and barbarisms of speech of middle Georgia lacked the raciness and the realism of Longstreet's *Georgia Scenes* and the comedy and character delineations in Thompson's *Major*

Jones's Courtship. This disparity was due in part to Johnston's familiarity with belles-lettres and to the fact that the passing of time and the Baltimore environment in which he was then living softened his memories of the original crudeness of the pioneer era. Even so, *Dukesborough Tales* affords a trustworthy insight into what Johnston called "The Grim and Rude, but Hearty Old Times in Georgia."

The last of the humorists with a similar background who wrote of rural and small-town life in the pattern set by Longstreet, Thompson, and Johnston was Charles Henry Smith, who was known throughout the South as Bill Arp, after the rustic character of that name whom he created. Smith was born in 1826 in Gwinnett, one of the newer counties which had been created in middle Georgia in 1818. He attended the University of Georgia for three years, read law privately, was admitted to the bar, and practiced law in Rome after his removal to that northwest Georgia city until 1877, when he retired to his plantation near Cartersville. He attracted attention as a humorist in the 1860's through his Bill Arp letters to President "Abe Linkhorn" and to Artemus Ward.

Smith first conceived of Bill Arp, whose prototype he had met in Rome, as a braggart in the tradition of Longstreet's boisterous frontiersmen who, despite his small size, boasted that he "could out-run, out-jump, out-swim, out-rassle, out-ride, and out-shoot anybody in Chulio."[18] Later, however, he depicted Arp in the more civilized role of an uneducated but witty, satirical, and homespun commentator on the Southern point of view during the Civil War and the first years of the Reconstruction. Arp spoke the vernacular language commonly employed by Georgians of the middle and lower classes, and he voiced their sentiments about President Lincoln, the Yankees, Tammany Hall, and Governor Joseph Emerson Brown during the war years. He also echoed their protests against the usurpation of power by the Federal officials in Georgia during Reconstruction in their exploitation of the freed Negroes who, he said, had agreed to resume their work on the farms for fair wages. Smith wrote, with some show of bitterness, through his spokesman Bill Arp: "Our ploughs are standing in the fields idle, our farms will go untilled, and

---

[18]Chulio was a rural settlement between Cartersville and Rome.

the land swarms with agents who are bribing the poor negroes away under the promise of higher wages, and under the sanction of a Bureau as rotten as the promises of Pharoah." [14]

Smith lightly regarded his Bill Arp letters, but at the request of Metropolitan Records Office in New York, he agreed to the publication of a collection of them in 1866 under the title *Bill Arp, So-Called, A Side Show of the Southern Side of the War*. He stated in his preface to the volume that he doubted whether the contents were worthy of being placed before the public in book form since he had written them in a humorous vein to relax the minds of his readers from their serious absorption in the war, and that he did not think they would survive the time and the conditions which had called them forth. Written against the background of the Civil War and Reconstruction, the letters of Bill Arp were tinged with a sectional point of view which identified them with the political enmities of the times in which they were written. *Bill Arp, So-Called* falls below *Georgia Scenes*, *Major Jones's Courtship*, and *Dukesborough Tales* in graphic description, character delineation, spontaneity of humor, and breadth of appeal, but it continued the reputation of the Georgia writers of the Old South as humorists and is of value in Harris' cultural heritage for the light which it throws on Southern thought under the strain of sectional warfare and the political and economic problems which the Reconstruction measures made acute.

In his own stories which dealt with the white population in the Old South, Harris was indebted to each of these Georgia humorists, but he owed less to Longstreet, Johnston, and Bill Arp than he did to Thompson, as will be shown later in this study. It is sufficient to say here that there are marked similarities between Thompson's Major Joseph Jones of Pineville and Harris' William H. Sanders of Shady Dale. Both were typical representatives of the uneducated but commonsensible middle class of Georgians known as Georgia crackers, but in the best connotation of that word.

The least known of all the writers who contributed to Harris' literary heritage was Joseph Addison Turner, who was born on his father's Putnam County plantation on September 23, 1826. Harris never knew Longstreet and his contacts with Johnston were limited to Johnston's visits in Atlanta to fill lecture engagements. He did not

---

[14]Charles H. Smith, *Bill Arp, So-Called* (New York: Metropolitan Records Office, 1866), 8.

come to know Thompson until 1870 when both were on the editorial staff of the Savannah *Morning News*, and it was not until after 1876, when Harris joined the editorial staff of the Atlanta *Constitution*, that he came to know Bill Arp, who was then living in Cartersville and contributing articles to the *Constitution* on farming and kindred topics. Turner, however, was the one literary person whom Harris knew in his boyhood and to whom he was indebted for the opportunity to begin his career in both journalism and literature. In 1862 Turner employed thirteen-year-old Joe Harris as a typesetter on *The Country-man*, a semiliterary newspaper which he had just begun to publish on his Putnam County plantation some nine miles from Eatonton, and the boy lived on this plantation into his seventeenth year.

Turner was both a planter and a lawyer, and in an era when authorship as a profession was looked down upon in the South he aspired to be the author of a literature that was indigenous to the South in theme and style. In spite of all the frustrations which he encountered, he pursued his ambition with ardor and determination as a poet, essayist, novelist, literary critic, and editor of four magazines. Measured by literary standards which prevailed in middle Georgia in his time, he was a man of culture. He was conversant with classical, English and American authors, and he loved literature for the pleasure he derived from reading it and as the means whereby he hoped to achieve both fame and fortune through his own works.

Although Turner failed to realize his grand dream of becoming a successful author of a literature which would portray the manner of life peculiar to the South, he did succeed in communicating to his young protégé a love of literature that was not merely entertaining for its exaggerated humor. He also encouraged Harris to be persistent in his efforts to develop his natural talent for writing and counseled him to concentrate on native Southern subjects.

During the years 1862 to 1866, when Harris was directly under Turner's literary tutelage, sectional feelings in the South ran high. Turner had followed a moderate course during the heated debate over slavery and had opposed secession, but after the war had actually begun he became intensely partisan and made *The Countryman* his personal organ for his unequivocal support of the Confederacy. As an inevitable consequence he indoctrinated the young boy in the narrow concept of a Southern literature which was entirely sectional in its viewpoint and motivated by a propaganda objective. Even so, when

one takes into account the low status of literature in Georgia as well
as in the entire South in the years from 1862 to 1866 and the
absorption of its people in the war, Harris was fortunate to have had
a man of Turner's sincere devotion to literature and experience as a
writer to counsel him in the first stage of his own literary apprenticeship. Nor could he have found a more congenial atmosphere in which
to further his youthful aspiration than that which Turner's quiet,
isolated plantation afforded him. Time would resolve the sectional
influence which Turner had exerted upon him. He would continue to
concentrate his writings upon Southern subjects, but with an enlarged
vision he would remove the geographical boundaries which Turner
had drawn around them, free them from sectional bias and political
propaganda, and imbue his regional stories with a national perspective.

Religion and education contributed their refining influence in the
evolving culture which was Harris' heritage. Churches, principally
Methodist and Baptist, were organized in the rural communities as well
as in the villages and courthouse towns, and they had a civilizing
effect upon the barbarisms which Longstreet had graphically portrayed
in his *Georgia Scenes*. Reverend John Duncan, a Methodist circuit
rider, preached with great emotional fevor at the Turnwold community's Philadelphia Methodist Church whose services were attended by
Harris when he lived on Turner's plantation. Augustus Baldwin Longstreet also preached there after he had become president of Emory
College at Oxford, Newton County. Jesse Mercer and Adiel Sherwood,
two eminent Baptist ministers who were instrumental in the founding
of Mercer University at Penfield, preached at Eatonton and conducted
revival meetings there and in the middle Georgia area.

In 1819 Joseph Addison Turner's father William, one of the Virginia small farmers who had earlier migrated to middle Georgia and
settled permanently in Putnam County, helped to organize Union
Academy near his plantation. It was, in his son's description of it,
"one of the first and best in Middle Georgia. It was built when the
country around it was almost an unbroken forest, and while the
swamps and neighboring woods were yet retreats for the deer and the
wolf." [15] Union Academy marked a cultural advance in teaching

[15]Joseph Addison Turner, "William H. Seward as a Schoolmaster in Georgia,"
The Plantation (June, 1860), 226. A file of *The Plantation* is available in the
Joel Chandler Harris Memorial Collection, Emory University, Atlanta, Georgia.

personnel and subjects over the primitive backwoods schools such as Longstreet had described in "The Turn Out" and Johnston in "The Goosepond School." The trustees employed as its first rector or principal young William H. Seward from Union College, Schenectady, New York. Its curriculum was an inclusive one for a school in a pioneer settlement, for the trustees contracted with Seward to teach "the Latin and Greek languages, theoretical and practical Mathematics, Logic, Rhetoric, Natural and Moral Philosophy, Chemistry, Geography, and English Grammar." [16]

Although no school of college level was established in Putnam County, Adiel Sherwood conducted in his home near Eatonton a private school which was a direct forerunner of Mercer University, and by 1836 five colleges had been founded near Putnam. They were Franklin College at Athens, in Clarke County, chartered in 1785 but not put in actual operation until 1801; Mercer University at Penfield, founded in 1833; Oglethorpe College at Midway near Milledgeville, Baldwin County, in 1835; Emory College at Oxford, Newton County, in 1836; and Georgia Female College at Macon, Bibb County, also in 1836.

All of these colleges, with the exception of Franklin which was founded and financially supported by the state in its program of public education, were church-related and controlled by their respective fostering denominations—Mercer by the Baptists, Oglethorpe by the Presbyterians, and Emory and Georgia Female College by the Methodists. Handicapped in their operation and growth by the lack of adequate facilities and financial resources, they nevertheless set up and maintained courses of study which were taught by capable professors and which were in keeping with the best traditions of liberal arts education. Their stabilizing and refining influence was felt throughout middle Georgia, and until after the Civil War they gave to that section a cultural distinction enjoyed by no other region of the state.

Harris' cultural heritage had had its beginning in the rough, barbarous but vigorous, and boisterous civilization of frontier society. Under the influence of the Christian religion, education, and the social impact of the planter class, it evolved through a period of more than sixty years of hard labor and toil into the stable social and economic order which prevailed at the time of Harris' boyhood in Putnam County. However provincial, isolated, and tranquil the way of life

[16]*Ibid.*, 225.

which characterized its people may have appeared to an outsider, it was to them a source of pride and satisfaction, and they would not have exchanged it for the civilization of any other section of the country. Along with their cultural progress they had retained in essence those pioneer qualities of strong individuality of character, of independent convictions and picturesque language, of the democratic mingling of all classes irrespective of wealth and social position, and of a fondness for hearty and broad humor.

In reading Harris' numerous stories with a Putnam County setting, one is aware of the powerful and permanent impact which all of these traits made upon him. These qualities were in the ascendancy among the people whom he knew in his boyhood, and in his maturity he had reasons of a personal nature to evaluate them as a force sufficient to regulate men's lives in general and his own in particular.

2

BOYHOOD IN EATONTON

Eatonton, Harris' birthplace, was situated in a sparsely settled agricultural region and isolated by a distance of some twenty miles from Greensboro, Madison, Monticello, and Milledgeville. Founded in 1807, the same year that Putnam County was formed from a portion of Baldwin, it numbered only 379 whites and 347 blacks twenty years after it had been founded. Among the whites there were six physicians, seven lawyers, and thirteen families who owned four-wheeled carriages, an indication of the wealth and social status which these families had attained.[1] Even in its pioneer period, however, its citizens had been civic minded and generous in their support of public enterprises. With evident pride and satisfaction in its material and cultural progress, Adiel Sherwood, a pioneer Baptist minister and educator who had lived near the town, wrote that in 1829

Eatonton contained a Court House which cost 6000 dollars, Jail, two Academies, Brick Masonic Hall, a branch of the State Bank, and one of the finest houses of worship in the upcountry. In this, which cost $6000, the Baptists, Methodists, and Presbyterians worship. To the Meeting House is attached a fine toned Bell, weighing three hundred pounds. A good bell is a great convenience in a village. The Academies and the Meeting House are situated in a most beautiful grove. With the Academies is connected a Library, which cost 600 dollars, and which has since been enlarged, and a Philosophical Apparatus purchased in London for 2500 dollars.[2]

Its people continued to make civic progress as the years passed and as their material prosperity increased. In 1849 the Eaton Manufacturing Company established a cotton factory capitalized at seventy thousand

[1] Adiel Sherwood, *Gazetter of Georgia*, (Philadelphia: J. W. Martin and W. K. Bodin, 1829), 105.
[2] *Ibid.*

dollars on Little River, about three miles from the courthouse.[3] Travel to and from Eatonton was by stagecoach until the Central of Georgia Railroad Company built a branch line to it in 1853.[4] The Methodists built their own meetinghouse in 1857, and by 1860 some of the planters who lived in the village had erected fine homes in keeping with their wealth.[5] Although the white population of Eatonton had increased from 379 in 1827 to only 478 in 1860, the number of Negroes had increased during the same period from 347 to 1,531, of whom 1,519 were slaves and 12 were free.[6]

The outward appearance of Eatonton at the time of Harris' boyhood was not unlike that of the other small county-seat towns in middle Georgia and throughout the antebellum Deep South. When the town was first laid out in 1807, four acres were reserved at its center for the courthouse. Facing this square were merchandising houses, offices of the professional men, and homes of some of the planters. One of the largest and finest of these homes was occupied by Michael Dennis, reputed to have been Putnam County's wealthiest man. For the accommodation of travelers there were three hotels, the Barnes House, the Planters Hotel, and the Eatonton Hotel, which was owned by Dennis. On the streets adjacent to the courthouse square there were other planters' homes, one of which was the handsome two-story home of Andrew W. Reid. Often in close proximity to the homes of the wealthy planters were the small but attractively kept homes of the middle-class families and the modest cottages of the poor. Majestic old trees lined the village streets and served as an appropriate setting for some of the finer homes.

In the comparative isolation of their town, the people of Eatonton went quietly about the routine of daily affairs without any sense of urgency or haste. The hard labor and the crude manners which had been part of the pioneer environment were now behind them. Their fields were fertile and yielded substantial harvests of cotton and corn. The climate was temperate and the seasons changed gently and almost imperceptibly.

[3]George White, *Statistics of the State of Georgia* (Savannah: W. Thorne Williams, 1849), 480.

[4]Eatonton *Messenger*, Uncle Remus Edition, August 22, 1927.

[5]Adiel Sherwood, *Gazetteer of Georgia* (Macon: S. Boykin; Atlanta, J. Richards, 1860), 110.

[6]U.S. Census Office, *Eighth Census of the United States: 1860*.

Although life ran evenly and peacefully as Harris observed it during his boyhood in the 1850's, the most thoughtful among its older citizens discerned the signs of the times and were disturbed by the rising tempo of the national debate over the issue of slavery. This was especially true of the planters who believed that the stability of their social and economic order depended upon the preservation of the institution of slavery. While it was true that the slaveowners more often than not were humanitarian in their treatment of the slaves, the Northern abolitionists were forcing the issue, and the planters were aware that the day of ultimate decision could not be forever postponed. The hotheads among Georgia's political leaders were resolved to maintain the South's traditional system within the Union if they could, but apart from it through secession and open warfare if they must.

It was in this outwardly somnolent atmosphere that Harris spent the first thirteen years of his impressionable youth. Although several of the characters in his fiction are clearly autobiographical to those readers who are familiar with the facts in his life, he made no specific references either in his letters or press interviews to the circumstances of his birth and of his impoverished childhood. In a letter which he wrote from Savannah in 1870 to a friend, he said, "My history is a peculiarly sad and unfortunate one. . . ." [7] The first statement which he authorized for publication, as late as 1886, concerning his personal background was merely that he had been "born in the little town of Eatonton, Georgia, on December 9, 1848, under the humblest sort of circumstances." [8] In a rare interview, which he granted to a newspaper reporter in 1900, he spoke warmly but in general terms of his gratitude to the people of Eatonton for their kindness to him during his boyhood. "It is a great blessing," he said in reminiscent mood, "for a young fellow in the clutches of poverty to be raised among such people as those who lived in Eatonton when I was a boy, and whose descendants still live there. I have not the slightest difficulty in the world in referring all that I have ever done or hope to do to the kindly interest which the people of Eaton-

---

[7] Julia Collier Harris, *The Life and Letters of Joel Chandler Harris* (Boston and New York: Houghton Mifflin Company, 1918), 78. Hereinafter cited as *Harris, Life and Letters.*

[8] Joel Chandler Harris, "An Accidental Author," *Lippincott's Magazine,* XXXVII (April, 1886), 418.

ton took in my welfare when I was too young to know of the troubles which inhabit the world by right of discovery and possession." [9]

In due time young Harris made that painful discovery, but it must be said that his initiation into an awareness of the troubles which inhabited the world in general and his own in particular did not come about through any word or action either directly or indirectly on the part of the people of Eatonton. They were kind and generous in their consideration of him, and his boyhood among them was a happy one.

Information concerning Harris' father is vague. According to one Eatontonian, Fannie Lee Leverette, he was an Irish day laborer who worked near the home of Joel's mother, Mary Harris, in Newton County, which adjoins Putnam. She stated in the account which she furnished Julia Collier Harris, Joel Chandler Harris' daughter-in-law and his biographer, that the pair became involved in a romantic attachment which her parents were unable to break despite their strenuous opposition.[10] Driven to make a choice between yielding to her parents or following her lover, she was said by Miss Leverette to have left home and gone to Eatonton to be with him. "The details of the days that followed," wrote Julia Collier Harris, "are meager and confused, and Mary Harris' story from this point until after the birth of her child and her desertion by its father, partakes of the nature of legend." [11] However, according to Miss Leverette, the child's father "left Putnam within a short time of his child's birth and was never again seen there." [12]

Even the exact place of Harris' birth is in question, but the consensus is that it was in the Barnes House, where Mary Harris is said to have been employed when her son was born, and a marker has been placed at the site where this hotel originally stood.

The distressful situation which the desertion of the boy's father created for Mary Harris was somewhat alleviated by a reconciliation between her and her mother, who came to Eatonton and lived with her prior to and after the birth of the child. She continued to be stead-

[9] "Joel Chandler Harris Talks About Himself," Atlanta *Daily News*, October 10, 1900.
[10] Julia Collier Harris, *Harris, Life and Letters*, 5–8.
[11] *Ibid.*, 4.
[12] *Ibid.*, 7.

fastly loyal to her daughter even though the other members of the Harris family, especially Mary's only sister, never effected a reconciliation.[13]

Miss Mary, as the townspeople called her, was in her thirty-first year when her son was born. Putting aside what romantic feeling she once had for his father, she assumed a realistic attitude toward her situation. Because she had no reason to expect that the father would ever return or come to her aid in any way, she gave the child her own family name, and set about rearing him as advantageously as her resourcefulness would permit. No photograph of her is extant, if indeed one was ever made, but one person who knew her well described her as a resolute woman with dark hair, sparkling black eyes, and an aquiline nose. She was known to possess a ready wit, a fondness for reading newspapers and books, and a gift for entertaining children with stories of her experiences in the pioneer era of middle Georgia.[14]

Harris could have been severely handicapped at the very beginning of his life if the people of Eatonton had not taken a sympathetic attitude toward his mother's plight and responded in a practical way. Prompted by a humanitarian concern for the welfare of Miss Mary, her infant son, and her mother, Andrew Reid provided a small cottage for the family.[15] It consisted of only one large room with an attached shedroom which Joel later occupied as his own. This humble cottage fronted on Marion Street and was separated from Reid's home, which by comparison in size and appearance was a mansion, by only a garden and a hedge. It thus happened that in the democratic society which characterized the Eatonton of Harris' boyhood, poverty and wealth, untoward circumstances and favorable fortune existed in close physical proximity; and generosity of mind and a humanitarian concern prevented the raising of any barriers between the material and social extremes represented by the two families.

After Joe's mother became established in a home of her own, she began the task of creating as normal an environment as possible for her growing boy. Out of her concern for his religious training, she took him with her to the services of the Eatonton Methodist church

---

[13]Fannie Lee Leverette, Eatonton, to Paul M. Cousins, September 25, 1931.
[14]Fannie Lee Leverette, "The Mother of Joel Chandler Harris," Atlanta *Journal*, July 29, 1928.
[15]Julia Collier Harris, *Harris, Life and Letters*, 8.

of which she was a member. When he was nine she gave him a
Bible, one which she must have purchased at some financial sacrifice, for it was a large and handsomely bound edition. When the
Frank Leverette family came to occupy the Andrew Reid home,
the children made a path through the garden and hedge and kept
her supplied with newspapers and magazines. She is known to have
read Goldsmith's *The Vicar of Wakefield* in the hearing of her
young son, and it made an impression upon him far beyond that
of merely entertaining him.

When the townspeople learned that Mary Harris was a good
seamstress, they supplied her with all the tailoring work which she
could turn out, and she was thus able to provide the ordinary necessities for her family. One of her patrons was Joseph Addison
Turner, who maintained a law office in Eatonton with his brother
William. He lived on his Turnwold plantation, but Joel came to
know him when he called at his mother's home for the sewing she
had done for his family. Their casual relationship was eventually to
lead to a closer tie between the two which was to have a far-
reaching influence in determining the boy's future career in both
journalism and literature.

Joel easily made friends among the other Eatonton boys, to whom
he was known as Joe. When he became of school age his mother
was confronted with the problem of providing for his tuition at
one of the town's two academies. Once again Andrew Reid is said
to have solved her problem by paying the boy's entrance fees.[16] He
first attended the academy for boys and girls, where the teacher was
Kate Davidson from Vermont. His first day was an ordeal for him.
As he stood by Miss Davidson when she presented him as a new
scholar, he became frightened for, although among his boy companions
he was lively and talkative, he became shy, quiet, and extremely self-
conscious when he was in the presence of girls. His embarrassment
became even more apparent when he saw the poorly concealed merriment of the other girls and boys who were looking at him in his misery.
One of the girls who was present later said that he looked like a scared
rabbit peeping out from behind a cabbage leaf.[17] His almost tearful

---

[16]Julia Collier Harris, *Harris, Life and Letters,* 8.
[17]Louise Prudden. She married W. B. Hunt of Eatonton, who related the
incident to the writer in an interview.

experience was an early manifestation of his innate shyness in the presence of those whom he did not intimately know and he never overcame it.

Joe was later transferred to the academy for boys where he was in the company of those with whom he was accustomed to play. All accounts agree that he took very little interest in his textbooks, with the exception of English composition. John S. Reid, one of his teachers, recalled that he was the best writer in his class.[18] One of his academy schoolmates said that Joe was not a diligent student nor regular in his attendance but that he liked to read and that he had an excellent memory.[19] Under the fictional name of Joe Maxwell in one of his thinly veiled autobiographical books, Harris referred to his indifferent attitude toward his books when he was at the academy. "It would not be fair to say," he confessed, "that Joe was a studious lad. On the contrary, he was of an adventurous turn of mind, and he was not at all fond of the books that were in his desk at Hillsborough [Eatonton] Academy."[20]

Years later, in the summer of 1886, Harris received an invitation to attend a reunion of his former schoolmates at Eatonton. The pressure of his daily newspaper duties prevented acceptance, but the invitation inspired him to write some reminiscences of his school experiences. In keeping with the public image of him as a humorous writer, he played down any serious benefits which he may have derived from his schooling and gave an exaggerated account of his truancies.

Harris remembered that William A. Wilson, the teacher in charge, was an excellent instructor and also a strict disciplinarian, a trait which he said he discovered some seven or eight times a day. He also recalled that Wilson organized his high-spirited and mischievous scholars into military companies in imitation of the young men in Eatonton who were then drilling in preparation for service in the Confederate army and equipped them with uniforms and plumed hats. Joe's company was designated the Putnam Cadets, in which he was the Fourth Corporal. "I think they all made presentable soldiers," he wrote, "except the Fourth Corporal, who brought up

[18]Robert L. Wiggins, *The Life of Joel Chandler Harris*, (Nashville: Publishing House Methodist Episcopal Church, South, 1918), 14.

[19]John W. Adams, Eatonton, personal interview.

[20]Joel Chandler Harris, *On the Plantation* (New York: D. Appleton and Company, 1892), 14.

the rear. This officer kept the commander busy, and once brought himself into disgrace before a large company of spectators by informing Hudson Adams, in a loud voice, that it was not proper for him to turn his toes in on dress parade. Hudson was one of the lieutenants and he was properly shocked. So was the commander. As for the Fourth Corporal, he fully expected to get a trouncing— this undoubtedly would have been the result, but for the interposition of Lieutenant Adams, who was a brave and generous boy." [21]

Everyone in Eatonton knew Joe. His diminutive size and his pronounced red hair and freckled face set him apart from the others. His open friendliness, cheerful disposition, humorous turn of mind and quick wit, and his readiness at any time to engage in some prank or adventure all made him a favorite among his companions. In retrospect, he said the other boys were older and larger than he was and he wondered then and since why they were such good friends of his and why they always hunted him up when he failed to meet with them. Perhaps, he concluded, it was because he was so full of unadulterated mischief. One of them in later years said he and the other boys regarded Joe as their leader and looked to him to devise the schemes for their various escapades. When he failed to show up at the appointed time, they would go in search of him and would frequently find him sitting quietly on the steps of a Negro cabin, listening intently to some old Negro man who was telling him a legendary tale of his race.[22]

Under Joe's leadership the boys found village life neither dull nor monotonous. Scarcely a day passed, Harris later wrote about his boyhood in Eatonton, that they did not play some practical joke on Ike Nicholson, a good-natured Negro, and on another one whom they knew simply as "Free Joe" because he had no master. They knew the two Negroes would take no offense at their pranks and would join in the laughter created at their expense.[23] For a real adventure the boys would steal out the pedigreed, highly trained foxhunting dogs of Harvey Dennis and put them on the trail of the lowly rabbit. He admitted later that it was a mean trick but he said that he had no regrets, for he was sure Dennis forgave them

[21] Atlanta *Constitution*, July 20, 1886.
[22] John W. Adams, interview.
[23] Atlanta *Constitution*, July 16, 1885.

out of his understanding of the temptation which his dogs gave them to enjoy the lively thrill of an exciting chase.[24]

An element of mystery and awesome expectation always surrounded a visit which the boys occasionally dared to make to the home of Mrs. Betsy Cole, an old woman who lived on the outskirts of Eatonton. She had a local reputation as a fortuneteller, and her appearance lent color to the belief that she possessed a magical power of divination, for she had white hair, a long neck, and dressed in a peculiar fashion. Children were awed by the strange stories which they had heard about her, and the superstitious Negroes would not go near her lonely cottage after dark. Her only attendant during the day was Aunt Sally Pike, who solemnly declared that Miss Betsy turned into a spirit after sundown when she went outdoors to study the stars. The townspeople knew she was poor and lonely, and they saw to it that she did not lack for food or other necessities if she ever became sick. According to an Eatonton legend, when Mary Harris once visited her on a mission of charity she jokingly asked the old woman to study the stars for her. On her next visit, Miss Betsy is said to have told her that writings from her family were going to be read all over the world.[25]

Years later when Harris read in the Eatonton *Messenger* a notice of her death, he wrote an account of a boyhood visit in her cottage and of having seen her run her cards and employ other media in the performance of her clairvoyant art. He said that the tools of her trade consisted of a beautiful quartz stone, a pack of cards, and an unsurpassed knowledge of human nature. To some of the boys who went with him, he commented, she was a terror, but to others she was most friendly.[26]

There were few chores which Joe had to perform at home, and his mother, busy with her needle, placed no restraints upon his activities or whereabouts. So free was he that some of his elders felt he needed a restraining influence such as frequent applications of the rod could provide. He evidently had them in mind when, in his maturity, he wrote of his boyhood: "He was full of all sorts of pranks and capers, and there were plenty of people in the little town ready to declare that

[24]*Ibid.*
[25]Atlanta *Journal*, October 23, 1927.
[26]Atlanta *Constitution*, August 3, 1886.

he could come to some bad end if he were not more frequently dosed with what the old folks used to call hickory oil." [27]

The pastoral serenity of Eatonton in the 1850's was rarely disturbed by any unusual happenings, but when stated sessions of the court were held, the little town would come to life with activities both within the courthouse and on its surrounding square. Under the shade of the large trees, groups of citizens from all sections of Putnam County discussed the topics of the times. Lawyers gathered on the hotel verandas during the court's recesses and swapped stories of their experiences, especially those which had occurred in the rural settlements, and there was nothing to prevent young Joe Harris from mingling with the crowd.

What he observed was another cross section of middle Georgia life during the last decade before the Civil War: planters accompanied by slaves who looked after their masters' horses and carriages, small farmers of the middle class, plain folk from the outlying districts, lawyers, casual spectators attracted to the scene, perhaps a slave speculator. Joe was too young to have understood the meaning of any talk which he may have heard about politics, abolitionists' attacks on slavery, and threats of secession, or to have joined in the robust laughter which the humorous and earthy anecdotes of the lawyers produced. But the animated scene made an unforgettable impression upon him. Years later he would turn his recollections into stories of antebellum plantation society with Eatonton and Putnam County as their locale.

However seriously the older people of Eatonton may have been concerned over the mounting tension between the South and the North, Joe and his companions were as yet unaware of any portents of change. In their own small world they were more intent upon today's carefree pleasures than upon any forebodings of tomorrow's probable troubles.

"They were children," Harris wrote from the vantage point of his maturity, "when the demoralization of war was about to begin—when it was already casting its long shadow before it—and when their elders were discussing as hard as ever they could the question of State Rights, the true interpretation of the Constitution, squatter

[27]Harris, *On the Plantation*, 6, 7.

sovereignty, the right of secession—every question, in short, except the one at issue."[28]

It would be a mistake, however, to conclude that the boy confined his interests to humorous capers and pranks. He early developed a fondness for reading those books and newspapers which were in the range of his comprehension. He never made a reference to having read any of the volumes which were in the library attached to the academies, but his interest was stimulated through the kindness of one of the lawyers in town, a Mr. Deomatari, whom Harris described as a political refugee from his native Greece. On discovering that Joe liked to read, he let him ransack the boxes of books which he had brought with him. "Many of the volumes," Harris recalled, "were in strange tongues, but among them were some quaint old English books, and these the lad relished beyond measure."[29]

Newspapers were more easily accessible to him than books, and he formed the habit of reading them early in his career. In addition to those which the Leverette family gave his mother, there were others which he read in the Eatonton post office. As a convenience to the local citizens, postmaster S. S. Prudden placed the newspapers to which they subscribed on a shelf outside the wire enclosure which separated the post office area from the rest of the general merchandise store in which it was located. There was an old, broken-down sofa in the store, and young Joe curled up on it from day to day to read such papers as he could lay his hands upon.[30]

No newspaper was being published in Eatonton at the time, but among those which postmaster Prudden placed on the shelf were the *Southern Recorder* and the *Southern Federal Union*, both of which were published every Tuesday in Milledgeville, the state capital, some twenty miles away. Although they featured news happenings of statewide and national importance, they also carried local items of current interest to their readers in Baldwin, Putnam, and other contiguous counties. Both of these papers published announcements in their issues of March 11, 1862, that J. A. Turner, Esquire, had begun the

[28]Joel Chandler Harris, *Gabriel Tolliver* (New York: McClure, Phillips and Company, 1903) 13.
[29]Harris, *On the Plantation*, 6. Harris did not name any specific author, but Sir Thomas Browne was one of his favorites.
[30]*Ibid.*, 2, 3.

publication of *The Countryman*, on his plantation nine miles from Eatonton. These items aroused Harris' interest, for he knew Turner through his patronage of his mother's tailoring shop, and he waited impatiently to see a copy. When one came to the Eatonton post office he read it, he said, from "beginning to end, advertisements and all, and he thought it was the most entertaining little paper he had ever seen." [31] Among the advertisements the boy read was the following one which appeared in an inconspicuous place on page four: "Wanted: An active, intelligent white boy, 14 or 15 years of age to learn the printer's trade."

This brief advertisement, considered in the light of the impact which it made on Harris at the time, proved to be a decisive factor in determining his life's career. In the previous December, 1861, he had become thirteen years of age, and it was time, as he later expressed it, for him "to be up and doing." But what kind of profitable employment could a boy of his age find in the little town? Moreover, he was then also caught up in the sobering effect which the war was having upon the lives of its people. The enthusiasm with which they had greeted the smashing victory of the Confederates over the Federals in the battle of Bull Run and the hope which it had inspired of a quick end of the war had given way to some doubts about the ultimate success of the Southern cause.

The seriousness which was apparent among all the people in the town brought the boy to a realization that playtime should be over for him, and he seized the opportunity to learn the printer's trade which the advertisement in *The Countryman* offered. Without delay or consultation with anyone, he borrowed a pen and some paper from postmaster Prudden and wrote Turner that he would like to work for him as an apprentice.[32] "I wrote the editor, whom I knew well," Harris said in recalling the details of his first employment, "and the next time he came to town he sought me out, asked me if I had written the letter with my own hand, and in three words the bargain was concluded." [33] He then put his few personal possessions in his small, paperbound trunk, and when Turner called for him on his way to his Turnwold plantation, the thirteen-year-old boy bade his mother

[31]*Ibid.*, 14.
[32]John W. Adams of Eatonton told the writer in a personal interview that he was present in the post office when Harris wrote the letter.
[33]Atlanta *Daily News*, October 10, 1900.

and grandmother good-bye, and "set forth on what turned out to be the most important journey of his life." [34]

Harris was never again to make Eatonton his home, except for two brief intervals when he was unemployed, but he would always remember the pleasing impression which the physical features of the town of his boyhood had made upon him. Harris' genius, like that of Mark Twain, was nostalgic, and in retrospect he remembered the town's virtues rather than its faults. Forty years after he had left for Turner's plantation, he wrote the following poetic-prose description of Eatonton:

You go down to the old town from the city, and you say to yourself and your friends that you are enjoying the delights of the country. You visit it from the plantations and you feel that you are breathing the atmosphere that should be found in the social life of a large, refined, and perfectly homogeneous community. But whether you go from the city, or from the plantations, you are inevitably impressed with a sense of the attractiveness of the place; you fall under the spell of the old town—it was old even in the old times of the sixties. And yet if you were called upon to define the nature of the spell, what could you say? What name could you give to the transient beauty that hovers about and around the place, when the fresh green leaves of the great trees are fluttering in the cool wind and everything is touched and illumed by the tender colors of spring? Under what heading in the catalogue of things would you place the vivid richness which animates the town and the landscape all around when summer is at its height? And how could you describe the harmony that time has brought about between the fine old houses and the setting in which they are grouped? [35]

He would also remember the cultural currents which ran beneath the surface of the town's outward repose, a quality of its life which casual visitors from a more aggressive and competitive society might easily mistake for inertia and indifference to progress. In the fall of 1880 Bill Arp, who was then contributing feature articles to the Atlanta *Constitution* at the same time that Harris was its associate editor, made a brief visit to Eatonton. He was not favorably impressed by what he had seen, and on his return he called by Harris'

[34]Harris, *On the Plantation*, 14.
[35]Harris, *Gabriel Tolliver*, 36, 37.

editorial office and in the course of their conversation he remarked with a sigh that the people of Eatonton had plenty of time.

Bill Arp made his observation somewhat in jest, but Harris was not blind to its serious implications, and it led him to write an editorial in which he emphasized that Eatonton's tranquil manner of life was not because of indolence on the part of its people but of the cultural refinements which they had gradually evolved. It was true, he wrote, that the people there did have plenty of time, that it had been so in the beginning and would be so in the end. "It was not the fruit of indolence," he insisted, "but of system; the fruit of the methods of patience and steadiness. . . . The early settlers of the town gave to their children a discipline of industry and economy as rigid and severe as the Puritans, but it was tempered by a refinement as genial and as sunny as favorable fortune could make it. The tree of hospitality planted by the Bledsoes, the Branhams, the Shorters, the Flournoys, the Adamses, and the Reids, has grown and spread until the whole community moves in its shadow." He emphasized that Eatonton was a town of culture and refinement before Marthasville (later renamed Atlanta) had been founded, that there was no social development without repose, that the society of cities was processional, merely a series of shows, and that Eatonton still held "in fee simple that rare elegance of method and demeanor, which we hastily call refinement, but which is inherited rather than acquired." He wished that Bill Arp had remained in Eatonton long enough to have gone fox hunting with Harvey Dennis, for if he had done so, Harris said, he would not have spoken of Eatonton with a sigh.[36]

Harris found in the Eatonton of his boyhood a congenial atmosphere in which to give expression to his own innate love of boyish pranks and amusing capers. In retrospect, however, he could see influences of a far deeper import which that culture had contributed to his well-being. He could trace his love of nature to the serene beauty of the town's landscape and surrounding fields and woods. He could see, too, that integrity of character was a truer standard by which to judge an individual's worth than by his material wealth, that neighborly kindness in a democratic society was a finer heritage than false pride in an aristocratic family background, and that Christian charity toward the poor and the unfortunate was a virtue that gave hope and

[36]Atlanta *Constitution*, November 21, 1880.

purpose to life. When he lived in the post-Civil War environment of Atlanta and felt the impact of the forces that were changing the South from its agrarian simplicities to the complexities and stresses of modern industrialization, he turned in spirit to the pastoral scenes of his youth and to the cultural refinements which had characterized its people.

At Turnwold he would enlarge the range of his experiences through his initiation into the lore of Southern plantation life and acquire a knowledge of it that would eventually enable him to become its foremost literary historian.

3

TURNWOLD PLANTATION

In all probability, Harris made the journey which he called the most important in his life about the middle of March, 1862, for the advertisement for a boy to learn the printer's trade did not appear in *The Countryman* after the issue of March 11. Although the distance from Eatonton to Turner's Putnam County plantation was only nine miles, he found there a world which was entirely different from the village environment to which he had been accustomed. He was to live on this plantation during four of the most eventful years in the history of the South, 1862 to 1866, and the intimate knowledge of plantation life which he acquired while there proved to be as valuable for him in his literary career as did the four years, 1857 to 1861, for Mark Twain when he was a pilot on the Mississippi River. Out of the memories of their personal experiences, they preserved for future generations two of the most colorful eras in American culture, both of which were ended by the Civil War.

While he was at Turnwold, Harris learned far more than the printer's trade, and therein lay the significance of that journey, not only for Harris himself but also through him for literature in the South during the post-Civil War era. Therefore, in order to have a proper perspective for an evaluation of Harris' contribution to America's literature, it is essential to point out some of the positive and negative influences which were brought to bear upon him during the four years he was to spend at Turnwold. This chapter, then, will deal with some of the personality traits of Joseph Addison Turner as they embodied for Harris the individuality of character which was an important feature of his middle Georgia heritage, with Turner's concept of a Southern planter, and with plantation life as Harris actually came in contact with it. The next chapter will be concerned with Turner's singular devotion to literature for its own sake, with his overmastering ambition to become a distinguished

Southern author, and with the encouragement he gave his young compositor to develop his talent for writing. It will also discuss the effect which Turner's crusade for a strong regional literature had upon the youthful literary aspirant.

Turner was only thirty-five years of age when he began publication of *The Countryman* on his plantation and employed young Joe Harris as a compositor, or printer's devil. A wide variety of interests, however, had already claimed the attention of his restless and ambitious mind. Before he founded *The Countryman* he had taught school, engaged in the practice of law, published at his own expense in the interest of Southern literature three volumes of romantic poetry and four short-lived literary magazines, and actively engaged in politics, all in his search of a congenial vocation. When Harris became directly associated with him in 1862, Turner had become widely known throughout middle Georgia as a lawyer-planter with scholarly interests. There were those who regarded his political activities as a matter of course for a lawyer, but there were others who looked upon him as an eccentric because he wrote poetry and followed literature rather than law as a profession.

Turner maintained an independent stand on the current issues of his day. No one ever came in contact with him without being either favorably or unfavorably influenced by him, for he was never reticent or restrained in the expression of his views. Harris had not been closely associated with any mature man before he went to Turnwold, and Turner made a profound impression upon him. He once described him as a man "whose strong individualism was the delight of his friends and the despair of his enemies." [1] Friend and foe alike, however, respected his keen and able mind, the integrity of his character, and the honesty of his convictions. He was known to be a good friend to have at court, for he could turn biting satire against those whose principles he opposed.

Turner was fully aware that his independent stand on any important issue whether religious or political had made him a controversial figure, but his awareness neither disturbed him nor diverted him from following a course of action which he believed was right, even though in doing so he knew he might be unpopular. "I have been accused of eccentricities and oddities peculiar to myself," he wrote

[1] Atlanta *Daily News*, October 10, 1900.

as early as his twenty-first year. "The fact is I dislike to do as anyone else has ever done. If there is any possibility of taking any other
road than that taken by the multitude, that path I am certain to
follow." [2] It must be said of him, however, that he acted from conviction, not from a chance whim of the moment or from a mere
desire to be different.

An early manifestation of his individualism in religion occurred
when he withdrew his membership from the Philadelphia Methodist
Church, of which his father and mother were devout members,
strictly orthodox in their beliefs. In a review of his early religious
experience he stated that in his thirteenth year he was "seized with
a fit of religious excitement" under the preaching of Reverend John
Duncan whose efforts were directed, he said, toward arousing the
emotions of his hearers. But in less than ten days after the emotional
excitement had died down he grew tired of the church and ashamed
of himself for what he then considered and still conscientiously believed to have been the folly of fanaticism.[3] Although he withdrew
his membership from the Philadelphia church, he continued to attend
its services and to teach a Bible class there until, as he put it, "Lincoln's War" disrupted it.

In the years that followed, he never recovered from his aversion
to revivalist preaching such as prevailed in the days of the circuit
rider, nor did he ever again identify himself with any religious body.
Harris also attended the services of the Philadelphia church with
Turner's family and he recalled that he had once heard Turner himself give a sermon from its pulpit and said that it was a good one.[4]

In order that the readers of *The Countryman* might clearly understand his attitude toward the orthodox religious beliefs commonly
held by middle Georgians, Turner published the following militant
statement of his position: "In religion, too, let everybody understand
that *The Countryman* is what self-styled 'orthodoxy' calls 'heterodox': and not only is it 'heterodox,' but it glories in its 'heterodoxy'—

[2]*Turner's Monthly* (February 1848), 28. The February number of *Turner's
Monthly* is available in the Atlanta Historical Society, Atlanta, Georgia.

[3]Turner, "Notes of Autobiography at Twenty-three," MS. Journal. Turner's
manuscript journals were in the possession of John DeJarnette Turner when
the author had access to them. They are now held by his daughter. A micro-
film copy is available in the Joel Chandler Harris Memorial Collection at Emory
University, Atlanta, Georgia.

[4]Atlanta *Daily News*, October 10, 1900.

which it understands to mean progress in religion, civilization, and refinement—in short, freedom from the cruel dogmas of so-called 'orthodoxy'—those dogmas whose tendency, it believes, is to degrade the Almighty in the eyes of his creatures, and to make men cruel, vindictive, and revengeful." [5]

When the Macon *Index* took him to task for his heterodox beliefs and intimated that he was a Hardshell (Primitive Baptist), he published the following bristling reply: "You may call him Hardshell, heretic, knave, scoundrel, infidel, atheist, or devil! If he can only succeed in doing what is right, that is all he cares for." [6] In the same issue of *The Countryman* he expressed what was for him a moderately charitable opinion of the Baptists, whom he had once held to be "contracted, ignorant, and bigoted," [7] by saying that although he differed with them in their views on baptism and communion he admired "their form of church government, their love of liberty and independence, and their firm and unyielding adherence to what they believed to be principle." [8]

It is highly probable that Harris set these statements of Turner into type. The effect which they may have had upon him is, of course, conjectural. Although he had attended the Methodist church in Eatonton, he did not become one of its members, and, in fact, he never subscribed to the creed of any one church until a short time before his death.

Turner also pursued an independent course in politics. At a time when the nation was becoming increasingly divided over the slavery issue, he was a Union Democrat and opposed secession. In taking this position he incurred the enmity of the extremists in Georgia who as early as 1851 were clamoring for a break with the Union. On recalling the hostility toward him which his opposition had aroused, he wrote in his journal on February 14, 1865: "We can well remember that in the year of 1851, we could hardly walk the streets of Eatonton without insult because we were a Union man." The enmity, however, did not change his position. In 1856 he wrote to Miller, Orton, and Mulligan, New York publishers whom he was endeavoring to interest in publishing one of his manuscripts. He emphasized that he was not identified with the Southern extremists in the heated debate over slavery: "I

[5]*The Countryman*, June 24, 1862.
[6]*Ibid.*, July 12, 1862.
[7]Turner MS. Journal, August 25, 1850.
[8]*The Countryman*, July 12, 1862.

am not now, and never have been denominated a fire-eater, nullifier, disunionist, or secessionist. I have stood politically arrayed against these. . . . I am now and always have been a Union man."

In the historic 1858–60 sessions of the Georgia legislature, to which he had been elected in 1857 on an independent platform to represent Putnam County in the senate, he sponsored a resolution for the appointment of a joint commission of Northern and Southern representatives to work out a peaceable dissolution of the Union, but the time had passed when the voice of moderation or conciliation had a chance to be heard, much less to prevail. "I felt," he later wrote with reference to the overwhelming secessionist spirit which dominated the session, "that an attempt to stem the tide of popular fury roused by [Robert] Toombs and Tom Cobb, would be like tossing a feather before the whirlwind." [9] It was no surprise, therefore, when on January 19, 1861, the convention which Governor Joseph Emerson Brown had called to meet at the capitol in Milledgeville to consider the course which Georgia should take voted 218 to 89 to secede from the Union.

Whatever the ultimate consequences might be, Georgia had committed itself to a course and a cause from which there could be no turning back. Turner, who had openly and consistently opposed secession, never wavered in his loyalty to the Confederacy after the war began in April. His brother William volunteered for active service and he himself attempted to do so, but an attack of necrosis in his right thighbone when he was seven years old had left him permanently lame and disqualified him for army duty. Also, his friends persuaded him that he could be more useful at home. During the war he manufactured hats at Turnwold for the Confederate army and made patriotic addresses. And by means of his editorials in The Countryman he urged the farmers to grow food for the army and heartened the morale of the folks at home by his faith in the courage of the Confederate soldiers and in their ultimate victory.

However, Turner was under no illusion as to the real reason, as he saw it, why the South was waging war. He quite frankly declared that the first object of the war for the South was to preserve the institution of slavery, though it was fashionable, he said, to deny it and to insist that the fighting was for independence. "We wished to have independence," he stated without any hedging or apology,

[9] The Countryman, February 13, 1866.

"to govern ourselves because we desired to perpetuate the institution of slavery, and we desired to perpetuate that because we regarded it as the foundation of our social and industrial system, and the source of our prosperity. . . . Had secession depended on our vote alone, there would have been none of it. As it is, however, we stand by the act, and are willing to share all the responsibilities." [10]

In standing by the act, Turner used *The Countryman* to support the Confederacy vigorously and wholeheartedly and to glorify the War for Southern Independence. As a compositor on *The Countryman*, Joe Harris set Turner's fervently patriotic articles in type. His family had owned no slaves and he himself was too young to understand the social, economic, political, and moral issues involved in the war or to evaluate the effect which a defeat for the Confederacy would have on the plantation civilization. However, Turner's spirited support of whatever was Southern and his equally spirited antagonism to whatever was Northern was contagious, and, as might have been expected from Harris' close proximity to Turner during the war years, he became thoroughly imbued with Turner's highly partisan and sectional viewpoints, especially in his preference for Southern over Northern authors.

Turner also possessed a middle Georgian's fondness for humor. He wrote in his *Autobiography* that he was compelled by his nature to be an inveterate joker. "If I can see a chance to put in a little fun," he said, "I will lay every other consideration aside, and indulge my humor, repartee, or joke, even at the risk of offending my best friend." If, however, anyone took offense at his wit or repartee, Turner was sure to ask his forgiveness, for he insisted that he intended no malice or sting in his humor. [11]

Although Turner continued the tradition established by Harris' predecessors for their humorous writings, his own particular brand of humor differed from theirs in that it consisted of quick repartee, irony, and satire rather than of the antics and pranks of rustic characters. Consequently, his humor more nearly resembled that of his English namesake Joseph Addison than that which appeared in Longstreet's *Georgia Scenes* or in Thompson's *Major Jones's Courtship*. In keeping with this trait of his personality, he liberally in-

[10]*Ibid.*, January 31, 1865.
[11]*Ibid.*, February 13, 1866.

serted puns, witticisms, and humorous anecdotes in *The Countryman* to relieve, he said, the tensions of the people from the de-
pressing atmosphere of the war, but in reality they were a kind of
safety valve for the mercurial temperament of Turner himself. It
would be some years before Harris comprehended the significance
of Turner's editorials on religion, politics, and the war, but the
witty puns and funny anecdotes made an immediate appeal to him
because of his own humorous nature.

Before Harris went to Turnwold he had never known anyone
like Turner. Fresh from his play in the streets of Eatonton and its
environs, he came to look upon the editor of *The Countryman*
as a man of learning, of scholarly attainments through the books
which he had published, and as an aggressive champion of the
South's ideals and institutions in its war against the North. Moreover,
Turner's strong individualism gave the youth an insight into that particular characteristic which had prevailed in the pioneer period of
middle Georgia and which still existed in the society of his own day.

Also, through his observations of Turner in the role of master of
Turnwold and through his own contacts with plantation life, Harris
acquired his knowledge of the plantation mores which he was to depict
in his stories of that era. Turner held the idealistic concept that the
Southern planter was the noblest type of man who ever lived. "The
Southern planter," he wrote only two years before Harris came under
his direct influence, "in many respects bears a considerable resemblance
to the ancient English baron, surrounded by his liege subjects, all dependent on him for whatever they have of happiness or unhappi-
ness." [12] In 1850 Turner had married Louisa Dennis, daughter of the
wealthy Michael Dennis of Eatonton, and the following year had purchased for $9,910 the thousand-acre William Alexander plantation
which adjoined the Turner family home place.[13] Early in 1852 he and
Mrs. Turner occupied their new home. At first he gave it the name of
Merry-Dale but later changed it to Turnwold. Happily married and the
master of his own plantation, he proposed to settle down to enjoy the
life of a country squire and, in keeping with his twofold ideal of the
life of a Southern planter, "to cultivate corn, cotton, and literature."
As he contemplated his situation in 1852, every prospect pleased him
and only the abolitionists were vile.

[12]*The Plantation* (March, 1860), 150.
[13]Turner MS. Journal.

The house itself was as old as the one which his grandfather, Joseph Turner, Jr., had purchased from Edmund Lane in 1808, after he and his family had moved to Putnam County from Dinwiddie County, Virginia, in 1793 and in which Joseph Addison had been born.[14] Turner wrote in his journal that at first the grounds surrounding it were in a rundown condition, but to make them more attractive for his children he had laid out walks and gardens, planted flowers and shrubbery, and set out trees on both sides of the driveway which led to the public road. When Harris arrived there in 1862, the place presented an attractive appearance. The house had two stories, but, situated in an open space on a slight elevation, it was less imposing than the nearby Turner family residence in its natural setting in a grove of noble old trees which gave it an air of dignity and repose. On the left of the hallway as one entered from the front there was a large family room in which Turner wrote, kept his books and the numerous magazines to which he subscribed, and selected the material which he approved for printing in *The Countryman.* Across the hall there were two smaller connecting rooms, in the second of which there was a concealed stairway leading to the upper story which had the same arrangement as the lower. Behind the "big house," but connected with it by a passageway, was the kitchen, and in the backyard there was a storehouse where supplies for the family and the slaves were kept. The home was comfortable and sufficiently large for the Turner family, but Harris saw nothing about it, either without or within, to give him the impression that it was a lordly mansion, for it had no massive white columns, no broad porch, no overhanging balcony, no winding stairway, and no elaborate furnishings. Although it fell far short of what Turner would have made of it if his wealth had permitted, he became very much attached to it, for it symbolized to him the home of a literate and independent Southern planter who had leisure to indulge in his literary interests, to engage in gentlemanly field sports, and to view with satisfaction his fields of corn and cotton.

The home dominated the rest of the compact little domain over which Turner presided. On its western side were the cabins for his slaves and hired hands, and he had converted the cabin which was

[14]Mrs. Dennis Turner, Milledgeville, Ga., from the Turner family records in her possession.

nearest his home into a printshop for *The Countryman*. Behind
the house there was a large spring, which became the setting for
a number of Harris' stories. Beyond this, there was a tannery and
the building in which Turner manufactured hats for the Confederate army from the fur-bearing animals which abounded in the
swamps and fields. To the east there was an open field which extended to the woods where his father's home was located. Facing
his home was Phoenix Academy, the successor of Union Academy,
in which Turner himself had once taught.[15] This environment was
entirely new to Harris, but he soon adapted himself to it and
entered into the routine of plantation activities with the same degree of zest that had characterized his boyish adventures in Eatonton. No phase of plantation life escaped his observant eye.

From the writings of both Turner and Harris it is evident that
Turner conducted his plantation as a benevolent master. He put
into effect the same kind of amicable master-slave relationship
which he described as having existed on his father's plantation when
he himself was a boy. In writing of that relationship he said he
remembered with what love and veneration he used to regard
some of his father's gray-headed Negroes who dandled "Young
Master" upon their knee and spoke words of kindness which thrilled
through his heart as no other words ever did save those spoken by
his beloved parents.[16] As he grew older, the sons of his father's
slaves were his companions in play, hunting, and fishing, and in
a mood of homesickness when he was a student at Emory College
he wrote in his journal of the "true friendship as it exists between
the white and the black children who have been reared together." [17]

When Turner became a master in his own right, he manifested a humanitarian concern for the welfare of his slaves. He once refused to
re-employ an overseer whom he thought had been too hard on the
field hands. "Upon the whole," he wrote in his journal, "he has made
me a pretty good manager, and has always tried to please me. He has
sometimes been rougher with the negroes than I like; but he always

[15]The original home in which Turner was born is still standing (1966),
but it is in a dilapidated condition. However, Turner's own home has been
renovated, and it now appears more like a planter's country home than it
did when Harris lived at Turnwold.

[16]*The Plantation* (March, 1860), 150.

[17]Turner MS. Journal, September 10, 1845.

changed his course when I told him to do so." [18] Confident of the loyalty of his slaves, he did not impose any strict discipline upon them,[19] nor did he permit the dreaded patrollers to search their quarters for slaves who had run away from other masters.[20] As a result of the considerate treatment of his own slaves, he had no cause to fear any uprising on their part toward him during the war,[21] nor did any occur.

Furthermore, Turner made it possible for his slaves to earn a measure of economic independence. He allotted to those who had the initiative to earn money of their own a certain number of acres on which they could grow such crops as they pleased, and at harvest-time he paid them in cash the market price for what their labor had produced. In his reminiscences of his Turnwold days, Harris stated that some of the Negroes had grown as much as two bales of cotton on the land allotted to them and that others had made good crops of corn, both of which Turner bought from them. In addition, so Harris wrote, he encouraged them to make baskets, horse collars, brooms, foot mats, walking canes, axe handles, and other items from the materials which the plantation afforded. At the Christmas season he loaded on a wagon and took to Eatonton whatever they had made, and turned over to the individual makers the proceeds from the sale of their articles.[22]

Neither was life on the Turnwold plantation as Harris observed it all labor and toil in the fields for the slaves. He described the Christmas season as the happiest time of the year for them. No work was done on Christmas Day. The Negroes, dressed in their best clothes, gathered in the yard in the rear of the "big house" early in the morning, and while they waited for their master and mistress to make their appearance, they frolicked in holiday mood and joined with Big Sam as their leader in the singing of plantation songs. "No musical director," Harris wrote in recalling the scene, "ever had a more melodious chorus than that which followed the leadership of Big Sam. It was not a trained chorus, to be sure, but the melody which it gave to the winds of the morning

[18]*Ibid.*, December 7, 1853.
[19]Atlanta *Constitution*, August 8, 1885.
[20]Harris, *On the Plantation*, 49, 50.
[21]*Ibid.*, 50.
[22]*Ibid.*, 121.

was freighted with a quality indescribably touching and tender."
When the Turners appeared, the Negroes greeted them with ex-
pectant shouts of "Chris'mas gif!" Turner then gave the storehouse
key to Harbert, his right-hand man among his slaves and directed
him to distribute gifts. "For each of the older ones," Harris recalled, "there was a stiff dram apiece, and for all, both old and
young, there was a present of some kind. The presents were of a
substantial character, too." It was a happy time, he said, in spite of
the war and he himself was as happy as any of the rest.[23]

The number of slaves Turner owned has been stated to have been
as many as 125, but from the record which he kept in his journal
it is clear that he never at any time owned more than 25 and that
was at the end of the war when all of his plantation enterprises
were at the height of their operation.[24]

In keeping with the impression given by some antebellum writers
of romantic fiction, it would be pleasant to believe that plantation
life at Turnwold was in the grand manner of Southern aristocracy.
But such was not the case. It is true that his home was above the
average in the Turnwold community in size and appearance and
that there was a sufficient number of yard and house servants to
perform the conventional duties involved in the daily routine of a
planter's home and enough laborers to cultivate his fields of corn
and cotton advantageously. However, despite Turner's idealistic concept of the life of a Southern planter, the kind of plantation life
which Harris saw at Turnwold was not wholly romantic.

One of the principal reasons why Turner was unable to translate
his grandiose dream into actual achievement was that he was con-
stantly harrassed by debt. In November, 1858, he wrote in his journal
that he was thinking of borrowing $15,000, for which he said he
could give a mortgage on his land and his twelve slaves, whose
combined worth he estimated to be between $25,000 and $50,000.
In January, 1860, he wrote that he was so hard pressed by his
debts that the only recourse open to him was to sell his slaves, but
somehow he managed to retain them.

In July, 1861, only four months after the war had begun, he
summarized his financial condition in a journal entry as follows:

[23]*Ibid.*, 118–21.
[24]"Turner MS. Journal, July (no day stated), 1865.

"Am in debt probably as much as my property is worth, and probably more, during these war years, as property has declined in value." When the war ended in 1865, the total number of persons, including his own family, his slaves and hired hands, and those employed in operating his auxiliary enterprises, who were dependent upon him for support could not have been less than fifty. For a year after his slaves had been freed, he unsuccessfully endeavored to operate his plantation by contract labor, and by the summer of 1866 he was completely insolvent.

Until the Federal soldiers invaded Turnwold in the fall of 1864, life on the plantation ran evenly and peacefully from day to day. Since *The Countryman* was issued once a week, Harris' duties as a compositor required only a portion of his time, and he used his leisure to explore various phases of his plantation surroundings. He talked with old George, one of Turner's hired hands then in his late seventies, as he mended shoes in his cabin, made baskets, and did other odd jobs. He became acquainted with the house and yard servants, listened to their play, work, and religious songs and heard them speak the language which was peculiar to them. In the evenings he read the books Turner gave him from his library, and sometimes alone or with some of Turner's children he went to Harbert's cabin, where he and the children were entertained by Aunt Crissy, fat, jolly, talkative, and superstitious, who told them legendary stories of her race.[25]

At other times he went rabbit hunting as he had in Eatonton, and at Turnwold the sport was not only exciting but profitable since Turner paid him twenty-five cents a dozen for the skins and used the fur to make hats.[26] For the most part, Harris' associates at Turnwold were men, and they frequently took him into the recesses of the swamps in their search for coons and other fur-bearing animals. On occasion, they let him accompany them on a fox hunt. He never forgot the thrill of hearing the sound of the horn and the yelps of the dogs as they picked up the trail of the elusive fox nor the mounting excitement of dogs and hunters as the capture became imminent. "Time and the world must have stood still," he afterwards wrote as he recalled the experience, "while those rare spirits

[25]Harris, *On the Plantation*, 104, 105.
[26]*Ibid.*, 51.

rode through the frosty weather, their hounds footing it across the hills, or in full cry after old red fresh from the Turner old fields." [27]

In his rambles over the countryside and in the woods Harris occasionally met with runaway slaves from other plantations, and through conversation with them he learned of the harsh and cruel side of plantation life. There were also times when in his boyish curiosity he went along with the patrollers and their trained track dogs who were following runaways. In retrospect, however, he wrote that "his curiosity with regard to them was soon satisfied, and he was better contented when he was spending his evenings at home with his books, or in listening to the wonderful tales that Mr. Snelson [the foreman of *The Countryman*] told him." [28]

It was not until the last week in November, 1864, that Turnwold felt the impact of actual warfare for the first time. In July, Sherman had laid seige to Atlanta. After he had captured and destroyed that strategic city, he struck out on his relentless and devastating march to the Georgia coast. A detachment of his troops under the command of General Henry Slocum invaded the Turnwold community and, pillaging and burning at will, reduced the once peaceful and prosperous community to shambles. During their occupation some of the Federal troops entered Turner's home, appropriated some of its contents, caused consternation among the Negroes, and completely disrupted the orderly routine of the plantation activities. Although many other homes in the vicinity were ransacked and burned, neither Turner's home nor any one of the buildings which housed his various enterprises was burned. The office of *The Countryman*, its press, type, and supplies were left intact. His relatively light losses were attributed by those plantation owners whose property had been either confiscated or destroyed to the fact that he had maintained a sense of humor in dealing with the invaders. Whatever he may have thought, he prudently exercised restraint in the face of humiliating provocation. All that he could do under the circumstances was to watch the tragic scenes that were being enacted before him as an unwilling but necessarily passive spectator.

Young Joe Harris, then nearing his sixteenth birthday, shared in the general excitement. One day he was in the building where the hats

[27]Atlanta *Constitution*, September 7, 1890.
[28]Harris, *On the Plantation*, 50.

for the Confederate army had been stored before their delivery when a German trooper with the Federals became angry with him because Harris refused to let him take as many of the hats as he could load on his horse. In his anger, the soldier was in the act of setting fire to the building when a Federal officer entered and gave the irate trooper a paddling with the flat of his sword. In recalling the incident some years later, Harris said that the scene had been as humorous to him then as a circus performance.[29]

In the belief that all of the Federal troops had resumed their march after they had occupied Turnwold and nearby plantations for ten days, Harris walked aimlessly one day down the road which led to Milledgeville and stopped to rest on a rail fence which ran alongside the road. Idly musing on the confusion which he had witnessed during the invasion, he was brought out of his reverie by the appearance of a contingent of the departing troops. As they slogged by his reviewing stand in ankle-deep mud on the misty, cold November day, they made him the target of their jests.

> Jump down, Johnny, and let me kiss you good-by!
>
> He's a bushwacker, boys. If he bats his eyes,
> I'm goin' to dodge!
>
> If there was another one of 'em a-settin' on the fence,
> on t'other side, I'd say we was surrounded!
>
> Hello, Johnny! Where's your parasol! [30]

The experience had a disenchanting effect upon the boy. Since March, 1862, he had been setting in type Turner's brave editorials about the impregnability of the South. The excerpts which Turner had reprinted in *The Countryman* from other Southern papers had confirmed his impression that the War for Independence on the part of the South was a glorious cause endowed with all the elements of high romance. He was, therefore, not prepared for the grim reality of war which he had witnessed. Instead of streaming banners, martial music, and the triumphant shouts of Confederate victors, here were Northern soldiers plodding by him in disorderly fashion on a muddy road and making him the object of their jibes as he sat alone atop a

[29]*Ibid.*, 226, 227.
[30]*Ibid.*, 229.

rail fence. What glory could be attached to the smoldering ruins of burned homes, plundered storehouses, a countryside laid waste, and a people left stunned and desolate by invading Federal soldiers? How could what he had seen actually be real?

The experience made a lasting impression upon Harris, one that was later on to color the stories which he would write about the war era. The scene which he had witnessed as a boy was still vivid in his memory in 1892, and he wrote of it as follows: "That the Federal army should be plunging through that peaceful region after all that he had seen in the newspapers about Confederate victories, seemed to him to be an impossibility. The voices of the men, and their laughter, sounded vague and insubstantial. It was surely a dream that had stripped war of its glittering trappings and its flying banners. It was surely the distortion of a dream that tacked on to this procession of armed men, droves of cows, horses, and mules, and wagon loads of bateaux." [31]

After all the soldiers had passed, Harris walked across a field toward Turnwold and on his way he saw an old Negro woman shivering in a fence corner in the cold November air. He noticed that near her there was an old Negro man lying on the ground. In reply to his question as to who he was she told him that it was her old man. "What is the matter with him?" he asked her. "He dead, suh! But, bless God, he died free." [32]

Both experiences had put him in a frame of mind to realize that the Turnwold plantation would never be the same again. There was a strange stillness in the Negro quarters. Harbert and some of the slaves whose work had kept them closely associated with their master and mistress had remained, even though Turner had told all of them they were free, but some of the others had gone away with the Federal troops. [33]

Although Joe was too young at the time to have comprehended the historical significance of the chaotic and revolutionary scenes which he witnessed during the last week in November, 1864, from the vantage point of his mature years he clearly saw that the events of that fateful

---

[31] *Ibid.*, 229, 230.
[32] *Ibid.*, 231. In a footnote which Harris appended to his account of the incident, he stated that it had had many adaptations but that it had occurred just as he had given it.
[33] *Ibid.*, 230.

week had foreshadowed the end of a civilization which had been peculiar to the South. In time, he would relive in memory his various experiences on the Turnwold plantation and make them the source of his most significant literary work.

In the meantime, while Harris was at Turnwold, as if in preparation for the time when he would begin to draw on his memories for these stories, he was to receive the necessary training in the art of developing a competent writing style under Turner's demanding but helpful instruction. In *The Countryman* he had at hand a medium in which he could publish, with Turner's approval, his experimental compositions in various literary forms.

4

PROLOGUE TO A LITERARY CAREER

Harris' purpose in going to Turnwold was to learn how to set type for *The Countryman*. In the long run, however, the cultural influences which Turner brought to bear upon him while he was there proved to be far more significant than any practical instruction he received. Nowhere else in Georgia during the boy's formative years could he have been associated with a man of Turner's wide acquaintance with the standard authors of Greece, Rome, England, and America, nor with one who had persisted through frustration after frustration to realize his ambition to become a distinguished author himself. "Ever since I had a wish," Turner wrote in his thirty-third year, "I have wished to be a writer of articles, the perusal of which would not be confined to a few partial friends, but which would be conned over by everybody that took up the book, or paper, or magazine in which I wrote." [1]

Turner had given up teaching and the full-time practice of the law, with its possibilities of political preferment, to devote his time, energy, and money to the accomplishment of his ambitious wish. In 1847 he published a volume of poems, *Miscellaneous Poems, Original and Translated*, under the name of Frank Kemble, the first of the numerous pseudonyms he employed from time to time. This first venture was a failure, and he himself later referred to the volume as his "first folly" and to the poems as "juvenile productions" which he had written in his teens. In January, 1848, he launched, entirely on his own and at his own expense, a literary magazine called *Turner's Monthly, A Miscellaneous Journal and Review*, in which he appealed to Georgians to support his effort to promote the writing of an indigenous literature by subscribing to his monthly. "We have the talent in our state," he confidently asserted. "All that is wanted is that this talent should be excited to action, and properly developed. This

[1]*The Plantation* (June, 1860), 215.

50

depends upon your willingness to support our enterprise." [2] To his great disappointment the appeal brought an indifferent response, for in the February number he acknowledged only twenty-three paid subscribers, and he was obliged to discontinue *Turner's Monthly* with the March number even though the price of a year's subscription was only $1.50.

Having failed to gain literary recognition through his independent efforts, Turner began to send his manuscripts to established periodicals, and he received enough acceptances that he felt justified in writing in his journal that by the time he was twenty-four he would be known in America and in Europe "as one of the most distinguished writers in Georgia." [3] The *Southern Literary Messenger* published his poem, "All Things Speak of God," in its September, 1848, issue, and *Godey's Lady's Book* carried another of his poems, "My Mocking Bird," in its August, 1849, issue.

In the years from 1848 through 1852, poems, articles, and book reviews by Turner appeared in *De Bow's Review*, the *Southern Literary Messenger*, *Godey's Lady's Book*, and *Peterson's Magazine*.

In his review of Judge Henry R. Jackson's *Tallulah and Other Poems*, which the *Southern Literary Messenger* published in March, 1852, Turner wrote eloquently and enthusiastically, for that Georgia poet had written the kind of literature which he had advocated in his *Turner's Monthly*. He noted with great satisfaction that the poems contained "none of the would-be transcendentalism of the Boston school of Poesy—no seeking to mystify the author's meaning with oddities, quaintness, or affectation of expression, so as to make the ideas seem grand, or to make it appear that there is an idea where there is none." He was aware, he said, that the *North American Review* had not written Jackson a passport to Parnassus, but in his opinion Jackson's poems belonged alongside those of Bryant and Longfellow. [4]

Up to this point in his quest for literary fame, Turner had produced literature that conformed to his idea of belles-lettres and, considering his strong Southern sentiment, he had kept what he had written relatively free from objectionable sectional bias. After 1851,

[2]*Turner's Monthly* (February, 1848), 29.
[3]Turner MS. Journal, July 29, 1849.
[4]*Southern Literary Messenger*, XVIII (March, 1852), 179–84.

however, he became deeply involved in the rising tempo of the
debates over slavery, and his articles became so proslavery and so
anti-Northern that not even *De Bow's Review* or the *Southern Literary Messenger* would accept them, nor would Northern publishing houses agree to bring out his books. Forced to depend upon
local concerns for the publication of his articles, he published in
September, 1853, a magazine, *The Tomahawk*, in which he said he
"wielded his blade for democracy." He issued only one number and,
since it had no subscribers, he solicited the aid of E. J. White of
Milledgeville, Georgia, to help him dispose of the copies. One sentence in his letter to White expressed the attitude which he felt
existed in Georgia toward authorship as a profession: "Really, the
pursuit of letters in Georgia is hardly considered an honorable one,
and I am afraid you will associate me with some newspaper drummer
getting a gentleman by the button and holding on until he subscribed to get rid of the bore." [5]

No discouragement, however, prevented Turner from continuing
his pursuit of letters. In 1857 he succeeded in getting S. H. Goetzel
and Company of Mobile, Alabama, to publish a volume of his poems
which were not political in theme nor partisan in treatment, *The
Discovery of Sir John Franklin and Other Poems*. During 1858 and
1859 he concentrated his literary attention on the writing of *The
Old Plantation*, his *magnum opus* as a poet. He frankly stated in his
preface that his poem was modeled after Goldsmith's *The Deserted
Village*, and he followed his model too closely for the poem to
possess any marked degree of originality. It turned out to be an
idyllic portrayal of life in the old plantation South, based upon the
local history of the Turnwold settlement, its rural people and their
manners, and its pastoral scenery.

He composed the poem when the clouds of sectional strife were
growing darker and more ominous. And he said that it would have
been to his advantage with the critics to have made no mention in
it of Negro slavery, but he justified his inclusion of the divisive
subject by saying that he could no more write a poem depicting
Southern manners, customs, and institutions and leave out this vexed
question than one could attempt to describe the scenery of Switzerland and not mention the Alps. He claimed, however, that he had

[5]Turner MS. Journal, October 9, 1853.

not treated the controversial subject in an offensive manner, and he expressed the hope that his poem might do some good toward extinguishing at least "one spark of animosity between the two *sections*—(unhappy word!)—of my much loved country. . . ." Indeed, except for two relatively brief, emotional passages, one of which denounced a "beardless youth" [William H. Seward] for repaying with hatred the kindness which the patrons of Union Academy had shown him when he had taught there and the other which hotly admonished the Northern abolitionists to cease their interference in the affairs of the South, he did not attack the North. On the other hand, he magnified the idyllic qualities which he identified with the Southern plantation to a degree that obscured its dark realities.[6]

The swiftly developing drama of the North-South conflict over slavery brought Turner out of his concentration on the romantic features of plantation life to a consideration of the imminent threat of its destruction by civil war. Since the South had no periodical whose major objective was to defend slavery, he resolved to establish one of his own in which he would set forth the Southern position and answer the attacks against it by the Northern newspapers and magazines. To that end he made an arrangement with Pudney and Russell of New York to publish for him *The Plantation: A Southern Quarterly Journal.* With his flair for including all areas of knowledge in his literary periodicals, Turner stated in his Prospectus in the initial number in March, 1860, that he would include articles on literature, law, politics, art, religion, and science, but he made it emphatically clear that the special feature of *The Plantation* would be "a defense of Negro slavery—total, unqualified, unreserved—in a moral, social, and political point of view." In his Salutatory he promised that he would blend the literary and the political in such a way as to make his quarterly as readable and as influential as was the *Atlantic* on this side of the ocean and *Blackwood's* on the other. Once again Turner grasped at his elusive dream of literary fame.

The first number was all that Turner promised it would be in its

---

[6]In his note which he prefixed to his original preface when he published the poem in *The Countryman,* October 27–December 15, 1862, Turner stated that on completion of *The Old Plantation* in 1859 he had offered it to Harper's but that they had declined to publish it, probably, he said, because it was so strongly proslavery. In 1945 Henry Prentice Miller edited the poem and the Emory University library reprinted it in its series of *Sources and Reprints.*

inclusiveness. He wrote each of the sixteen articles which made up
its 221 pages. "Thoughts Suggested by John Brown's Raid," the
first of three articles in which he defended slavery and attacked its
opponents, was the most violent and unrestrained. In it he unleashed
his wrath against Emerson for the defense which he had made of
John Brown in his Tremont Temple, Boston, address.

The other pieces consisted of his poems, sketches of famous Georgians, informal essays on nature and various pleasant aspects of old
plantation life, and an Editor's Table. These were free from political
animosities and reflected his earlier concern with a belles-lettres type
of literature. Turner recognized, for instance, the literary potential
inherent in the work and religious songs of the plantation Negroes,
and he inserted one of his own compositions, "Hoe De Cotton," in
his essay "Cotton on the Plantation," but he did so with an apology
for its dialect. It did violence to his conscience, he said, to put into
print anything "so murdering the King's English" as a song written
in Negro dialect. He pleaded, however, in extenuation of his crime,
that these Negro melodies had become rather an institution in the
land and that they were "generally admitted" even by those who
opposed them.[7] In the same article he charged the South's neglect of
literature to its subservience to cotton. "Let us leave such low things
as literature," he wrote in satirical vein, "to Yankee pedagogues and
itinerant booksellers! . . . Give us a literature built upon cotton, and
we will be the most literary people in the world." [8]

In the June, September, and December issues of *The Plantation*,
Turner toned down his articles on slavery and made the magazine's
contents more literary, but Georgia's secession from the Union sealed
off any further contacts by Turner with his New York publishers,
and *The Plantation* became a casualty of the impending war. Born
of sectional political strife and national disunity, the journal reflected
the temper of the Southern mind in 1860 in its impassioned pro-
slavery articles, but in its other features it revealed Turner's sincere
appreciation of literature of proven quality. And it was his supreme
individual effort to promote the cultural development of the South
at a time that was the least propitious for him to succeed in his
laudable endeavor. Even so, Bertram Holland Flanders' study of the

---

[7] *The Plantation* (March, 1860), 138.
[8] *Ibid.*, 152.

magazines which were published in the South before the Civil War evaluates *The Plantation* as "one of the most ambitious journalistic undertakings made by any man in the Old South" and describes Turner as "a cultivated Southerner, well qualified to make a success of such a literary undertaking if he could have had time and the proper backing of those in his section." [9]

When Harris first went to Turnwold in March, 1862, Turner had just started his latest literary venture, that of publishing a weekly newspaper on his plantation. Fortunately for Harris, Turner's life-long devotion to literature, his determination to make a name for himself as a writer, and his ingenuity as an editor, all combined to make *The Countryman* a successful publication. Indeed, it occupies a unique place in the history of American journalism. "In 1862," Turner wrote in his *Autobiography* (1866), "I did what has never been done before—established a newspaper upon a plantation, and called it The Countryman. Of the reputation of that paper, I trust I may be allowed to be a little proud." [10] This modest statement was in reality his gentlemanly way of saying that he was enormously pleased with the success of his unusual venture, for his plantation newspaper had subscribers in every state of the Confederacy, and the editors of other Southern newspapers were unanimous in their praise of it. With the exception of its first and second issues, Harris was a compositor on its staff, and, later, under Turner's supervision he published in it his first paragraphs, essays, poems, and book reviews.

Turner had entertained the idea of establishing a newspaper on his plantation as early as 1857. At that time his literary fortunes were at their lowest ebb because of the fact that no publishers would accept his articles on account of their extreme pro-slavery contents. However, he was known throughout middle Georgia as an able writer on contemporary political issues, and in January, 1857, he received an offer from James G. Gardner of Augusta to become the editor of the Augusta *Constitutionalist*. But Gardner withdrew his offer when Turner stipulated a salary of $3,000 a year. He then proposed that Gardner employ him as the literary editor of the *Con-*

[9]Bertram Holland Flanders, *Early Georgia Magazines* (Athens: University of Georgia Press, 1944), 156.
[10]*The Countryman*, February 13, 1866.

stitutionalist; in that capacity, he said, he could continue to live at Turnwold and write reviews of new books for his newspaper. On second thought, however, he dismissed the idea as one scarcely worth Gardner's serious consideration, and, remembering the lack of support by Georgians for his own literary enterprises, he sadly and resignedly commented: "But I suppose there is no use talking about such a department in a Southern newspaper." He concluded his letter to Gardner by saying that some time during the year he might start a small journal on his plantation to publish his own writings.[11] On January 25 he made an entry in his journal to the same effect: "Am becoming afflicted with the idea of issuing a small journal from this place." At the time, however, he did not enforce his intention by any definite action and the idea lay dormant in his mind for more than five years.

With the beginning of the Civil War in April, 1861, Turner found himself in a state of complete literary isolation at Turnwold. Entries in his journal reveal that he made what was for him a valiant effort to reconcile himself to the enforced idleness of his pen, but not for long. To have some medium to publish his articles which other publishers had rejected and through which he could express his thoughts on the war, he revived his earlier scheme of publishing a journal on his plantation. The difficulties which he had to overcome in carrying out his resolve would have seemed insurmountable to any practical journalist. He had at the time no printing press, no paper, no ink, no type, no typesetters: he was already heavily in debt, money was becoming increasingly scarce, prices were inflationary, and the minds of the people who might possibly subscribe were intent upon the war.

But Turner was not a practical journalist. When some idea that offered a prospect for his literary advancement occurred to him, neither his past failures nor any consideration of future frustrations could stop him from an attempt to realize his purpose. Therefore, he went into action, and by the late fall of 1861 his plans had begun to take definite shape. On December 20 he wrote a letter to S. A. Atkinson of Augusta inquiring where he could buy a foolscap press and explained his unusual request by saying: "I am indulging a quixotic freak to publish a Essayist—not a newspaper—on my

[11]Turner MS. Journal, January (no day stated), 1857.

plantation, to be devoted to—everything generally." [12] On the same day he wrote to R. J. Reagan of Augusta relative to the purchase of supplies and stated why he intended to publish his Essayist on his plantation: "I would not have the newspaper printed away from my supervision, so that I could not read the proof. I would not trust Faust himself to do that." [13]

The press in Augusta proved to be too expensive for him, but he located an old Washington handpress and the necessary supplies in Greensboro. By January 29, 1862, he had moved them to Turnwold, employed John T. Wilson of Madison to supervise the printing for him, and on March 4 the first issue of one hundred copies of *The Countryman* was run off.[14] Its contents were made up of three of his Frank Kemble poems, articles on farming, appeals to support the Confederate army, news items of interest to Putnam County readers, and advertisements of local interest. Among the advertisements was the one which Joe Harris read about the need for a boy to learn the printer's trade.

Having in mind his former failures as an editor, Turner proceeded cautiously with his latest enterprise. In his Prospectus he made no grandiose promise in regard to the scope of *The Countryman*. He simply said that it was a country paper and that it would serve the interests of the country people. With the issue of April 17 he reduced its form to quarto size, introduced more items of a literary nature, and wrote a new and enlarged prospectus in which he said he proposed to model *The Countryman* after Addison's *The Tatler*, Johnson's *The Rambler* and *The Adventurer*, and Goldsmith's *The Bee*. He promised to fill it with essays, poems, sketches, agricultural articles, and choice miscellany, assured his readers there would be nothing in it which was dull, didactic, or prosy, and expressed the hope it would help to relieve their minds of the engrossing topic of war.

The Countryman attracted paid subscribers throughout the Confederacy, and after only three months of its publication Turner had

---

[12]*Ibid.*, December 20, 1861.

[13]*Ibid.*

[14]Turner was known in middle Georgia as "The Countryman" through this name which he had signed to the articles he had written for the Milledgeville newspapers. In naming his newspaper *The Countryman*, he closely identified himself with it in the minds of its readers.

made of it both a financial and a journalistic success. Since 1847 he had striven in vain to win recognition as a prose writer and poet, but his frustrations were now at an end, for as the editor of *The Countryman* he had at last found his true metier. The success of the paper rekindled his creativity and made him more independent and individualistic than ever before. He no longer had to go hat in hand to Northern magazine editors and publishing houses and beg them, as it were, to publish for him. He could now write and publish what he pleased without any regard to possible adverse critical reaction. He dropped the editorial "we" and adopted a less formal style which was more nearly like his native middle Georgia conversational speech, yet which retained his penchant for orthodox grammar. In short, Turner made *The Countryman* his personal organ, and its success was due solely to his innate love of literature, to the many-sided traits of his colorful and individual personality, to his ingenuity and resourcefulness as an editor during the war years, and to his ability as a competent writer. It was during the four years that Turner was enjoying his only successful literary venture that young Joe Harris was under his direct influence.

Throughout the four years of its publication, *The Countryman* was everything that Turner promised it would be. Freshness, aliveness, and variety characterized its contents. Its columns contained useful items of information for country people during the war such as substitutes for salt and quinine, instructions on how to make tallow candles, and lists of prices current in the Augusta market. Its humorous paragraphs and amusing anecdotes were set off against the serious news from the battlefronts and the casualty lists of Putnam County soldiers. For those who were interested in field sports, there were articles about dogs and hunting. Turner's provocative editorials on dancing, religion, and politics evoked favorable and unfavorable responses from individuals and other newspapers, all of which he published with evident relish. The items which he reprinted from newspapers outside Georgia kept his readers informed about the progress of the war, and his editorials which voiced faith in the ultimate success of the Confederate cause lifted their morale when the war news was adverse. For his readers who owned few books, there were literary articles from his own pen, as well as travel sketches, essays, poems by Southern authors, didactic paragraphs, and other selections which he made from the books in his own library. Through the four years of its publication there was not one dull or conventional issue.

In the fall of 1864 the Confederate army was in such need of fresh reinforcements that the conscript officers in Georgia made an effort to round up every available man who was physically fit to bear arms and who was not exempt from military service by Confederate law. In response to an inquiry from Lieutenant William B. Watts, the conscript officer in Eatonton, concerning the military status of his employees on *The Countryman*, Turner replied by sending him a letter in which he gave his lameness as grounds for his own exemption and then named the seven members of its staff and the military status of each one. In the list there was the following notation concerning Harris: "Compositor—Joel C. Harris—19 years old. Weighs only about 100 pounds. Frail and feeble. Not fit for military service. Exempt under state and confederate law, as a compositor." [15] Turner was in error about Harris' age, for at the time he was only fifteen years and ten months old. Nor is there any evidence that he was in feeble health. Turner was probably of the opinion that the boy's small stature and light weight for his age would not permit him to endure the hardships of army life.

Turner suspended the publication of *The Countryman* from June 30, 1865, to January 30, 1866, as a result of the restrictions which Federal military authorities in Macon imposed on what he considered to be the freedom of his editorial utterances. He had published in the issue of June 6, 1865, an editorial in which he advocated, among other things, state sovereignty in all domestic affairs, including the right of secession, and no punishment of the so-called "rebels" who had acted under the sanction of their state governments. He republished this "Platform" in the issues of June 13, 20, and 27, whereupon the Federal officers, who regarded his statement as being openly disloyal to the Federal government, arrested him and took him before General James Wilson in Macon where he said he was "subjected to very rough TALK, amounting to grossest insult."

Turner charged that they had suppressed *The Countryman* by imposing such restrictions upon what he could say that he could not

[15]Turner MS. Journal, October 29, 1864.

accept them.[16] He therefore suspended publication for the next six months. When he resumed publication, he adopted the innocuous motto, "Devoted to the Editor's Opinion," and thereafter he restrained himself from running afoul of the Federal officers.

By some means which only Turner could have devised, he managed to continue to publish *The Countryman* each week through the spring months of 1866, but the tone of his editorials revealed that his former resilient spirit in the face of adversity had at last been broken beyond recovery. The South, whose patriarchal way of life he had exhibited as the master of Turnwold and romantically portrayed in his poem, *The Old Plantation*, and his journal, *The Plantation*, was now prostrate in defeat and subjected to military rule. With the old plantation regime destroyed and with no prospect that it could ever be restored, he no longer had a cause to defend nor a satisfactory manner of living to set forth in his writings. It was true that his thousand-acre plantation was still intact, but its uncultivated fields and silent cabins were sad reminders of what to him had been better and happier days. Reluctantly yielding to the inevitable, he permanently suspended *The Countryman* with the issue of May 8, 1866. In his final editorial, "Adieu!" he wrote that *The Countryman* was "a representative of independent country life, and of the home of the planter. These are gone, and *The Countryman* goes with them."

The Countryman was unique in the history of American journalism in the antebellum South not only because it was successfully published for four years on a remote Georgia plantation but also because it was, as Turner intended that it should be, an exact reflex of Southern life during the Civil War and as such had historical value. Whatever may have been the eccentricities of its editor and however he may have failed in his effort to stimulate literary creativity in the South, Turner had a genuine love of literature that was rare in the South of his own day. On the other hand, he had in his young compositor Joel Chandler Harris one who caught his enthusiasm, and he provided the boy with the opportunity to develop the literary talent which he discerned that he possessed. In time, Harris would accomplish for literature in the South what

[16]*The Countryman*, February 13, 1866.

Turner had dreamed of doing, but without the narrow sectional prejudices and geographical limitations which the latter had prescribed for it.

It seems likely that not long after Harris had learned to set in type the articles for *The Countryman* which others had composed, he began to submit some of his own compositions to Turner, but he declined to publish any of them until the boy had demonstrated an improvement in his writing style. To that end, Turner published in *The Countryman* an open letter "To a Young Correspondent," which he intended to be not only for Harris' benefit but also for other beginning writers who had sought his counsel. In his own career he had "scribbled, scribbled, scribbled" without anyone to discipline him in his writing style, and out of his long and hard experience he had learned the essentials of effective writing. In his letter he pointed out the weaknesses in his young protégé's prose style.

I am reluctantly compelled to decline your article, but return it to you. Take it, and keep it carefully until you are older, and you will thank me for rejecting it.—Your fault is that of all young writers, you employ too much language to convey your ideas. Your article contains some very good ideas, but they constitute only about one fourth of your piece, while the other three fourths are mere words. The only use in the world you have for words is to serve as a medium for conveying your ideas, and the fewer words you use the better. Your language should be the plainest and the simplest possible.—You have an exuberant fancy. Curb that, and cultivate your judgment. Above all, study simplicity and artlessness of style. I do not intend this for rebuke but for instruction. I am doing you a kindness, and would be treating you with great injustice, were I to publish your article.—Do not let what I say discourage you. I have been rejected hundreds, if not thousands of times, by publishers, but never allowed this to overcome me. . . .—You have a talent for writing, and I advise you to cultivate it. There is a glorious field just ahead of you for Southern writers. I publish this instead of writing to you privately, so that all my young friends and correspondents may profit by it.[17]

To curb his youthful exuberance was difficult for Harris, and

[17]*Ibid.*, October 27, 1862.

Turner did not permit one of his articles to be published in *The Countryman* until he had been at Turnwold for almost eight months. It appeared in the issue of December 1, 1862.

Mr. Countryman: In looking over an old newspaper, I find the following recipe for making black ink, which may prove valuable to you as well as to your readers owing to the scarcity of the fluid. Will you give it a trial and report result?

J. C. Harris
(The recipe then followed.)

With this carefully written, prosaic, but singularly appropriate article of only forty-five words, Joel Chandler Harris began his career as an author. Turner's counsel to write with simplicity and artlessness was already having its effect and it was instruction which Harris never forgot. These qualities were to characterize his prose style as an editor and author and to give his fiction a mark of distinction.

Harris' next article in *The Countryman* was an essay, "Grumblers," in which he voiced his protest against faultfinders whom he described as those "delicate morsels of humanity who cannot be pleased, who are so fastidious and dissatisfied that all the world cannot reconcile them to their lot." His observation was an early expression of the constructive philosophy which was basic in his attitude toward the problems of life and revealed his reflective turn of mind.

In moods of loneliness he contemplated the serious aspects of human nature. "It was just lonely enough," he wrote in one of his reminiscences of his years at Turnwold, "to bring me face to face with myself and yet not lonely enough to breed melancholy. I used to sit in the dusk and see the shadows of all the great problems of life flitting about, restless and uneasy, and I had time to think about them." [18] It was an attitude of mind which foreshadowed his mature outlook on life. In the quietness of thought he would continue to see the restless and uneasy shadows of the problems of life as they concerned him personally, of the South in the throes of its readjustment to a new era, and of human nature in its virtues and its weaknesses.

In 1863 Turner published in *The Countryman* such other essays

[18]Atlanta *Daily News*, October 10, 1900.

by Harris as satisfied his meticulous requirements in language and grammar, but he made no restrictions upon the young man's choice of subjects, and all of them were of a serious nature as their titles indicate: "Sabbath Evening in the Country"; [19] "Death"; [20] "The Progress of Civilization"; [21] "Hypocrites"; [22] and "Prodigality." [23] During the same year Turner also inserted some of Harris' first humorous paragraphs on items of current interest which he read in the various newspapers which came to the office of *The Countryman* as exchanges. Turner himself had a great fondness for puns, and Harris' apt play on words in his paragraphs so pleased his sense of humor that he published fourteen of them in the issue of April 13, 1863. Of these the following two were typical:

Tell me, Dutchman, how many he's does it take to contend wtih the scolding women of the Yankee Congress?

Vorhees is enough for all of dem. *Countryman's Devil.*

Why are the women all opposed to the *stay* law?

Because a great many of them consider *stays* their chief support. *Countryman's Devil.*

These first experiments by Harris of a humorous nature attracted the attention of other editors, but, knowing Turner's addiction to puns, they mistakenly ascribed them to him, although they bore the signature *Countryman's Devil.* Turner, however, informed them that if they only knew what a smart devil *The Countryman* had they would not have credited the "sharp sayings" to him. Despite their juvenile quality, these paragraphs' brevity and spontaneity revealed a side of Harris' nature in contrast to the serious mood reflected in his essays, and they gave promise of the really brilliant paragraphing which he was later to do on the Savannah *Morning News* and the Atlanta *Constitution.*

The book reviews which Harris wrote for *The Countryman* give a better insight into his literary possibilities than do either his essays

[19]*The Countryman*, February 17, 1863.
[20]*Ibid.*, March 3, 1863.
[21]*Ibid.*, March 23, 1863.
[22]*Ibid.*, September 1, 1863.
[23]*Ibid.*, September 15, 1863.

or his paragraphs. They reveal that he had been reading rather widely from the books which he had borrowed from Turner's library of about eleven hundred miscellaneous books (exclusive of his three hundred law volumes),[24] which Harris stated as having been "especially rich in the various departments of English literature." [25] In the issue of *The Countryman* for June 14, 1864, Turner included Harris' review of a volume of poems by Henry Lynden Flash, a popular Southern romantic poet who was then living in Macon, where he edited the Macon *Daily Confederate*. Turner was so pleased with the boy's review that he featured it on the entire first and second pages and in two and a half columns of the third page. He evidently overlooked the exuberance of its style in his admiration for Harris' spirited defense of Southern authors in general and for the jaunty enthusiasm with which he extolled the virtues of Flash's poems in particular.

Harris began his review by declaring that it was time the South should "atone for her former coldness to her sons of song," and he then gave a biographical sketch of Flash with emphasis on his service to the Confederacy as a member of General Joseph Wheeler's staff. He said that he would follow Dryden's advice "upon the delicacy of writing criticisms upon living men" and that he would therefore quote from Flash's poems and from the criticisms which other reviewers had made of them. He took particular note of the adverse review which the New York *Saturday Press* had made of the volume and countered with an attack of his own on that Northern paper. "There was a time," he indignantly asserted, "when our Southern readers received such things as they were written, and made the *Yankee* wiseacres the basis of their judgment," but he went on to say that a careful reading of Flash's book would scatter all ideas of meeting with "vapid nonsense" as the *Saturday*

[24]On September 10, 1863, Turner made the following entry in his Journal: "Counted my books today and found that I had about 1100 miscellaneous vol's, and about 300 law vol's. This is more than I thought I had." His collection was broken up after his death, but references in his Journal and in his extant publications show his familiarity with Horace, Virgil, Xenophon, the Greek New Testament, Shakespeare, Sir Thomas Browne, Walton, Milton, Swift, Addison, Steele, Dryden, Pope, Johnson, Goldsmith, Burns, Dickens, Thackeray, Scott, Tennyson, Irving, N. P. Willis, Halleck, Bryant, Poe, Cooper, Richard Henry Wilde, Henry P. Jackson, Simms, Griswold, Longstreet, Longfellow, Emerson, Harriet Beecher Stowe, Prentiss, and with many other standard authors.

[25]Atlanta *Daily News*, October 10, 1900.

Press had been pleased to call one half the volume. Throughout his lengthy review there were allusions to N. P. Willis, Poe, Tennyson, and Bulwer.

Although the review revealed how thoroughly Harris subscribed to Turner's sectional prejudices against Northern authors during the war and his equally partisan approval of books written by Southern authors apart from their literary merit, it also revealed Harris' growing acquaintance with English and American authors and his developing confidence in himself as a writer. Even when its faults have been discounted, the review was a creditable performance for the boy of only fifteen, whose education had been of a desultory nature, and who two years before he wrote it had been playing in the streets of Eatonton. It foreshadowed the effective work which he was later to do as a critic of Southern and American literature when he had gained a larger perspective of those qualities which gave a book genuine literary distinction and could overlook the geographical location of its author.

In his review of Reverend Rufus W. Griswold's life of Edgar Allan Poe, Harris again manifested his loyalty to a Southern author. He characterized Griswold's biography as "one of the most miserably gotten-up affairs, perhaps, that ever intruded itself upon the reading public of America" and said that there was "enough of nonsensical mediocrity, patronizing inferiority, and ridiculous envy in it to damn it forever in the mind of any reader of taste." He then gave specific instances from the biography to justify his condemnation of it. Out of his indignation he wrote scornfully of Griswold's "critical ability" and his "analytical astuteness" and closed his satirical review by expressing the hope that "even yet we may have an edition of the works of that great genius honorable alike to his memory and to us as an honorable people." [26]

Judging from the number of poems which Harris contributed to *The Countryman*, it seems that during his literary apprenticeship his chief ambition was to be a poet. As might have been expected of a boy of his age, he drew the inspiration of his first poems from the books which he had been reading, especially those by Flash, Poe, Bryant, Byron and Tennyson. Highly romantic in incident and tone coloring, they dwelt rather morbidly upon such subjects as death, the

[26]*The Countryman*, February 13, 1866.

grave, and love in its unhappy and tragic aspects. In "Nellie White" the moon shone drearily upon her grave;[27] in "Ruanne" two friends drank life to the lees and found its dregs to be bitter.[28] "Accursed" was the melodramatic story of a man with sin in his heart who had been driven by remorse of conscience to take his own life on learning that the woman whom he had wronged had died.[29] "Murder" was a tale of terror in which even a screech owl shivered in affright at the sight of a murdered man's red blood on the green grass.[30] The lovely but disconsolate young heroine in "Moselle" died of a broken heart upon realizing her miserable mistake in having married an old man for his gold instead of her young lover for his love.[31] In the excess of the romantic qualities of melancholy, despair, hopeless love, and terror with which Harris saturated his juvenile poems, he outdid those whose works he was imitating. His works, however, gave evidence of his lively imagination which, with more experience, he would learn to control.

While Harris was at Turnwold no one of his poems dealt with the plantation scenes which he daily observed and only one of them, "The Battle Bird," [32] had any connection with the war. In a prefatory note he said that the poem was based on a story which he had heard of a mocking bird singing amid the din of the battle of Resaca. After having described the singular incident, he made it prophetic of the coming of peace to a nation at war. His interpretation was also prophetic of the conciliatory influence that he was to exert in restoring goodwill between the North and the South during the years that followed the war.

Since the fortunes of Harris were bound up with those of Turner, the only course left open to him after the final suspension of *The Countryman* in May, 1866, was to return to his mother's home in Eatonton and try to make a connection with some other newspaper whereby he could earn a livelihood. He was only seventeen but his four years at Turnwold had given him more maturity than might ordinarily be expected of a boy his age in middle Georgia. He had

[27]*Ibid.*, September 27, 1864.
[28]*Ibid.*, January 17, 1865.
[29]*Ibid.*, March 28, 1865.
[30]*Ibid.*, April 18, 1865.
[31]*Ibid.*, February 20, 1866.
[32]*Ibid.*, April 18, 1866 (dated Turnwold, 1864).

acquired a liberal acquaintance with English and American authors from the books in Turner's collection, and under Turner's instruction he had learned the essential elements of a clear and concise prose style, even though he had not yet mastered them. He had also derived his concept of literature in the South from Turner's social and political propaganda articles. Moreover, while he was there he had observed the operation of plantation life at Turnwold under favorable auspices, but he had also come to see the harsh and cruel features of the regime. He had also seen the end of that regime, and he himself had become involved in the economic paralysis and general chaos which had prevailed immediately after the end of the war. All of these scenes and experiences were stored up in his mind.

It would be some ten years, however, before he would begin to revive his memories of the plantation and translate them into poems and stories. During this interval he was diverted from his early literary aspirations by the necessity of earning a living—as an employee on the staffs of various Georgia newspapers.

5

A JOURNALISTIC ODYSSEY

Although Joe Harris had become proficient as a typesetter during his four years on the staff of *The Countryman*, he had no immediate prospect that any other newspaper in Georgia in the summer of 1866 would employ a boy of his age. Two years earlier he had made an inquiry about the possibility of securing an appointment on a Columbus, Georgia, newspaper in the belief that such a connection would afford him a larger opportunity to further his budding literary aspirations, but he had been advised to stay where he was on account of the uncertainty of the times under war conditions.[1] Even though the war had ended, conditions were more uncertain in 1866 than they had been in 1864. Business in Georgia and elsewhere in the South was at a standstill, and well-established newspapers were struggling for survival.

Therefore, much sooner than Harris had dared to hope, he received an offer from the Macon *Telegraph* to become a typesetter on its staff. In all probability the offer came to Harris through Turner's friendship with William A. Reid, formerly of Eatonton, who was the owner and editor of the *Telegraph*. This offer to join the *Telegraph* was an unusually attractive one for Harris. For one thing, Macon was less than forty miles from Eatonton and, since he had never gone outside his native Putnam County, he would still be in the kind of environment with which he was familiar. A more important consideration in the boy's mind was the fact that the *Telegraph* was a daily newspaper which from its beginning had encouraged the development of a native Southern literature, and he foresaw in his connection with it not only an opportunity to earn his livelihood but also to publish in it his literary compositions. He therefore accepted the offer with hopeful anticipation and went to Macon by train. The exact date of his arrival there is uncertain, but it is likely that he wrote the

[1]Julia Collier Harris, *Harris, Life and Letters*, 55.

brief article which appeared in the *Telegraph* on May 12, 1866, in which he appealed to the Central of Georgia railway to arrange a more convenient schedule between Eatonton and Macon so that passengers enroute to Macon would not have to lay over an entire day in Gordon.

When Joe Harris went to Macon he began the first phase of his initiation into a more complex world than the one which he had known on Turner's plantation. Living in a city instead of in the country called for an adjustment that was not an easy one for the innately shy boy to make. He soon discovered that the work of getting out a daily edition of the *Telegraph* was far more demanding on the time of its staff than was the leisurely process involved in getting out a weekly issue of *The Countryman*. What surprised him even more, however, was his discovery that the *Telegraph* employees frequently indulged in playing pranks and practical jokes on each other and that they engaged in other forms of frolicking which Turner would have frowned upon among his own employees. Then, too, he noticed that his new associates drank with evident relish the cold beer and champagne which the proprietors of the twelve drink and food emporiums on Cotton Avenue, Cherry and Mulberry streets sent them on the hot summer days and nights. He had not been accustomed to such hilarity as he was now observing, for Turner, who was a strict advocate of temperance, would have summarily discharged any member of his staff who drank any intoxicating beverage on his premises.

When Harris was with the *Telegraph*, the personal element characterized American journalism, and his odd personal appearance immediately attracted the attention of his new and convivial associates. Heretofore, none of his companions either in Eatonton or at Turnwold had ever made him conscious of his red hair and freckled face, his shyness, and his awkwardness in the presence of strangers, but all of these personal characteristics served to excite merriment on the part of his older and seasoned associates on the *Telegraph*. They therefore made the naive apprentice from the hinterland the object of their goodnatured banter and jests. On August 6, Harry J. Neville, the city editor, referred to him in his column, "Things About Town," as "an enthusiastic young friend from Putnam at present sojourning here," and in his column on September 4 he humorously dubbed him "Pink Top" from "Old Put," the first of the many nicknames which his red hair was to inspire among Georgia journalists.

Although Neville and the other older men on the staff soon became fond of this unsophisticated boy and assumed a kind of paternal attitude toward him, they could not resist the temptation to play a joke on him. Perceiving that he stuttered when he became excited and knowing that he was totally innocent of the effect which alcoholic beverage would have upon him, they conspired one night to get him to drink several glasses of strong beer one right after the other. The result was all that the conspirers could have wished, and Neville so thoroughly enjoyed it that he published the following humorous account of it in his column:

An enthusiastic young friend from Putnam, but at present sojourning here, was induced the other night to swaller four or five glasses of beer in rapid succession. Noting that he was looking a little swivel-eyed, we asked him if he thought the German liquid was intoxicating. Throwing his head back and blinking considerably, he replied: "C-a-n-'t s-a-y z-a-c-t-l-y t-i-s t-s-i-c-a-t-i-n, b-u-t m-a-k-e-s a f-e-l-l-e-r'-s t-o-n-g-u-e a-w-f-u-l t-h-i-c-k." If the young man wishes to speak German fluently, in a short time, we would advise him to drink lager daily.[2]

Having himself played numerous tricks on others, Harris took no offense at this one played on him. However, although Neville had not named him in the published account, he knew that readers of the *Telegraph* in Eatonton and in the Turnwold community would readily identify him as the "young friend from Putnam," and he was concerned with the effect which the published story would have on his reputation among his home folks. In response to the boy's earnest entreaty, Neville published a partial correction in which he still further embarrassed him by directing his retraction specifically to the girls in Turnwold toward whom the timid boy had never shown the slightest romantic interest. "For fear some of the fair Turnwoldians should consider him 'demoralized,' we make the correction with pleasure. Although our young friend *had* been taking a social glass of beer, we assure the demoiselles of Turn-

[2]Macon *Telegraph*, August 5, 1866.

wold that it had nothing to do with his speech. *He stammers naturally when the least excited.*" [3]

Although the older men did not regard Harris seriously, he found in Bridges Smith, another boy about his age who was also with the *Telegraph*, a congenial companion. Smith was later to become mayor of Macon and one of its leading citizens, and Harris was to become one of the nation's outstanding journalists on the staff of the Atlanta *Constitution*, but the friendship which they formed when they were boys lasted throughout Harris' life. In his reminiscences of their boyhood associations, Smith recalled that when Harris first came to Macon he was "a timid, shrinking stripling of a boy" and that, although he was only a copy boy, he was far more capable and efficient than an ordinary, old-fashioned printer's devil.[4] In another reminiscence, Smith said that this timid boy soon became a favorite with the printers. "Not," said Smith, "that he mixed with them or frolicked with them—in those days of old-time printers frolicking was a sin often indulged in—or that he had much to say. . . . He talked very little, and at the odd times when he was not busy with his work of taking proofs and aiding the foreman in his duties, he was either reading or writing." [5] Smith also recalled that when Harris had completed his apprenticeship as a typesetter he accompanied him one Sunday afternoon to the engine house on Third Street where he went through the formal ceremony of becoming a member of Typographical Union No. 64. Harris was so frightened, however, at the necessity of having to repeat the obligations involved that Smith doubted if the boy was actually aware of the words he was repeating.[6]

Harry Neville was completely a newspaper man, and if he knew of Harris' literary ambitions he did little to encourage him to develop them. He gave the boy simple routine assignments, one of which was to write the customary "puffs" in appreciation of the generous supplies of food and drink which the saloon proprietors sent the staff with their compliments. They must have felt amply rewarded for their generosity when they read in the *Telegraph* the boy's enthusiastic puffs of which the following is a typical ex-

[3]*Ibid.*, August 9, 1866.
[4]*Ibid.*, July 4, 1908.
[5]*Ibid.*, July 6, 1908.
[6]*Ibid.*

ample: "Fred Brainard seems to have the knack of knowing when all hands are thirsty, and Henry's appearance with a bucketfull of cool lager at a late hour on Saturday night was hailed with manifestations of delight. All partook freely and the "New Idea" was voted a good institution." [7]

In his spare time, however, Harris continued to compose poems as he had done at Turnwold and submitted them to Neville, who supervised his work. Neville included one of them, "Little May," in his column on September 4, but he evidently did so more out of his desire to please the boy than out of his own appreciation of its literary merit, as his foreword to the poem would suggest: "Our young friend, 'Pink Top' from 'Old Put' furnishes us with the following sweet lines." The poem consisted of five stanzas in which Harris extolled the beauty and the virtues of his imaginary Little May, but if he had actually met her she would have charmed him into a bashful silence. The lines were after the manner of some of Flash's sentimental poems, but even so they were a decided improvement over the morbid and ultraromantic poems which Harris had contributed to *The Countryman*.

But Harris was not content with writing puffs to please the Macon saloon keepers, and, since Neville regarded his poems lightly, he turned to reviewing current magazines and books for the *Telegraph* as he had previously done for *The Countryman*. The two bookstores in Macon, Patrick and Havens and J. W. Burke and Company, supplied the *Telegraph* with the latest books and periodicals with the same motive that prompted the drink and food establishments to send its staff satisfying refreshments, and Neville gave Harris a free hand in writing his reviews, always, of course, with the proper acknowledgments.

Harris' reviews clearly revealed the extent to which he had been indoctrinated by Turner's partisan preference for Southern writers. He wrote of John Esten Cooke's *Surry of Eagle's Nest*: "It is a work that Southerners will long read and like, because of their great deeds, of their great men, and of that which redounds to their great honor." [8] His glorification of this Southern novelist and of Southern heroes was no doubt intensified by his recollection of the devastation

_____
[7] *Ibid.*, July 8, 1866.
[8] *Ibid.*, June 7, 1866.

which he had witnessed in the Turnwold community and by the fact that in the summer of 1866 Macon was under Federal military rule. General Howell Cobb had been in charge of defending the city, but because he lacked a sufficient force to resist the invading enemy he had surrendered it to General Wilson on April 19, 1865. The surrender, however, had not prevented the federal troops from inflicting heavy damage on certain sections of the city. They had pillaged many homes, burned two blocks on Mulberry Street, and set fires elsewhere.

Of all the magazines which Harris reviewed for the *Telegraph*, the one which most enthusiastically claimed his attention was the *Crescent Monthly*, published in New Orleans by William Evelyn, a former Confederate officer. This new periodical, "Devoted to Literature, Art, Science, and Society," was another brave effort to establish a cultural periodical in the old South. At the time of its founding, New Orleans was under Federal military government, and the South as a whole was enduring the woes of the Reconstruction. Therefore, the environment was not favorable for the launching of a predominantly Southern magazine. Evelyn's motivating purpose, however, differed from Turner's in establishing *The Plantation*, in that he proposed to avoid partisan politics and to rise above sectional prejudice in his cultural enterprise. In his introductory note he stated that although the *Crescent Monthly* would endeavor to be a faithful representative of the Southern region, it would depend for patronage upon merit alone and would not ask for sympathy because it was a Southern work.[9]

Harris saw in the *Crescent Monthly* a promising medium for the cultivation of the latent literary talent in the South, including his own. The May number in particular excited his admiration. "We are glad, at length," he wrote of it, "to witness the culmination of a Southern magazine. In the *Crescent* we have such a one. It is capital, and is likely to be a literary magazine that will develop and foster Southern talent to an extent that will show to the world that the Southern mind has more genius than it has ever had credit for. We advise all to subscribe."[10]

[9]*Crescent Monthly*, 1 (April, 1866), 7. A file of the *Crescent Monthly* is available in the Howard-Tilton Memorial Library, Tulane University, New Orleans.
[10]Macon *Telegraph*, May 26, 1866.

In his review of the August number, Harris again revealed the degree to which Turner's Southern bias had influenced him. In his review of that number he said that Evelyn deserved the support of the Southern people in his literary venture in their behalf because he had come to the South from England and had staked his life and fortune on the "Lost Cause." Taking his cue from the appeal which Turner had made for Southern people to support *Turner's Monthly* and his quarterly, *The Plantation*, Harris said it was time for Southerners to declare their independence of Northern literature. They could do so by supporting the *Crescent Monthly*. "Our people have patronized Northern literature," he wrote out of his sense of urgency for immediate action, "until there has been formed among them a Puritanical way of thinking which we fear will be hard to eradicate. Let us begin at once. We have *talked* of a Southern literature long enough. To possess a literature peculiar to ourselves we must ignore such periodicals as Harper and Leslie, and support such periodicals as the one under review."

Harris continued to beat the drums for Evelyn in the September twenty-second issue of the *Telegraph* in which he defended him against the charge that he had unfairly criticized a Prussian officer who had served in the Confederate Army. His last reference to the *Crescent Monthly* was on October 4, and thereafter there was no personal reference in the *Telegraph* to "Pink Top" from "Old Put" nor was there any article attributable to him.

In the evident belief that a connection with the *Crescent Monthly* would offer him a more advantageous opportunity to develop his literary talent than the *Telegraph*, he completed, in the fall of 1866, an arrangement with Evelyn to become his private secretary. Evelyn had never seen Harris, for his appointment had been made through correspondence, and when the small, red-headed, freckled-faced boy of only seventeen years entered his office and said that he was Joel C. Harris, Evelyn was understandably astonished.

Harris' association with the *Crescent Monthly* proved to be even more disappointing in a literary way than had been his brief stay with the *Telegraph*, for Evelyn published no signed article from the boy's pen in his magazine. In the December, 1866, number there was a poem, "In the Garden," which was signed by the single initial "H." In its tone of melancholy regret it was similar to the romantic poems which he had published in *The Countryman*, and in the March, 1867, number there was a prose article, "Extracts from a Literary Note Book," also signed "H" which, if Harris wrote it, could have been suggested by Turner's "Extracts from My MSS." The evidence, however, is insufficient to justify an assumption that Harris wrote either one, and he himself never made any reference to them as his compositions. The New Orleans *Times*, however, did publish two of his poems. The issue of January 20, 1867, carried his "The Old and the New" under the pen name "Cosmopolite," and in its issue of the next day his "Sea Wind" appeared but without signature attached. Harris subsequently published both of these poems under his own name. In their restrained sentiment and artistic technique they showed a marked advance over his earlier poetic compositions, and they indicated that poetry was his chief writing interest. If he submitted articles to the *Picayune* or the *Crescent*, the two other leading newspapers in New Orleans, neither of them carried any contributions signed by him or any which he ever later identified as his own.

As the months passed, it must have become increasingly clear to Harris that the move from his native pastoral environment in middle Georgia to New Orleans had been a mistake. From the very beginning of his residence there he had felt strangely alone in the metropolis with its population of over two hundred thousand, and his loneliness was intensified when he went to his attic room in a home near the St. Louis Cathedral. Forty-two years later he vividly recalled his desolate feeling on Christmas morning in 1866. "He was in a city far from home," he wrote, "and not at all happy in his new surroundings. He hung up his stocking, nevertheless, and woke to find it empty, and no wonder! Santa Claus could not have found him without a map of the town, and even then he would have needed a guide to show him the way to his small room in the top of a French boarding-house under the shadow of a great cathedral." [11] His sense of loneliness was further increased by the fact that he saw no familiar faces, and the speech which he heard was vastly different from that which he had heard spoken by the plain people in Put-

[11]*Uncle Remus's Home Magazine*, XXIV (December, 1908), 6. The *New Orleans City Directory* for 1867 listed Harris' residence in a private home at the corner of Rampart and Canal streets and his occupation as a clerk.

nam County and by the Negroes in Eatonton and on Turner's plantation.

Moreover, New Orleans itself, with its historical background, its blend of different cultures, and its picturesque features, seems to have made no permanent impression upon him. If he ever attended any of the performances which were available to him at the Academy of Music, the Opera House, the St. Charles Theatre, the National Theatre, or any of the literary lectures which were open to the public, he never thereafter made any mention of them. In only one of his stories, "A Belle of St. Valerien," did he use New Orleans for a setting, and even in that story the reference to the city was only an incidental part of the narrative. He increasingly found that his duties as Evelyn's secretary were only routine work and unproductive of any creative writing on his part. The simple truth was that the boy's enthusiasm for a literary career had taken him too fast and too far from the people and the scenes he knew best, and in May, 1867, he made the sensible decision to return to Eatonton. If his experience of some six or seven months in New Orleans had any practical value for him, it taught him never to leave Georgia again, no matter how attractive an offer to do so might be.

While Harris was in New Orleans, Turner in Eatonton had hit upon a scheme which, if enacted into law, would restore a measure of financial prosperity to the then impoverished South. He had envisioned a policy of "Reconstruction and Relief" whereby the Federal government would compensate those whose property had been destroyed by the war in an amount commensurate with their losses. His immediate difficulty, however, was that he had no medium through which he could advocate his policy, but, as formerly, whenever an idea for publishing his views germinated in his mind he assiduously cultivated it. On March 11, 1867, he wrote to former Governor Joseph Emerson Brown, whose reconstruction measures he had vigorously opposed, in an effort to solicit financial aid and influence in the promotion of his objective. "I would like very much," he wrote Brown, "to be at the head of an influential Georgia press to advocate Reconstruction and Relief. But the war has left me without means to gratify my wish." He suggested that Brown, whom he knew to be wealthy, form a stock company with some other wealthy men, purchase either the Middledgeville *Federal Union* or the *Southern Recorder*, and make him its editor in which capacity he said he could render the state some service.[12]

Brown made no response whatever to Turner's proposals, whereupon, with his usual disregard of the financial obstacles to overcome, Turner resolved to establish a paper of his own in Eatonton. He endeavored to persuade James P. Harrison, who had been in his employ on the staff of *The Countryman* but who was then the owner and publisher of the *Monroe Advertiser* in Forsyth, Georgia, to give up his paper and assume the management of the one which he proposed to establish in Eatonton. Harrison declined the offer, but Turner wrote him on June 13, 1867, to enlist his aid in securing the necessary printing equipment. "If the paper is to be started," he said in his letter, "it ought to be done immediately. I presume your brother could obtain outfit [for a country paper] in Macon. Joe Harris is here—a No. 1 printer—and is anxious to secure a position on it." [13] Although Turner's purpose to set up his newspaper fell through for lack of financial backing, his endeavor to do so turned out advantageously for Harris, for when Harrison learned that he was again in Eatonton and looking for employment he offered him a position on his *Monroe Advertiser*. Harris accepted the offer gladly, even though to join the staff of a weekly newspaper after having been connected with the daily Macon *Telegraph* and the literary *Crescent Monthly* may have seemed to him at the time to have been a demotion.

Harris felt more at home, however, than he had in either Macon or New Orleans, for Forsyth was a small town with a population in 1860 of only 608 whites and 773 Negroes, and it had not grown appreciably by 1867. Like Eatonton, it was the courthouse town in a predominantly agricultural county, located twenty-eight miles from Macon on the Central of Georgia railway to Atlanta. The former slaveowners and their freed slaves were in the slow and still uncertain process of readjustment to their radically changed race relationship. Both in Eatonton and at Turnwold Harris had observed at firsthand the various features of antebellum plantation life, and

[12]Turner MS. Journal.
[13]*Ibid.*

now in Forsyth he had the opportunity during the early years of Reconstruction to observe conditions during the transition from the old
regime to a new one.

The *Monroe Advertiser* was a weekly newspaper, and Harris' apprenticeship on *The Countryman* had prepared him for his assignments on it. With only one helper, J. T. Manry, a young country
boy from near Forsyth with whom he shared a room in the Harrison home, he set up the copy by hand, prepared the forms, ran off
the editions on a Washington handpress, and attended to their mail-
ing. Unlike *The Countryman*, the *Monroe Advertiser* was not in any
sense a literary journal, and it merely reported news items of interest to the people of Forsyth and Monroe County.

Since Harris' work in getting out the weekly newspaper required
only a portion of his time, he soon became acquainted with the
young men his own age in the little town, and one of them, John
W. Evans, recalled that they could always count on him to devise
some kind of humorous prank for their entertainment. On Sundays
he went with them to the Baptist church, and Evans remembered
an incident that occurred at one of the Sunday services. Joe, so Evans said, made rotary motions on the outer side of the pew on which
they were sitting as if he were grinding an organ and at the same
time audibly imitated organ notes. Much to his embarrassment and
his companions' amusement, he continued to make his grinding motions and audible sounds after the congregation had finished the
hymn. Evans also recalled that Joe was very shy and quiet when
girls were in their company.[14]

J. T. Manry later recalled the impression which Harris had made
on him the first time he saw him in the office of the *Monroe Advertiser*. He wrote that "Mr. Harrison called 'Joe,' to an undersized, boyish looking individual only 19, and here stood before us, with a
smile, one of the reddest-headed, freckled-faced boys I had ever seen.
The freckles were as large as the proverbial turkey egg, and the hair
was a fiery red." Manry also recalled that whenever Joe met a strang-
er his face would flush and he would stammer badly, and that Joe
was one of the quietest persons he had ever met. He remembered,
too, that Harris chose books from the town's circulating library for

[14]John W. Evans, Forsyth, personal interview.

him to read and would often make him stand on a chair and recite doggerel poetry.[15]

Harris had been in Forsyth less than a year when Joseph Addison Turner died in Eatonton on February 29, 1868, at the age of forty-one. In the literary history of the antebellum South his achievement was a minor one, but he had a capable and energetic mind, possessed a genuine love of literature that was rarely equaled by Georgians of his time, and crusaded for a Southern literary renaissance based in native materials. His extant publications and manuscript journal are important to the literary historian for the light they throw on the social, economic, political, religious, and cultural life of Georgia between 1847 and 1868. Moreover, he gave young Joe Harris, the half-orphaned child of poverty and obscurity, the impetus and the plantation background to become eventually Joel Chandler Harris, internationally known as the literary interpreter of both the Old and the New South.

With the death of Turner, the most powerful personal connection between Harris and the old plantation South was broken. A reservoir of pleasant memories remained from which he would later draw, but by 1868 the South had begun to recover from the paralyzing effect of the destruction of its old social and economic order and was moving forward in the direction of a new civilization, although as yet it was dimly seen and without a forceful leader, and Harris began to move with it. His brief sojourns in Macon and New Orleans had taken him out of the isolation of Turnwold and had given him a larger perspective of literature in the South. His major interest at the time was in poetry, for while in Forsyth he concentrated his time on the preparation of a volume of works by representative Southern poets which he proposed to publish under the title "Gems of Southern Poetry." In Harris' copy of Turner's *A Cotton Planter's Manual*, Thomas H. English, former curator of the Joel Chandler Harris' Memorial Collection at Emory University, found 161 items which Harris had collected for his proposed volume, one of which was a copy of a letter which he had written to another young Georgia writer, Sidney Lanier. Although he abandoned this project, probably because it proved to be too ambitious an undertaking, English states

---

[15]Shreveport (La.) *Journal*, March 8, 1930.

that Harris helped to supply James Wood Davidson with material for his anthology *The Living Writers of the South,*[16] which was published in 1869 and which included two of Harris' poems, "The Old and the New" and "Agnes." Davidson also wrote a rather effusive sketch of Harris in which he described him as one of the South's most promising poets. "As a poet," Davidson said, "Mr. Harris has the true principles of the poetic art. He recognized the twaddle and looks to legitimate art to accomplish its own mission." [17] The commentary indicated that Harris was then beginning to formulate his own independent standard for evaluating the worth of poetry in the South, one that was based solely on the literary merit of a poem.

Harris made no contributions of a literary nature to the *Monroe Advertiser,* but his humorous paragraphs attracted the attention of other newspapers in Georgia, and in the fall of 1870 he was offered a position as associate editor of the Savannah *Morning News* at a salary of forty dollars a week. The salary in itself was a compelling inducement for him to accept, but an even greater incentive was the opportunity to become connected with one of the state's most influential daily newspapers. There were personal reasons, however, why he regretted to leave Forsyth. He felt indebted to Harrison for employing him when he had returned from New Orleans to Eatonton with no prospects of securing work on any newspaper. Would Harrison feel that he was ungrateful? Then, too, he had found in Harrison's sister, Mrs. Georgia Starke, a sympathetic and understanding friend who more than anyone else had given him the confidence to overcome those personal handicaps of which he had become more and more conscious as he had grown older. He did not wish to appear disloyal to Harrison nor ungrateful to Mrs. Starke and other friends in Forsyth who had been kind to him, but the time came when he had to make a decision to go to Savannah or stay in Forsyth. J. T. Manry recalled that he had taken a letter from the *Morning News* to Harris and that Harrison gave his consent for him to accept the offer from that newspaper. "No time was to be lost," Manry said, "and Mr. Harris confided to my care the packing of his trunk, to be expressed later. He wrote me on his arrival in Savan-

[16]Thomas H. English, "Joel Chandler Harris's Earliest Literary Project," *Emory University Quarterly* II (October, 1946), 176–85.
[17]James Wood Davidson, *Living Writers of the South* (New York: Carleton, 1869), 236–39.

nah a nice letter . . . sending me a copy of 'Josh Billings' Family Tree,' just published." [18]

Professionally, Harris' move to Savannah was the most advantageous one he had made since he had left Turnwold in the summer of 1866. The *Morning News* had been founded in 1850 by William Tappan Thompson. In 1868 J. H. Estill had become its owner and had made it a spearhead in Georgia for a vigorous attack on the radical element which was then in control of the state's government, and by the time Harris joined its staff in the fall of 1870 it had risen to a position of popularity and influence throughout the state.

Harris' primary assignment on the *Morning News* was that of a paragrapher. His daily column, which he first called "State Affairs" and later changed to "Affairs in Georgia," consisted of humorous comments on personalities and events of current interest which he garnered from the state's daily and weekly newspapers. Out of his own instinctive bent for humor, Harris discerned the comic aspects in the everyday happenings among everyday people, and humor-loving Georgians in the 1870's needed no footnotes to explain the topical allusions in his paragraphs. The following typical examples taken at random from his column found a ready response from the readers of the *Morning News.*

An apocryphal paragraph is going the rounds to the effect that there is many a man in Heard County who has not had a dram in twelve months.

A suffrage-slinger in Rome named Sam Rambo recently caressed his wife with a panful of fire-coals. The authorities of that city have gone so far as to put Sam in jail. This country is coming to a pretty pass when a free American citizen can't amuse himself with his own wife.

A colored couple in Putnam County whose combined age is one hundred and eighty-two years, were united in wedlock recently. They said the reason they were so precipitate about the thing, they didn't want their parents to find out.

An Atlanta man who hilariously tempted his mother-in-law to hold a fire-cracker while he called the children is now temporarily boarding with his uncle.

A Wilkinson County man who went out the other day with a colored person and a small fice dog for the purpose of breaking up a small settlement of yellow jackets, has sent in his resignation as elder of the Church.

[18]Shreveport (La.) *Journal*, March 8, 1930.

No mention is made of any subsequent action of the negro or the dog.

Why should the spirit of mortal be proud? A Macon man on his way home from church on Sunday made an attempt to recover a lady's handkerchief in the street. Instead of doing so, he sat down violently alongside of it, splitting his pantaloons from mainsail to bowsprit. The snort he gave as he took his seat went to the heart of more than one mourner in the procession.

A Wilkinson County man who remarked in an argumentative way at breakfast the other morning, that there were several women of the complexion of his wife's brother in the Lunatic Asylum has appealed to the authorities for protection. He says he would rather be caught in a cyclone than to attempt to board at home.

A McDuffie County man broke his arm in two places and put out the eye of a grass widow recently in endeavoring to drop some molasses candy which he had picked up.

Harris' column soon won for him a reputation as Georgia's foremost newspaper humorist. His paragraphs were widely quoted and the Atlanta *Constitution* published the following fictitious sketch of his literary ancestry as a humorist:

JENKS CONUNDRUM HARRIS

His earliest progenitor is supposed to be a Frenchman, a fellow known to fame, a chap named Rabelais. His next notable ancestor in direct line was one to whom Jenks bears strong physical resemblance, a jolly buck answering to the title of Sir John Falstaff.[19] Another progenitor of note was a sort of harlequin, who flourished at the time of Queen Elizabeth. His name was Mark Twain.

Harris exudes, drools, eats, breathes, looks, imagines, and gesticulates humor. He, indeed, murmurs jokes, even in the tender hours of love, "which the same" he is very fond of.

But we must stop. The very suggestion of Harris sets our paper capering with laughter, our table to cutting up didoes, our pen to dancing a sort of Highland fling.[20]

As a humorist, Harris came upon the Southern scene at the right time. Georgia and the rest of the South were still smarting under the sting of military defeat and the harsh measures of Reconstruc-

---

[19]Harris had gained considerable weight for his short stature since going to Savannah, hence the reference in his appearance to that of Falstaff.

[20]Atlanta *Constitution*, April 23, 1873.

tion. His humor, like that of Bret Harte, Josh Billings, Artemus Ward, and Mark Twain, had the effect of relieving the tensions which were uppermost in the minds of his readers.

Harris' public image was now one of a carefree, jolly fellow whose every thought turned to humor. What the public did not know, however, was that he had gone through an agonizing experience of self-examination during his first months in Savannah. He brooded over whether or not he had been disloyal to Harrison in leaving the *Monroe Advertiser* for the *Morning News* and ungrateful to his other friends in Forsyth. His innate shyness made it difficult for him to adjust to his new environment in Savannah where once again as in New Orleans he was among strangers. Moreover, he had become highly sensitive about his awkwardness when he was among girls and women, and particularly so on account of the numerous references in the Georgia press to his personal appearance, especially to his red hair, even though he knew that in the era of personal journalism such references were intended to be humorous and not to be taken seriously. What troubled him most deeply, however, was that he had now discovered by right of possession some of the difficulties which inhabit the world as they applied to him. Foremost among these personal problems was his evident realization of the extent to which the adverse circumstances of his early years had set him apart from the normal social pattern. Despite his growing reputation as Georgia's most gifted young humorist, he fell into moods of morose introspection which depressed him to the depths of despair.

Having no one in Savannah in whom he could confide, he again turned to Georgia Starke. In his letters to her he laid bare his heart as he had not done to anyone before or ever did to anyone thereafter. In his letter of December 9, 1870, his twenty-second birthday, he wrote that he had never known what a real friend was until he went to Forsyth and that it was no wonder he looked back on his life there with the most sincere regrets that he had been compelled to give it up. "My history," he confessed to her without being specific, "is a peculiarly sad and unfortunate one—and those three years in Forsyth are the very brightest in my life. They are a precious memorial of what would otherwise be as bleak and as desolate as winter." [21]

[21]Julia Collier Harris, *Harris, Life and Letters*, 78.

Still in a depressed mood but finding some relief in his confessional letters, he wrote Mrs. Starke again on December 18 and dwelt at length on the torture of mind which his extreme sensitiveness had caused him. He did not expect, he said, to make any new friends in Savannah. "You see," he wrote her, "I am conservative in my disposition and suspicious of new faces. . . . I have an *absolute horror* of strangers. . . . The truth is, I am morbidly sensitive. With some people the quality of sensitiveness adds to their refinement and is quite a charm. With me it is an affliction—a disease—that has cost me more mortification and grief than anything in the world—or everything put together." He went on to say that the least hint, a word, or a gesture was enough to put him almost in a frenzy, and that the slightest rebuff tortured him beyond expression so much that he said he had "wished a thousand times that I was dead and buried and out of sight." Having in mind no doubt the jocular references in the press to his unusual features, he said his dearest friends had no idea how often they had crucified him.[22]

As the months passed, Harris gradually became better adapted to Savannah, and as his assignments became more numerous and responsible, he had less time for a gloomy analysis of his history. He also grew less sensitive about his looks and his various humorous nicknames. And the success of his column of humorous comments on everyday happenings in the lives of everyday people, both white and black, helped to buoy up self-confidence in his journalistic ability. He gained weight, wore clothes that improved his appearance, and no longer gave the impression of being "the greenest, gawkiest-looking specimen of humanity our eyes had ever rested upon," as one of his colleagues on the *Morning News* described him when he first saw him.[23]

If the most important journey which Harris ever made from the standpoint of his career in literature was the one with Turner from Eatonton to Turnwold in 1862, the most important event of his life in its effect upon his personal happiness was his marriage to Esther LaRose in 1873. Among the other boarders at the Florida House in Savannah when Harris began to reside there in the fall of

[22]*Ibid.*, 83, 84.
[23]*Ibid.*, 94.

1870 were Captain and Mrs. Pierre LaRose, French Canadians who had recently moved to Savannah where Captain LaRose was the owner and operator of the steamer *Lizzie Baker*. Early in 1872 their daughter Esther, then seventeen, joined her parents after graduation from the Catholic convent school in St. Hyacinthe, near Montreal. Never before had the shy and bashful Joe Harris had any romantic attachment for any girl. However, he saw in Esther a living embodiment of all the charms and virtues which he had fancifully ascribed to Little May in his "sweet lines" to her in the Macon *Telegraph*. Her youthful beauty, vivacious spirit, enjoyment of humor, and her social graces completely captivated him. Their mutual love resolved the differences in their geographical and cultural backgrounds, and after a courtship of little more than a year they were married on the evening of April 20, 1873, by Bishop Perisco of the Catholic church at his residence with only Esther's parents in attendance.

By the time of his marriage Harris had demonstrated to himself that he had the ability to succeed in the newspaper field. If any doubt remained, it was dispelled by the complimentary notices which his contemporaries of the Georgia press wrote about him and his work. But what he most needed was serenity of mind and the assurance which a normal home life could give him by its undisturbed continuity, and these he found in the home which Esther, despite her youth, helped him to establish. He would always be shy and uncomfortable when he was among those whom he did not intimately know, but, fortified in his home life by the perceptive and congenial companionship of his wife, he would never again yield to black moods of despair induced by a backward look at his unfortunate past.

During the entire period of Harris' connection with the *Morning News* he was so preoccupied with the preparation of his "Affairs in Georgia" column and with his other assignments of a general nature that he had very little time to devote to his literary interest other than an occasional poem to commemorate a local event.

Harris' daily column, "Affairs in Georgia," grew steadily in popular favor from its inception in 1870. By 1876 it had established him as Georgia's foremost humorist. He had also become well adjusted to his Savannah environment, and in all probability would have been content to remain indefinitely with the *Morning News* but for a serious outbreak of yellow fever in Savannah during the last week in August, 1876. The first cases were reported on Monday, and by Wednesday thirty-nine cases and nine deaths were officially known. By the first of September the number of deaths had increased to twenty-three, and the entire city was in a state of consternation and panic. The Savannah physicians held a joint meeting and advised all who could do so to leave the city at once. Motivated by his concern for the welfare of his wife and their two young children, Julian LaRose, aged two, and Evelyn, aged one, Harris decided to take his family to the high elevation of Atlanta where he intended to stay until the Savannah health authorities declared that it was safe to return.

On September 14, 1876, the Atlanta *Constitution* carried the following news item of their arrival in Atlanta: "Colonel J. C. Harris, of the Morning News, wife, two daughters [*sic*] and bilious servant, are registered at the Kimball." On September 17 the *Constitution* warned that there was little hope the yellow fever epidemic would disappear for another three weeks and advised all refugees to continue to stay away from Savannah.

During the waiting period, Harris accepted temporary employment on the Atlanta *Constitution*, which was to become permanent, through a change in the ownership of the *Constitution* and the reorganization of its staff. His journalistic odyssey was now at an end, for henceforth he would continue to live in Atlanta. His ambition to become an author of Southern literature, which had first been awakened at Turnwold but which since then had been almost dormant, if measured by any appreciable achievement, would soon be quickened into new life by a combination of circumstances which he could not have foreseen when he had left Savannah.

6

PERIOD OF TRANSITION

In the fall of 1876 Harris found himself in an urban environment that was pulsating with energy and dominated by the spirit of material progress. Atlanta was making a remarkable recovery from the almost total destruction inflicted upon it during the summer and fall of 1864. The major portion of the city which had not been consumed by fire had been "blown up, torn down, or otherwise destroyed." No other city during the war was so nearly annihilated.[1]

If, however, Atlanta had suffered more severely from the scourge of war than had any other city in the Confederacy, its resurgence from rubble and ashes had been more rapid, more spirited, and more substantial. Within a relatively short time, many of the refugees from the siege had returned, new citizens had moved in, and by 1870 the city's population had grown to 21,879.[2] In 1868 the federal government had made Atlanta the capital of Georgia and its officials occupied a handsome new building at a corner of Forsyth and Marietta streets. Also, near the capitol on Marietta Street, DeGive's Opera House had been built in 1869 and remodeled and enlarged to a seating capacity of 1,600 in 1871. During the same year some four hundred new commercial and residential buildings were erected,[3] and in 1876 the revitalized city could boast of having nine banks, of being served by six railroads, and of having twenty-eight churches of the Jewish, Protestant, and Catholic faiths.[4] The bold, dynamic, and imaginative civic enterprise which motivated its citizens in rebuilding the city between 1870 and 1880 made that decade one of the most

[1]"Atlanta, Fulton County, Georgia," *House Miscellaneous Document*, 47th Cong., 2nd. Sess., No. 42, pp. 157–62.

[2]U.S. Census Office, *Ninth Census of the United States: 1870.*

[3]Thomas H. Martin, *Atlanta and Its Builders* (Atlanta: Century Memorial Publishing Company, 1902) 2, 70.

[4]*Atlanta City Director*, 1876.

significant in Atlanta's history, for it was in that period that the famed Atlanta spirit was born.

The pride of Atlanta and the most tangible evidence of its rebirth and vitality was the Kimball House, the hotel in which Harris and his family stayed during his temporary employment on the *Constitution*. It bore the name of its founder and builder Hamilton Ingalls Kimball, who had been born in Maine and had made his way to Atlanta in 1867 by way of Chicago. He was one of the first of the many "foreigners" who came to Atlanta after the war and by their contributions to its civic development gave this Southern city the reputation of being the New York of the South.

During the weeks that Harris temporarily stayed at the Kimball House, he began to feel the impact of the aggressive spirit which pervaded Atlanta. He was again confronted with a problem of readjustment to a city environment in which trade and material progress had become the watchwords of its most prominent citizens.

By the fall of 1876 the Atlanta *Constitution* had attained a position of financial stability and statewide influence such as it had not hitherto known. Founded on June 16, 1868, only four years after Sherman had reduced the city to rubble, it had experienced a stormy and at times a financially precarious existence. Clark Howell, Sr., in his history of the paper, set forth the circumstances of its founding and the origin of its name. "The state of Georgia at that time," he wrote, "was in the hands of 'carpetbaggers.' Ex-slaves, only a few years before in bondage, were sitting in defiant authority in our legislative halls, overriding the state constitution itself, plunging the state hopelessly in debt, and under the authority of military bayonets, utterly ignoring the constitutional guarantees to the people. In this crisis the Constitution was born; and out of these conditions it took its very name—the CONSTITUTION." [5]

Carey W. Styles, its first editor, was an ex-Confederate officer, and he sharply and vigorously condemned the restrictions which Congress was imposing upon Georgia and the conquered South. J. R. Barwick, who succeeded him in 1869, was more moderate and conciliatory in his editorial pronouncements. "The South," he wrote, "cherishes no feeling of hostility to the government. It only asks an equal measure of justice in protection of its rights and property.

[5]Atlanta *Constitution*, September 26, 1917.

... Passion has had sway long enough. ... It is high time the North and the South should address themselves in unison to a correction of the many ills growing out of the war." [6] In a subsequent editorial he called for an adequate educational program for the Negroes in the South in the interest of the common welfare of both races. He emphasized that it was an obligation of the Southern white people to instill in the minds of the Negroes, in his words, "correct ideas of the views and the purposes of the Southern people toward their race. We must develop a spirit of confidence and trust in our humanity to and interest in them." [7]

In an atmosphere of sectional conflict between a punishing North and a resentful South, the *Constitution* fought for a restoration to the people of their constitutional rights, and, despite its lean financial resources, managed to survive the difficulties which arose during its first critical years. In 1872, however, it became involved in a bitter rivalry with the Atlanta *Herald*. The *Herald* began publication on August 22 of that year. Its founders, Alexander St. Clair-Abrams and H. L. W. Craig, served notice in their first editorial statement of policy that they intended to make the paper far more than merely another conventional daily. Its aim, they asserted, would be to expose fraud and corruption, to denounce everything that tended to injure Georgia and the South and to promote whatever tended to their prosperity, and to be independent of all political parties.

In short, they declared that their purpose was to make the *Herald* "the liveliest, raciest, and most interesting paper in Georgia."

On October 23, the *Herald* announced that Craig had retired from any further connection with it, and that Colonel R. A. Alston and Henry W. Grady had purchased a two-thirds interest. The addition of Grady to part-ownership and to its editorial staff was in itself a guarantee that the *Herald* would carry out its original policy of presenting the news and current issues in a lively, racy, and interesting fashion. He was only twenty-two years of age, but his unconventional and invigorating editorship of the Rome *Commerical* had already marked him as a new breed of Georgia journalist whose keen discernment of news values and ability to communicate them to the reader in a captivating manner would take him far in his pro-

[6]*Ibid.*, January 12, 1869.
[7]*Ibid.*, April 6, 1869.

fession. He made his aggressive spirit as an editor felt at once, for in the same issue the three owners published a signed, bristling declaration of policy to the effect that the *Herald* would be undaunted by threats, and that it reserved the right to say what it pleased, as it pleased, and when it pleased in the teeth of any partisan ties or opposition.

The more conservative and moderate *Constitution* accepted the challenge laid down by its bold, tough competitor, and the feud between the two Atlanta newspapers became the most bitterly fought and financially exhausting in the annals of Georgia journalism. Both papers indulged in sarcastic name-calling, bitter invective, and in charges and counter-charges. Each one publicly avowed that it would put the other out of business.

In its bid to outdo its older and more conservative rival for public support, the *Herald* began to deliver its editions to towns along the Atlanta and West Point railway by a chartered train which left Atlanta earlier in the morning than the daily scheduled one which the *Constitution* used to deliver its editions. The initial run on July 26, 1873, created such a favorable response from the towns along the route that the *Herald* chartered another train for the same purpose on the Central of Georgia railway for the towns between Atlanta and Macon. In response, the more conservative *Constitution* reluctantly, but of necessity, chartered its own engine and a mail coach to match the novel experiment of its publicity-minded but financially extravagant competitor. Since both newspapers came off the presses at about the same time, there was a race each morning to see which one of the special trains would leave the station first. Crowds gathered at each station along the route to greet the arrival of both trains, with E. Y. Clarke of the *Constitution* on one and Grady of the *Herald* on the other, and to express their unbounded enthusiasm for this journalistic innovation.

Both newspapers were publicly commended for their enterprising feats of journalism, but the financial returns proved to be far out of proportion to the extra cost involved, and their rapidly dwindling bank accounts compelled them to discontinue their chartered trains. The *Herald* was the first to call for a truce in what it stated in its issue of April 15, 1875, was their "insane" rivalry. Atlanta, it concluded, was simply not large enough to support adequately more than one newspaper and clearly intimated that the *Herald* would be that one paper.

In the months that followed, the *Herald* managed to survive one financial crisis after another, but the end was inevitable, for it had incurred obligations which it could not meet. In its issue of February 6, 1876, the *Constitution* carried among its legal advertisements one which stated that the *Herald* was to be sold. During its relatively brief existence of a little more than three years, it had fulfilled its promise of being the most interesting paper in Georgia. Its declared policy of opposing and attacking whatever it considered to be wrong either in public affairs or in prominent citizens had frequently involved it in heated controversies, but its spirited reporting of the news made it a consistently readable newspaper. It added color and zest to Georgia journalism, brought to the forefront the genius of Henry W. Grady as an imaginative, enterprising, and crusading editor, and made its competitor, the *Constitution*, then only in its seventh year of publication, better known throughout the state.

After the demise of the *Herald*, Grady made unsuccessful efforts to establish two newspapers in Atlanta, the daily *Courier* and the Sunday *Telegram*. He then went to New York to try his fortunes in metropolitan journalism, but this venture was a disappointment to him. He left New York and returned to Georgia to become the editor of the Augusta *Constitutionalist*. But before going to Augusta he stopped in Atlanta for a visit with friends and former associates.

In the meantime, on October 18, Captain Evan P. Howell had acquired from E. Y. Clarke his stock in the *Constitution*, and as its editor-in-chief he proceeded at once to reorganize its editorial staff. On learning that Grady was in Atlanta, Howell contacted him and made him an offer to become an associate editor of the *Constitution*. Grady hesitated at first to accept the offer and expressed doubt that the *Constitution* would employ him on account of the harsh criticism which he made of it when he was with the *Herald*. However, when Howell told him that he was now a part owner of the *Constitution* and in complete charge of its organization, Grady accepted the offer and joined its editorial staff on October 19, 1876.[8]

Harris was still in Atlanta because restrictions placed on the re-

[8]Raymond B. Nixon, *Henry W. Grady: Spokesman of the New South* (New York: Alfred A. Knopf, 1943), 120–27.

turn to Savannah of refugees from the yellow fever epidemic had not been lifted. Howell and Grady persuaded him to accept temporary employment on the *Constitution* and announced in its issue of November 21 that arrangements had been completed for him to become an associate editor on a permanent basis. Although Harris had not directly sought the appointment, it was one in which he had been interested when he was with the *Monroe Advertiser* in Forsyth. His assistant, J. T. Manry, remembered that when talk was going the rounds in 1868 about a new paper to be started in Atlanta he had overheard a conversation between Harrison, the editor of the *Monroe Advertiser*, and Harris to the effect that "Mr. Harris was to have a position" on the new paper.[9] Time and the recent turn of events in Savannah and Atlanta had at last brought about the fulfillment of that expectation.

No newspaper in the South in 1876 was more capably staffed than was the Atlanta *Constitution*, with Evan P. Howell as its editor-in-chief and Joel Chandler Harris and Henry Woodfin Grady as its associate editors. All three men were natives of Georgia and had a thorough knowledge of its people's political, social, and cultural mores and of their economic status. Howell, who was then thirty-six, had served the Confederacy as a captain of artillery with notable distinction in the battle of Atlanta and had also actively engaged in politics on both the local and state levels. Harris was only twenty-seven, but he brought to the *Constitution* fourteen years of practical experience on both weekly and daily newspapers, and his column in the Savannah *Morning News* had solidly established him as a humorist. Grady at twenty-six had proven his mettle as a journalist by his courageous and crusading editorship of the *Herald*. Since the *Constitution* now faced no competing paper in Atlanta, it was free to enter upon a constructive program for the rehabilitation of the South. Its field was unlimited: a new system of farming had to be devised; roads, educational facilities, and natural and cultural resources needed to be developed; and a better image of its people needed to be created. At this critical period, when the South's destiny was in the process of being determined, as Paul H. Buck in his *The Road to Reunion* states, the *Constitution* "rose to supremacy as the

[9]Shreveport (La.) *Journal*, March 8, 1930.

South's leading advocate of business enterprise and of friendship with the North." [10]

The regional supremacy which the *Constitution* achieved and the national influence which it progressively came to exert were due in large measure to Grady and Harris. Both had a passion for a revitalized South but each was concerned about a different phase of its progress. Grady envisioned an industrialized South which would change from a region of poverty to a land of undreamed-of prosperity and happiness for its people. With evangelistic fervor he went throughout Georgia and the South to proclaim the gospel of industrialization as the economic salvation of the South. Harris, on the other hand, was steeped in the cultural traditions of the old South, but he came to be a severe critic of its literary expression and a pioneer champion for the emancipation of its literature from its ultraromantic and sectional qualities and for its reconstruction on a realistic and artistic foundation. He was as concerned as was Grady for the prosperity of the South, but, being a child of the old, agrarian South, he advocated that its people should stay by the land but diversify their farming. It thus happened, as the historian C. Vann Woodward has pointed out, that on one side of the editorial desk of the *Constitution* Henry W. Grady was exhorting the South to exploit its treasure of natural resources, while on the other side Joel Chandler Harris was telling the South to develop its as yet untouched, unique, and original literary materials.[11]

Each in his own way according to his predominant interest made a significant contribution to the New South movement while he was an associate editor of the *Constitution.* Although each differed in cultural backgrounds, personality traits, and objectives in his efforts to rehabilitate the South, they became warm personal friends. In fact, their friendship antedated by some years their almost simultaneous appointment to the editorial staff of the *Constitution.* Harris said that it had its beginning when something he had written in the Savannah *Morning News* and something Grady had written in the Rome *Commercial* had drawn them together, that a correspondence

---

[10]Paul H. Buck, *The Road to Reunion* (Boston: Little, Brown, and Company, 1937), 186.

[11]C. Vann Woodward, *Origins of the New South* (Baton Rouge: Louisiana State University Press, 1951), 166.

had ensued, and that he had gone to Rome to meet him. In recalling the incident, Harris wrote that on his arrival in Rome he had inquired at the office of the *Commercial* where he might find Grady and that he had been "directed to a merry-go-round that had its tent pitched in the street. On one of the flying steeds Henry Grady was seated, and as soon as the machine could be stopped he came to greet me covered with dust and perspiration and glowing with health, strength, and enjoyment." [12]

This evidence of an exuberant spirit and of a zest for life was inherent in Grady's nature, and, with his added qualities of personal charm and an unbounded enthusiasm for a cause in which he ardently believed, he easily made a large circle of loyal friends, especially among the men who were engaged in various business ventures. Born in 1850 into a family of more than moderate affluence and fortunate social connections in Athens, he had attended the University of Georgia and the University of Virginia. He had displayed a flair for public speaking, and he was keenly interested in politics but exercised his interest behind the scenes, for he never cared to hold public office. An effective and fluent writer, he was, however, more persuasive with spoken words than with his pen.

Harris, on the other hand, although warmhearted and companionable in a group of his intimate associates, was extremely hesitant to meet strangers, especially those who were prominent literary figures. Perhaps his reluctance to do so grew out of his natural shyness and his consciousness of his humble origin and lack of formal education. He never attempted to make a public address but let his pen speak for him. However, he did possess the common touch, for he knew with sympathetic understanding the mind and the heart of Georgia's middle-class people and of those who were less fortunate, among both the poor whites and the Negroes. He watched with wary eye the rising tide of Southern industrialism, but he was never engulfed by it. While Grady was beating the drums for industrial progress, Harris was quietly but effectively pointing the way to a Southern literary renaissance and healing the sectional wounds left by the Civil War and Reconstruction. Both men were committed to a program of progress for the South, but from different points

[12]Atlanta *Constitution*, December 26, 1889.

of view, and the *Constitution* served as a medium for them to communicate their objectives to the South and to the nation.

Harris had been employed by the *Constitution* primarily because of his journalistic ability, and his transition from a full-time editor to a part-time author proceeded gradually over a period of four years. His first contribution to the *Constitution* was a column of humorous paragraphs similar to the one he had done for the *Morning News*, but he gave it a new heading, "Roundabout in Georgia," and it appeared in the issue of October 26, 1876, while he was temporarily employed. Of more significance, however, were two of his dialect sketches, "Markham's Ball" and "Jeems Rober'son's Last Illness," both of which appeared in the same issue. They were his first venture in writing dialect, and he wrote them not through his own initiative but at the request of Howell. Preceding Harris' employment on the *Constitution* Sam W. Small, a member of its staff, had been contributing a series of short dialect sketches in which he had used Old Si, an old-time Atlanta Negro, as his spokesman on current politics and sidelights of the local scene. The dialect which he attributed to Old Si was simply a jumble of misspelled words after the manner of Josh Billings and Artemus Ward, but the comments of the old man were amusing and they had become a popular feature of the *Constitution*. When Howell purchased an interest in the paper and reorganized its staff, Small severed his connection with it to establish two newspapers of his own, the *Sunday Herald* and the *Evening Telegram*, and the *Constitution* no longer carried his Old Si sketches. In response to its readers' requests for stories of a similar nature, Howell surveyed the members of his staff for someone who could possibly write them. One morning during an editorial conference he turned to Harris and said: "Joe, can't you write some dialect stories like the ones Small wrote?" "I don't know that I can," he replied, "for I have never done anything along that line, but I do know the old-time Middle Georgia Negro pretty well and I will see what I can do." [13]

His "Markham's Ball" followed the pattern set by Small in that he made a Negro character by the name of Uncle Ben his spokesman

[13]Personal interview with Clark Howell, Sr., son of Evan P. Howell, who said he was present at the staff meeting.

for some humorous comments on a recent celebration of a local political victory held at the Markham House, Atlanta's newest hotel. The sketch, however, was a clumsy piece of work, for it simply imitated the ones by Small. But the other one, "Jeem's Rober'son's Last Illness," bore the stamp of Harris' genius. In composing it he drew upon his recollections of the Negroes whom he had known in Putnam County and the dialect which he had heard them speak. The scene was the Union Station opposite the Kimball House; the two characters were an old Negro to whom he gave the name of Uncle Remus and a younger Negro from nearby Jonesboro who was waiting for his train to depart. The two struck up a casual conversation in which the Jonesboro man asked Uncle Remus about a mutual friend whom he said he hadn't seen for some time. "He ain't down wid de beliousness, is he?" "Not dat I knows un," responded Uncle Remus gravely. "He ain't sick, an' he ain't been sick. He des tuckn'n say he wuz gwinter ride dat ar roan mule er Mars John's de udder Sunday, an' de mule, she up'n do like she got nudder ingagement." He said that he had fooled with that mule before and that he had told Jim "he'd better not git tangled up wid er" but that Jim had allowed he was a "hoss-doctor" and had put the bridle on the mule and got on her. At this point in his narration, Uncle Remus, having employed the storyteller's art of creating suspense, warned his inquirer that it was time for him to catch his train which he said he had been told "goes a callyhootin'." But the other man insisted on hearing the rest of the incident. Whereupon, Uncle Remus proceeded with due solemnity to relate the sad outcome of Jim's ill-fated attempt to ride Mars John's obstreperous roan mule.

Without being aware of it at the time, Harris in his first Uncle Remus sketch was beginning to create a new and original character in American fiction, for he had endowed him with an individuality that set him apart from such stock characters as Old Si and Uncle Ben. Moreover, he had given him a certain natural dignity in keeping with his age, a keen knowledge of human nature, and the knack of telling a story effectively. Although his account of Jim's encounter with the mule had the element of humor after the manner of the tall tale, Uncle Remus kept the humor subdued by maintaining a grave countenance as he related the incident. The dialect was that which had been actually spoken by an old plantation Negro, not a poor imitation which had been contrived for humorous effect. The total impression was that of Uncle Remus speaking his own thoughts in his own language. The story also contained a suggestion of past plantation days in Uncle Remus's reference to Mars John.

Harris had written far better than he knew, for in letting the old man speak for himself he had made him a representative spokesman of his own race rather than merely a medium through whom Harris himself could make humorous comments on the current Atlanta scene. At the time, however, he did not concentrate on the development of Uncle Remus in this particular role but continued to experiment with various other characters in order to find a suitable successor to Old Si. In another sketch, "Politics and Provisions," two Negroes, one unnamed and the other one simply called Remus, expressed their disillusionment with the Republicans who, according to rumor, had promised to give those Negroes who voted the Republican ticket all the provisions and money they needed. The two Negroes had driven into Atlanta with a load of wood from the country but the unnamed one complained that no "'publican" would pay them more for it than a Democrat would and that he could buy very little provisions with the money he received at the "Freedmen's Bank." "Mount dis wagon, Remus," he said to his partner, "an' le's git out er dis." In this sketch Remus was only a secondary figure.

As soon as Harris got his hand in, so to speak, he turned out his dialect sketches with greater frequency, and during November and December, 1876, the *Constitution* published six of them. In one of them, "Uncle Remus and the Savannah Darkey," [14] he illustrated the differences in speech and attitudes of mind between those of the Negroes he knew at Turnwold and those of the coastal Negroes he knew when he had lived in Savannah.

In the process of writing these sketches, Harris gradually eliminated all of the characters with whom he had been experimenting except Uncle Remus. In doing so, he really began to create two different Uncle Remuses. One was a rather indigent old man who found it difficult to make ends meet by his own efforts. He became a familiar figure on Atlanta's streets in the vicinity of the Kimball House, the Union Station, and the editorial rooms of the *Constitution* where he

[14] *Atlanta Constitution*, November 18, 1876.

was always ready to recount his troubles to its reporters, to express his opinions on current politics both Republican and Democratic, the activities of the Ku Klux Klan and the Union League, or any other item of current events, and to ask for a dime to buy some tobacco or a dram. The other one was that of an old man who bore up under his troubles with a dignity which befitted his age, and whose wit and wisdom were inherent qualities of his race, and thereby foreshadowed the Uncle Remus of the folklore stories. Harris presented him in the sketches with appropriate fitness to the incident which he might be relating at the time.

During his composition of the dialect sketches, Harris began to revive his memories of his Turnwold experiences. Among them was his recollection of the songs which he had heard the Negroes on Turner's plantation sing, and in "Uncle Remus's Revival Hymn" [15] he recaptured this phase of plantation life which was familiar to him and characteristic of the deeply religious nature of the Southern plantation Negroes. In figurative language and with rhythmical cadence, "The Hymn" vividly pictured the sad plight of the unrepentant sinners on the Judgment Day. The first of its three stanzas, each with a hortatory refrain, was as follows:

> Oh, whar shill we go w'en de great day comes,
> Wid de blowin' er de trumpits en de bangin' er de drums?
> How many po' sinners'll be kotched out late
> En fine no latch ter de golden gate?
>> No use for ter wait twel ter-morrer!
>> De sun musn't set on yo' sorrer,
>> Sin's ez sharp ez a bamboo-brier—
>> Oh, Lord! fetch de mo'ners up higher!

On January 21, 1877, the *Constitution* published another Uncle Remus sketch with an Atlanta setting, "Uncle Remus's Church Experience," the only one that was to appear during the next nine months. In this character sketch Uncle Remus explained to one of the church deacons why he had quit attending its services. No, he said, he had not "unjined," he had "des tuck'n draw'd out." "I went dar," he solemnly declared, "fer ter sing, an' fer ter pray, an' fer ter wushup, an' I mos' giner'lly allers had a stray shinplarster w'ich de ole 'oman

[15] *Ibid.*, January 18, 1877.

say she want sont out dar ter dem cullud fokes 'cross de water."
Everything had gone along quietly and peacefully, he continued in
grave tones, until the first thing he knew a row had suddenly erupted
in the "amen cornder" over the disappearance of some money from
the collection box. It had spread from there to include the entire
congregation and the preacher. To escape from the mounting confusion, scuffling, and overturning of benches, Uncle Remus said he
had humped himself and scrambled out of the church only to be
arrested by a policeman and had to send for Mars John to bail him
out of jail. "Hit ain't no use ter sing out chu'ch ter me, Brer Rastus. I
done been an' got my dose. W'en I goes ter war, I wanter know w'at
I'm a doin'. I don't wanter git hemmed up 'mong no wimmen and
preachers. I wants elbow-room, an' I'm bleedzed ter have it. Des
gimme elbow-room."

On January 30, 1873, the *Constitution* announced that on the
previous day Sam W. Small had discontinued the publication of
the *Sunday Herald* and the *Evening News* and he was back on its
staff. Two of his Old Si sketches were published in that day's issue.
Since Harris had undertaken Howell's assignment to write some dialect stories as a substitute for those which Small had written for the
paper, there was now no necessity for him to continue the Uncle
Remus series. According to Small, Harris welcomed his release from
the assignment. "Mrs. Harris used to say," he wrote in his reminiscences of his newspaper association with Harris, "that Joe had rather
take a licking than grind out one of those stories," and Small himself
said that only Harris' affection for Howell and his loyalty to him
made him keep up the production of the Uncle Remus human interest
sketches.[16] It became increasingly evident, however, that during the
composition of the brief Uncle Remus stories Harris had begun to
consider plantation life as material for literature and that Uncle
Remus was taking shape in his imagination as a representative of
that era, not merely as a humorous Negro character in post-Civil War
Atlanta.

Although Harris' stories were undeniably superior to Small's, he
suspended their publication after Small returned to the *Constitution*,
and Howell then asked Harris to prepare in their stead "something

[16]Sam W. Small, "History of the Constitution," Atlanta *Constitution*, September 26, 1917.

light" for the Sunday editions. Left free to choose his own subjects, Harris began the composition of a series of light essays which in content and mood of reverie revealed his nostalgia for the pastoral scenes of his youth in Putnam County in comparison with the hurried pace of his Atlanta environment. His religious thinking was also disturbed by the impact which the current vogue of "higher criticism" was making on the validity of the Bible, although he had not identified himself with any church body. In his essay on "A Country Church," which he described as having been located in the quiet of the woods far removed from "the turbulence of trade and dust of the cities," he compared the simple and sincere faith of rural folk in his youth with the modern beliefs of city churchgoers who, he said, had come under the influence of Tyndall, Darwin, and Huxley.[17] In "The Old Plantation" he recalled the excitement of a fox hunt and heard again in memory the spirituals.[18] "The old plantation itself is gone," he wrote in nostalgic mood. "It has passed away, but the hand of time, inexorable and yet tender, has woven about it the sweet suggestions of poetry and romance, memorials that neither death nor decay can destroy."

Harris characterized these and his other light essays as ephemeral newspaper literature of the day, but they were important in his literary development because they revealed that the plantation regime, as he remembered it, was looming large in his mind as a source of literary material upon which he might draw for his own writings. He already had in Uncle Remus a character who offered him the possibility for the development of that material, but he had not yet firmly envisioned his role. Up to this point Harris had portrayed him for the most part as a humorous spokesman of his own views on the contemporary Atlanta scene, but in the "Revival Hymn" Harris had given him an old plantation setting, and in the reminiscent essays of his own boyhood in Putnam County he was beginning to revive his memories of that bygone era in Southern life. As the sketches proceeded, he began more and more to identify Uncle Remus with that era.

In "Uncle Remus as a Rebel" Harris illustrated the loyalty which he remembered that some of Turner's older slaves had exhibited toward

[17]Atlanta *Constitution*, November 25, 1877.
[18]*Ibid.*, December 9, 1877.

their master during the invasion of Turnwold by the Federal soldiers in the fall of 1864, and for the first time he had Uncle Remus voice his intention to return to his former antebellum home in Putnam County.[19] This was the first story which Harris had published in the *Constitution* for almost nine months, and he explained the old man's absence by saying that he had been living in the country where he had been trying his luck as a farmer. On his first visit to the editorial rooms of the *Constitution* after his return, he told the reporters that nothing had turned out right for him—his crops had been a failure and thieves had stolen his chickens and pigs. "I'm a-gwine ter drap farmin' sho," he gravely declared. "I'm gwine down inter old Putmon and live alonger Mars Jeems." When one of the reporters asked Uncle Remus if it were true that once during the war he had saved his master's life, he was obviously embarrassed, but at the insistence of his questioner he proceeded quietly to relate the dramatic incident and the role he had played in it. He said that after his Mars Jeems had joined the Confederate army and the overseer had been conscripted, his Ole Miss had put him in charge of the plantation. When the news came that the Federals were nearing the plantation, he had driven the stock to the woods and then had stayed near Ole Miss and her daughter Miss Sally to protect them from any possible harm. After he felt sure that all of the Federal soldiers had left the plantation, he had taken a rifle along with him and was on his way to the place where he had hidden the stock when he saw a puff of blue smoke burst from the top of a tall pine tree. He knew that it could have come only from the gun of a Yankee sharpshooter who had not gone on with the other soldiers. At that moment he had suddenly seen his returning master riding toward him, unaware of the danger. Looking up again into the pine tree, he saw that the Yankee sharpshooter was aiming his rifle directly at his Mars Jeems. "I disremembered all 'bout freedom," Uncle Remus said, "an' I jes raise up wid de rifle I had an' let de man have all she had." He concluded his recital by saying that his Ole Miss and Miss Sally had been so grateful to him they had promised to do anything for him. "Dat's w'at make me say w'at I do. I ain't gwinter be workin' 'roun' here . . . w'en I got a good home down yonder in Putmon."

Harris' problem at the time was to find an appropriate rather

[19]*Ibid.*, October 14, 1877.

than an arbitrary way of getting Uncle Remus back to his Putnam County environment, but it became increasingly clear that he was subordinating the post-Civil War-Atlanta Uncle Remus to the larger and more convincing portrait of Uncle Remus as a representative of the old-time plantation regime. In "Uncle Remus's Corn-Shucking Song" he moved a step nearer to that image in his recapturing of the high spirit of the plantation Negroes who sang while they shucked the ears of corn at harvest time before storing them in the barns. The song also contained Harris' first mention of folklore in connection with Uncle Remus in his brief reference to Mr. Fox and Mr. Rabbit.[20]

When Sam Small accepted an appointment as United States Commissioner to Paris in March, 1878, Harris again resumed his sketches of the Atlanta Uncle Remus in the *Constitution* with greater regularity. There were thirteen of them between March 10 and December 8 and one additional plantation song. In these sketches he continued to portray Uncle Remus as both a humorous and a serious observer of the trend of the times and as a sage counselor of his race during the years of the Reconstruction. Uncle Remus had never succumbed to the blandishments of the Northern organizers of the Union Leagues, for their glowing promises had meant very little to him in a material way, nor had he been intimidated by their scare threats that the freed slaves were in danger of being put back into slavery. In "Uncle Remus's Reminiscences," he admitted that he had once attended a secret meeting of the Union League in Atlanta out of curiosity, but that when he heard the speaker say that all the rebels, including his Mars John, were mean and lowdown, he had walked out and taken his son with him.[21] Then in a mood of wistful reverie, as if he were unaware that the *Constitution* reporters from whom he was expecting to receive a small handout were listening, he compared his present hand-to-mouth existence in post-Civil War Atlanta with what to him had been a more secure lot on the plantation in Putnam County. This freedom, he said, was all mighty nice for the younger Negroes but that old-timers like him hadn't got much good out of it, "an' sometimes w'en I'm a setting on Mars John's back steps,

[20]*Ibid.*, December 30, 1877.
[21]*Ibid.*, July 14, 1878.

sorter dozin' like, an' hear Miss Sally's voice soun'n fer all de worl' like Ole Miss had come back, hit makes me feel mighty cu'us, an' den sometimes I dream I hear de boys a hollerin' in de corn, an' de hoe-hands a singin' ez dey come up de lane from de new-groun', an' feel mighty happy ontwell I wake up an' members dat I dunno whar my vittles for de nex' day is comin' frum 'ceppin' I falls back on Mars John an' Miss Sally."

Freedom for Uncle Remus had not meant freedom from want. In the old days his food, clothing, and cabin, as simple as they were, had been provided for him. Not having been a field hand, he now found it impossible to earn his day by day necessities by farming, and he was too old to readjust his long-established rural way of life to the rapid pace of his new city environment. His desire to return to Putnam County was an illustration of the strange paradox which in many instances the old Southern plantation society had produced.

Harris had already experimented with various literary forms, poetry, the essay, and reviews of magazines and books, but ever since he had heard his mother read *The Vicar of Wakefield* to him when he was a boy, he had wanted to write a novel. In *The Romance of Rockville* he realized that ambition, and on March 7, 1878, the *Constitution* announced that it would shortly begin to appear in serial form in both the daily and weekly editions. The announcement said that the scene would be laid in Georgia and that the story would embody "the peculiar features of life and society in the South anterior to the war. It will, in short, be a study of Southern character. "The date of publication had to be set forward because Harris came down with a severe case of measles which confined him to bed for almost a month. His three children, Julian, Evelyn, and Evan Howell, the youngest, who had been named for the editor of the *Constitution*, all contracted the disease, and Evan Howell did not survive. The first installment, therefore, did not appear until April 16 and was published only in the weekly edition with the last installment in its issue of September 10.[22]

The setting of the story was the small village of Rockville in

[22]Robert L. Wiggins transcribed the complete novel and included it among his collection of Harris' early writings in his *The Life of Joel Chandler Harris*, 282–428.

Putnam County, and the characters represented a cross section of all the classes which had composed the democratic society in middle Georgia as Harris had known it during his boyhood. As an artistic performance, however, the novel was a failure. Harris himself confessed that he had written it hastily and that it was rambling and disconnected. With the exception of the strong-willed and plain-spoken Jane Perryman, his characterizations lacked originality and lifelikeness, but in his subsequent fiction he would overcome this fault. However, he would always find it difficult to compose a novel with a compact and suspenseful plot structure.

At intervals during 1879, Harris continued to write the brief human-interest stories in which Uncle Remus was the central figure, and in "The Old Man's Troubles" there was a suggestion that the old man had a knowledge of plantation folklore.[23] By way of explaining why he had looked so lonesome lately, he said that his Mars John and Miss Sally had been down in "Putmon" County for four days and that during their absence he had had to scratch around mighty lively to make his rations hold out. It had been necessary, he said, for him to paddle the canoe and do the fishing at the same time "an' w'en you bleedzed ter ketch de fish an' dassent turn de paddle loose ter bait de hook, den I tell you, Brer John, youer right whar de mink had de goslin."

Among Harris' assignments as an associate editor of the *Constitution* was the congenial one of reviewing the current literary magazines and books, and through these media he kept informed of literary trends in American fiction. Among magazines he reviewed were *Lippincott's, Scribner's Monthly, Galaxy* and *Atlantic Monthly*. Of the last named he wrote as follows: "The Atlantic is the most thoughtful, the most scholarly of all our magazines, and supplies more nearly than any other all the essentials that go to fit and fill the best literary taste." [24] He preferred those novels whose characters were wholesome and portrayed with what he termed "the unexaggerated humor of human nature." He expressed a distaste for those in which love affairs were of a tropical nature, even though there were no improprieties in them as he found true of *Clara and Bebe*, a novel which he said the Lippincotts had sent him. He wrote of it that the proper

[23]Atlanta *Constitution*, July 14, 1879.
[24]*Ibid.*, September 27, 1879.

parties were reported to love one another with a heat and lack of steadfastness that was little short of sheet lightning and that the curtain fell upon a picture of despair as big and as highly colored as a traveling panorama of the Chicago fire.[25]

In his account of how he came to write his first Uncle Remus folklore stories, Harris said that in reading an issue of *Lippincott's Magazine* some time in the 1870's he had come across an article dealing with Southern Negro folklore. "This article," he said, "gave me my cue, and the legends told by Uncle Remus are the result." [26] The legends themselves were not new to him, for he said he had heard them in Putnam County when he was a boy but he had had no idea of their literary value until he had read the *Lippincott* article. The technique for turning these legends into literature presented no difficulty. He already had in Uncle Remus an appropriate character to narrate the stories, and he merely had to satisfy the old man's desire to leave Atlanta and live again on the old plantation in Putnam County. From his memories of the visits which he had made at Turnwold in company with some of Turner's children when they had heard Harbert and others tell the legends of their race, he created the character of the little boy, the son of Miss Sally and Mars John, to whom the ancient legends were new and interest compelling. The dialect spoken by the old-time plantation Negroes presented no real problem, for Harris had been writing it in the Uncle Remus sketches for some three years.

When the various aspects of the story had fallen into harmonious relationship in Harris' mind, he wrote "The Story of Mr. Rabbit and Mr. Fox as Told by Uncle Remus," and the *Constitution* published it on the editorial page of its issue for July 20, 1879. With a few deft strokes Harris sketched the setting for the tale itself—Uncle Remus sitting on the piazza of his Miss Sally's plantation home, her six-year-old son sitting beside him with his head against the old man's arm and "gazing with an expression of the

[25]*Ibid.*, July 12, 1879.
[26]Joel Chandler Harris, "An Accidental Author," *Lippincott's Magazine*, XXXVII (April, 1886), 419. In his article, Harris did not state the specific number of *Lippincott's* to which he referred, but it could have been the one for December, 1877, in which "Folklore of the Southern Negroes" by William Owens appeared, 748–55. Among the six folklore stories which he gave in outline form was the tar-baby legend.

most intense interest into the rough, weather-beaten face, that beamed so kindly upon him." The boy gave such rapt attention to the story that he did not interrupt Uncle Remus with any questions while he told him how Mr. Rabbit had outwitted Mr. Fox by closing the door on the tip end of his tail and also by his refusal to stay for dinner with him because he had provided no calamus root with which to season the chicken.

In this first story Harris had at last placed Uncle Remus in a congenial environment and cast him in an appropriate role. He would revise Uncle Remus' dialect for greater accuracy as the series progressed and add other refining touches to his portrait as a kindly, gentle, and wise representative of the antebellum plantation Negro, but his stature as an original character in American literature was already beginning to be apparent. Venerable in features and age, he was eminently fitted to tell the little white boy the ageless legends of his race and to introduce him to a world of wonder and delight untouched by the hand of "turbulent trade." Harris would continue, however, to use the Uncle Remus of a postwar Atlanta environment for shrewd and humorous comments on the various aspects of contemporary affairs, but the other Uncle Remus was now firmly fixed as the teller of Negro folklore. Both Uncle Remuses were original and authentic characters, but, as Thomas English has pointed out, Harris never bothered to reconcile the two.[27]

With the publication of the first story, Harris made the transition from writing newspaper articles for daily consumption to the authorship of permanent literature, but it would be twenty years until he was free from the daily grind of turning out copy for the *Constitution* and could devote his entire time to his various literary projects.

[27]Thomas H. English, "The Twice-Told Tale and Uncle Remus," *Georgia Review*, II (Winter, 1948), 452.

7

SOUTHERN LITERATURE, NEW STYLE

In creating his first folklore story, Harris had discovered a rich mine of literary material which no Southern author had explored. The legends themselves were old and well known, but they took on a new meaning in Harris' setting. The response from the readers of the *Constitution* to his initial story was so favorable that Harris began to verify for their genuineness other legends which he had heard from the Negroes in Putnam County, and he did not publish his second one, "Brer Rabbit, Brer Fox, and the Tar-Baby," until November 16. Thereafter, they appeared in the Sunday edition of the *Constitution* through the issue of May 16, 1880. Meanwhile, he also continued to keep Uncle Remus before the public in his former roles as a humorous commentator on the current scene and as a singer of old plantation spirituals.

In the process of writing the Uncle Remus plantation songs and stories Harris recalled another trait of the old-time plantation Negroes, namely, their adeptness at putting into pithy sayings their down-to-earth philosophy. The following are some examples of the "Plantation Proverbs" which Harris attributed to Uncle Remus in the *Constitution* from time to time: "Mighty po' bee dat don't make mo' honey dan he want," "Ef you bleedz ter eat dirt, eat clean dirt," "Meller mush-million hollers at you fum over de fence," "Licker talks mighty loud w'en it git loose fum de jug," "Troubles is seasonin'. 'Simmons ain't good twel dey 'er fros'-bit."

Although Harris had no idea that the amusing sayings, plantation songs, legends, and proverbs which he was contributing to the *Constitution* would ever be considered of sufficient literary value to be republished in book form, he did begin during their composition to give serious thought to the status of literature in the South. As has been stressed in an earlier chapter, when Harris was under the direct influence of Joseph Addison Turner during the years of the war, he had enthusiastically subscribed to Turner's one-man crusade for the development of a Southern literature which adhered in subject matter and point of view to the old sectional political and literary emphases. The reviews of books and magazines which Harris had written for *The Countryman* had given evidence of his loyalty to Southern authors regardless of the lack of literary merit in their work, and he had encouraged Southerners to subscribe to the *Crescent Monthly* because it was a Southern literary magazine.

But the South as Harris had come to know it in Atlanta in the 1870's was far different from the South which he had known in the isolation of Turnwold during the years of the Civil War. He felt in Atlanta the stirrings of a new spirit, and he believed the time had come for the South to write a new kind of literature, one that would be regional in its material but without the old sectional qualities in its treatment. To that end, he began a series of editorials in which he advocated development of a literature in the South that would honestly represent its people both past and present and would reconcile sectional extremes.

The first of these editorials, "Literature in the South," was published in the *Constitution* on November 30, 1879. It is given below in full, not only for Harris' penetrating analysis of the reasons for the failure of Southern authors before 1879 but also for the revolutionary changes which he said Southern authors must make if they expected what they wrote to merit national recognition and acceptance as first-rate literature.

LITERATURE IN THE SOUTH

We saw a statement awhile ago to the effect that Mr. Paul H. Hayne proposed to leave Georgia and make his home at the North, because a professional literary man has no appreciation here. If any defense were necessary we would have no hesitation in defending Mr. Hayne against the suggestions and implications of his statement. He no doubt feels the need of literary fellowship but even stronger than this is the feeling that prompts him to enlarge his mental horizon, and to rid himself of the thousand and one special hindrances and trammels peculiar to the South and to the spirit of sectionalism that has fastened upon Southern thought. Fellowship is not necessary to the literary artist, but an enlarged vision, broad sympathies and national views are absolute essentials to perfect literary work. Perhaps we do not make ourselves understood. We mean that the work of a literary man, to be enduring, must be utterly and absolutely removed from all sectionalism or the prejudices to which sectionalism gives rise. Literary thought must move and adjust its creations upon a plane as high as the skies and as broad as the world. To draw in a reef or two, literature in America must be American in its broadest sense. It may come from the North or the South; it may be subjected to such modifications as result from social or climatic differences in the sections, and it may take tone and color from these, so much the better. The result must still be American, otherwise it will not survive. A refusal or a neglect to recognize these fundamental facts has smothered literary effort in the South for generations; so that if the accounts were to be made up tomorrow—if the genius of the nations were to sit in judgment upon us—we could not point to any one whose work is worthy enough to entitle his name to a place in the gallery of the immortals. A fugitive poem here and there and a stray oration would make up the sum of all we could venture to place on exhibition. The results of literary effort in the South are pervaded with the most intense sectionalism. Prejudices take the shape of egotism and we unblushingly allude to ourselves as the pinks of chivalry and our neighbors as the sons and daughters of every mean and unworthy impulse. In short we have gushed until the general effect of so much gush has reacted upon us. We are asked to support Southern papers because they are representative of Southern literature and we are asked to buy books for the same reason. Our poets arc all Southern poets and our novelists—such as we have—are all Southern novelists. Does a publisher fill a paper full of trash from the composition books of romantic schoolgirls? We must all applaud and buy for the benefit of Southern literature. Does Miss Sweetie Wildwood get together a lot of sickening doggerel? The newspapers must gush over the gush, not only for the purpose of building up Southern literature but because Miss Sweetie is a daughter of Colonel Wildwood. What is the result? Why, simply this, that the stuff we are in the habit of calling Southern literature is not only a burlesque upon true literary art, but a humiliation and a disgrace to the people whose culture it is supposed to represent. These are very harsh words; but they must be said some day, and the sooner they are said and accepted as the truth, the better for those who have an interest in building up a local literature. We must drop sectionalism and all the outlying and resultant prejudices, and along with them must go the selfishness and spite that have misrepresented us at home and abroad. The very spice and flavor of all literature—the very marrow and essence of all literary art—is localism. No literary artist can lack for material in this section. They are here all around him, untouched, undeveloped, and undisturbed; unique and original; as new as the world; as old as life; as beautiful as the dreams of genius. They must be run through the stamp mill. Where is the magician who will catch them and store them up? You may be very sure that the man who does it will not care one copper whether he is developing and building up Southern or Northern literature; and he will feel that his work is considerably belittled if it be claimed by either on the score of sectionalism. In literature, art and society, whatever is truly Southern is likewise truly American, and the same may be said of what is Northern. Literature that is Georgian or Southern, is necessarily American, and in the broadest sense. The sectionalism that is the most marked feature of our modern politics can never intrude into literature. Its intrusion is fatal and it is this fatality that has pursued, and overtaken, and destroyed literary effort in the South. The truth might as well be told: we have no Southern literature worthy of the name because an attempt has been made to give it the peculiarities of sectionalism rather than to impart to it the flavor of localism.

This bold statement by Harris was his own literary declaration of independence of those sectional views which he himself had held during the period of his literary apprenticeship. It also marked the culmination of the concept which he had begun to develop when he was in Forsyth—that the work of a Southern writer should stand or fall on its literary merit, not on the mere fact that it was written by a Southerner. Although he considered himself to be primarily a working journalist rather than an author of literature, he clearly perceived that there was no dearth of literary material in the South, and he insisted that the writer who proposed to deal with it must divorce himself from partisan politics and sectional prejudices. When Harris wrote the editorial his was a voice crying out in the long-established romantic tradition of Southern literature and calling for reform, but he at least was unconsciously preparing the way for his own true interpretation of Southern life and for other Southern writers of like purpose. No adverse criticism ever turned him aside from his declaration or caused him to compromise with it.

The favorable response on a national scale to the folklore legends as they appeared from week to week in the Atlanta *Constitution* confirmed the strength of Harris' stand for independence. In fact, they attracted such widespread interest that in a *Constitution* editorial of April 9, 1880, Harris stated his twofold purpose in writing them. They were the result, he said, of his desire "to preserve in permanent shape those curious mementoes of a period that will no doubt be sadly misrepresented by historians of the future." He therefore emphasized that he had been careful to retain the version which seemed to be most characteristic of the plantation Negroes and that he did not intend to include any which had not been verified by the memory of those who were most familiar with the "Negroes whose peculiarities invest the old plantation with the flavor of poetry and romance."

His other purpose, he said, was to preserve the dialect through the medium of which the legends had become a part of the domestic history of the Southern people. He confessed this had been a difficult undertaking for him, but he had endeavored by means of the dialect to convey the peculiar qualities of the old plantation Negroes. "If," he wrote, "the language in which the legends have been framed in the *Constitution* has given vivid hints of the really poetic imagination of the Negro; if it has embodied the quaint and rugged humor which was the most characteristic; if it has made clear a certain picturesque sensitiveness—a curious exaltation of mind and temperament—if this has been done, then the attempt to reproduce plantation dialect has been measurably successful."

To Harris' great surprise, the tales attracted the attention of scientific folklorists, among them J. W. Powell of the Bureau of Ethnology, Smithsonian Institute, and Herbert H. Smith. As a result, Harris said in the same editorial, he had found himself in a position which he had least expected, that of being regarded by eminent folklore specialists as an authority in the general field of folklore.

Since the scientific aspect of the legends had not been even remotely a part of his purpose in writing them, he said, he would gladly leave to the deductions of the scientists whatever scientific interest the plantation stories might possess. In closing his explanatory editorial, he humorously observed that some curious person had professed "to have traced our whole system of religion to India so that if the investigation of the origin of affairs proceeded as successfully as it had heretofore, we would presently discover that there was nothing modern but antiquity, and that the romances of

Uncle Remus were merely modifications of dime novels which had been composed by a desperate Chinese professor millions and millions of years ago."

The tales were reprinted in numerous newspapers outside the South, especially in the New York *Evening Post*. While Southern readers merely took them for granted because of their familiarity, Northern readers as well as the folklore scholars were intrigued with them. Not only were they interesting stories, charmingly told, but they also threw a new light on life in the old plantation South. As a result of this national interest, Harris received more than a thousand letters of inquiry concerning the prospect of their availability in book form. Since the letters were too numerous for him to answer personally, he requested the New York *Evening Post* in a letter of May 19, 1880, to say that D. Appleton and Company would shortly publish *Uncle Remus's Folk-Lore*, that it would be illustrated by Frederick S. Church, and that not all of the legends in the forthcoming book would have been previously published in the *Constitution*.[1]

Arrangements for the publication of the book were made with Harris by J. C. Derby in Atlanta. In his account of their negotiations, Derby wrote that he found Harris to be a very agreeable and intelligent gentleman, "although diffident in the extreme," but that the arrangement for the publication of the legends was quickly completed.[2] When the book was published the last week in November, 1880, it bore the more appropriate title, *Uncle Remus: His Songs and His Sayings*, instead of *Uncle Remus's Folk-Lore* as originally planned. In addition to thirty-four legends, nine of which had not been previously published in the *Constitution*, it contained nine of his old plantation songs, thirty-four of his plantation proverbs, twenty-one of his local Atlanta human interest sketches, and a revision of the sketch "Uncle Remus as a Rebel," in which it turned out that the Yankee sharpshooter whom Uncle Remus had felled from the tree to save his young master's life during the Civil War was none other than his Mars John. Even though he had been an enemy in war, he had been taken into the old plantation home, had been

[1] Julia Collier Harris, *Harris, Life and Letters*, 147.
[2] J. C. Derby, *Fifty Years Among Authors, Books, and Publishers* (New York: G. W. Carleton and Company, 1884), 438.

nursed back to health, and eventually had married Miss Sally. This proved to be the first of many of the stories which Harris was to write in which a Southern girl married a Northern man who had fought against the South.

Frederick Church drew the illustrations for the stories, but J. H. Moser, an Atlanta artist, drew those of Uncle Remus himself and those for the plantation songs and proverbs. All of the illustrations were geared to the concept that Uncle Remus was essentially a humorous character and that all of his stories and sayings were intended to amuse the reader. Since Moser had no particular individual to work from as a model for Uncle Remus, he pictured him as a conventional comic character with a wrinkled face, white hair and short beard, his spectacles pushed back on his forehead, and with an exaggerated grin to give the impression of hearty laughter. This portraiture did not capture Harris' own interpretation of Uncle Remus in his role of the teller of the folklore stories, songs, and proverbs, but it did please the publishers, who had advised Harris that his book would be included in their catalogue of humorous publications in an effort perhaps to capitalize upon the popularity of the humorous books which the American readers were then buying, notably those by Mark Twain. Both Church and Moser therefore failed to impart in their illustrations the deeper significance of the serious elements which lay beneath the humorous aspects in the character of Uncle Remus.

In his introduction to the volume, Harris made it clear that, however humorous it might be in effect, his intention had been a perfectly serious one. He also re-emphasized the statement which he had made in his *Constitution* editorial of April 9 that ethnological considerations had formed no part of the undertaking and that whatever the origin or allegorical interpretations of the legends might be, he had primarily intended them to be characteristic of the old-time Negro. No scientific investigation was needed to show why he had selected as his hero the rabbit, the weakest and most harmless of all animals, and brought him out victorious in contests with the fox, the bear, and the wolf. "It is not virtue that triumphs," he said, "but helplessness; it is not malice but mischievousness."

For the benefit of readers who were not familiar with plantation Negro songs, Harris explained that Uncle Remus' songs did not conform to the conventional rules of versification but depended for their melody and rhythm upon the quality of time and not upon the regularity of long or short, accented or unaccented syllables. He expressed the belief that Sidney Lanier had made this metrical peculiarity of the Negro songs the thesis of his *The Science of English Verse*. Of the brief character sketches with an Atlanta background which had not been reprinted in the Northern newspapers, he went on to say, mistakenly to be sure, that they were without any permanent interest but that he had included them in the book to present a part of the old time Negro character not permitted in the legends—"the shrewd observations, the curious retorts, the homely thrusts, the quaint comments, and the humorous philosophy of the race of which Uncle Remus is the type."

For readers outside the South who had never had any firsthand knowledge of the friendly relationship between the former slaves and their masters such as he had observed at Turnwold, he suggested a point of view with reference to Uncle Remus and the little boy. They should imagine, he wrote at the end of his introduction, that the stories were told by a Negro who was venerable enough to have lived through the period which he described, who had only pleasant memories of the discipline of slavery, and who had all the prejudices of caste and pride of family which were the natural results of the system.

The first story in the book differs somewhat from Harris' original version, as it contains several alterations made for the sake of greater historical accuracy in both the setting and the dialect. He changed the title from "The Story of Mr. Rabbit and Mr. Fox" to "Uncle Remus Initiates the Little Boy"; the age of the boy from six to seven years; the place where Uncle Remus told the stories from the piazza of the boy's home to the old man's cabin; and the time from yesterday to one evening. Among the dialect changes which he made were the following: Mr. to Brer; an' to en'; arter to atter; was to wuz; when to w'en; hear to yer; wrapped to wrop; that to dat; mustash to mustarsh. In making these and other dialect changes, he was motivated by his desire to retain the exact language which he had heard spoken. Each of the tales had a skillful introduction which stimulated the boy's interest in the story that followed. Sometimes Uncle Remus would adapt a legend to reprove the boy for some infraction of his family's code of conduct, and with the wisdom of his eighty years he would at times include such local allusions as he thought would enable the boy to comprehend more easily the meaning of the ancient legends. Whenever the boy questioned Uncle Remus to explain how the animals could act as they did, he had a ready answer: "Ez de tale wer gun to me des dat away I gin it unter you." [3]

Uncle Remus: His Songs and His Sayings was an immediate success. *The Critic,* in its issue of January 1, 1881, stated that by the end of December, 1880, only a month after publication, 7,500 copies had been sold; by the end of March, sales had reached 10,000 copies.

New York newspapers were enthusiastic in their reviews, each one praising the book for a different reason. The New York *Times* praised it as a valuable contribution to America's folklore. "Mr. Harris's book," its reviewer wrote, "is altogether excellent of its kind, and in preserving certain quaint legends and giving us exactly the sounds of the Negro dialect, he has established on a firm basis the first real book of American folk lore." [4] The New York *Evening Post* called it a notable work and deplored any treatment of it as a comic book intended primarily for the entertainment of juvenile readers. "So strong, indeed," its reviewer emphasized, "is our sense of the value of his [Harris'] work as a unique contribution to literature at a point where such a contribution is most needed that the comic aspect necessarily given to the book by its illustrations and by the look of dialect in print is to us distressing. The work is humorous to a high degree certainly; but it is not comic." In his lengthy appraisal, the reviewer went on to point out the historical value of the book by saying that it was not burlesque but painstaking portraiture—that changed surroundings and new conditions were working the rapid disappearance of the type of character which Harris had depicted. And he pronounced it to be the worthiest and most considerable contribution to the literature of Negro life that had yet been made. [5] The New York *Sun* commended its humor and saw in "Miss Meadows en de gals" the same relationship to the beasts

---

[3] Joel Chandler Harris, *Uncle Remus: His Songs and His Sayings* (New York: D. Appleton and Company, 1880), 100.
[4] New York *Times,* December 1, 1880.
[5] New York *Evening Post,* December 6, 1880.

in the fables that the social divinities sustained with mortals in Greek mythology.[6]

Literary magazines, both American and British, joined in the many-voiced chorus of critical approval. *Scribner's Monthly* praised the book as a work of superior literary art, the ultimate in its field. "Joel Chandler Harris," it said, "had recorded in a style so true to character and tradition, the folk-lore of the Ethiopian, that it is safe to say that no one will ever undertake to improve his work. It is as artistic in its execution as it is characteristic in its humor." [7] The *Literary World*, in London, found in the volume "a vein of humor, which to ourselves—and we doubt not to English readers generally—is entirely new, and which is at once amusing and interesting in a very high degree." [8]

Discriminating readers, irrespective of the geographical area in which they lived, perceived that this was a new kind of literature which had come out of the South. Instead of chivalric gentlemen, charming belles, and imposing white-columned mansions, there was a kindly, venerable Negro in his humble cabin, telling the ancient legends of his race to a little boy whose father and mother he called master and mistress. Instead of a lordly manor house with a retinue of servants and with its table groaning under the weight of all the viands that the Southern novelists of the old school could heap upon it, there was a one-room cabin with an open fireplace and an old Negro man roasting a yam in the hot ashes and sharing it with the little boy from the "big house." Nothing in the picture was blurred or distorted or exaggerated for comic effect, but all of its component features—the interior of the cabin, the open fire casting its lights and shadows on the weatherbeaten face of Uncle Remus and the boy, an ancient story evoking a new wonder—were harmoniously blended by a literary artist whose art was so true and unaffected that it appeared to be entirely artless.

Another notable aspect of the stories was that, although they were told by a slave in a setting of the antebellum plantation South, they contained no suggestion of racial tensions, partisan politics, or sectional prejudices. On the other hand, the total effect produced by the

[6]New York *Sun*, December 19, 1880.
[7]*Scribner's Monthly*, XXII (September, 1881), 786.
[8]*Literary World*, London, April 22, 1881, 250–52.

book was one of mutual understanding and goodwill that transcended racial and sectional differences and appealed to young and old, folklore scholar, literary critic, and general reader, independent of their race and geographical boundaries and even of time itself. Here was the delineation of a phase of life characteristic of the old South that could be trusted for its authenticity. The success of the book further confirmed Harris' editorial statement in the *Constitution* of November 30, 1879, on the status of a Southern literature free of the peculiarities of sectional politics and prejudices.

However much the shy and reticent author may have wished it to have been otherwise, the acclaim with which his book had been received made him a figure of national interest, and visitors of importance from outside Atlanta began to call at his office, not to see Joe Harris, one of the editors of the *Constitution*, but to meet Joel Chandler Harris, author of *Uncle Remus: His Songs and His Sayings*. One of these callers was young Walter Hines Page of North Carolina who was later to become eminent as a publisher and editor. In his travels throughout the South to learn more of its people, their needs and prospects, he stopped in Atlanta for an interview with Harris, and in a letter from there dated September 28, 1881, he gave his impressions of Harris and an evaluation of his first book.

"It was impossible to believe," Page wrote, "that the man realized what he had done. I afterwards discovered that his most appreciative friends had this same opinion; that Joe Harris does not appreciate Mr. Joel Chandler Harris. From merely looking at him one must be pardoned for fearing that he could not keenly appreciate anything. A little man, just turned thirty-one, I believe, with red, unkempt hair, a fiery, half-vicious moustache, a freckled face and freckled hands; and there is nothing striking about him—what strange habitations does genius choose among men! His eyes are all that belong to Mr. Joel C. Harris; all other things, hair, complexion, hands, chin, manner, and clothes are the property of Joe Harris." [9] Both the character of Uncle Remus and the dialect which he spoke were not the result of a studied effort on the part of Harris, Page wrote, but came from his associations with Negroes on a Southern plantation. He

[9]Burton J. Hendrick, *The Training of an American: The Early Life and Letters of Walter H. Page* (Boston and New York: Houghton Mifflin Company, 1928), 149.

said he had Harris' word for it that he could think in the Negro dialect, and Page thought that he could translate even Emerson and perhaps Bronson Alcott into it as well as he could tell the adventures of Brer Rabbit.[10] He was impressed by Harris' diffidence, his indifference to a life of society, and his protest against the interpretation of himself as a humorist. Page concluded his letter by saying that Uncle Remus was a permanent addition to literature, that by comparison every effort that had been made in the previous fifty years to embalm an old slave in literature receded into insignificance beside Uncle Remus, and that Harris had painted the whole structure of Southern life in the background of the stories.[11]

Time did not change Page's early enthusiasm for *Uncle Remus* or for the genius of Harris in his portrayal of Southern life in the stories. Writing some twenty years after his first meeting with Harris in Atlanta, he asserted that *Uncle Remus: His Songs and His Sayings* was "so great a piece of literature that if all histories and records of slave-life in the South were blotted out, a diligent antiquarian thousands of years hence could reconstruct it in its essential features from the three human figures that Mr. Harris has used—Uncle Remus, the little boy, and Miss Sally. . . ." [12]

Although *Uncle Remus* had a remarkably large sale, the purchase price of the volume was only one dollar, and Harris' share of the proceeds was not sufficient to make him conclude that he was on the way to wealth as an author. He did feel justified, however, in moving his family into a larger house than the one in which they had been living at 201 Whitehall Street since his permanent connection with the *Constitution* in 1876 and to which he had brought his mother from Eatonton to live with them. Consequently, in 1881 he rented a house at 214 Gordon Street (the number was later changed to 1040) in West End, which at that time was an unincorporated village outside the city of Atlanta but connected with it by mule-drawn trolley cars. Two years later he purchased the place through a loan of $2,500 from the Constitution Publishing Company.[13]

The property consisted of a frame dwelling on a lot containing a little more than five acres. The home itself was simple in its

[10]*Ibid.*, 150.
[11]*Ibid.*, 154.
[12]*Ibid.*, 332.
[13]Courthouse records, Fulton County, Georgia, dated November 13, 1883.

architecture and had a hallway which ran from the front to the rear. Harris later improved it by the addition of a second-floor room originally designed for a study; but he never used it preferring instead to write in close proximity to his wife and children. He also added a wide veranda in front where he enjoyed sitting and entertaining his friends during the summer season as was the custom in the South of his time. With his fondness for a rural environment, he planted trees and roses, grew seasonal vegetables in his garden, and established himself as The Farmer on a small scale. His place eventually became known as "The Sign of the Wren's Nest" from the discovery one day that a wren had built its nest in the mailbox at the end of the walk to the street.

The Harrises made this modest home in the suburb of Atlanta their permanent residence. It was there that their first daughter, Mary Esther, died in 1882, and it was there that their four other children were born, Lillian in 1882, Linton in 1883, Mildred in 1885, and Joel C., Jr., in 1889. Evan P. Howell, Harris' most intimate friend in Atlanta, lived in the same neighborhood, but Harris rarely ever visited with the Howell family on account of his extreme shyness. As the years went by and her husband's fame increased, Esther Harris protected him from the intrusion of strangers who admired his books and wished to see in person the creator of Uncle Remus. He never joined any clubs, and when he was not in his editorial office in Atlanta he spent his time at home puttering around among his rose bushes, reading, or writing in the midst of his family circle. After 1890 he attended the daily morning meeting of the staff of the *Constitution*, gathered up a bundle of exchanges, and returned home to write his assignments in order to escape the embarrassment of being interrupted in his work by curious visitors who, on seeing him busy at his desk, would exclaim, "So this is the great Uncle Remus!" [14]

Although Harris was extremely shy in his personal relationships other than with his family and intimate friends, he was far from being reticent in his editorial utterances. The national success of his first book of regional stories led him to continue his crusade for contemporary Southern authors to tell the truth about the South, even though his own harsh criticism of Southern writers in his first editorial on regional literature had provoked adverse criticism from those who

[14]Clark Howell, interview.

felt that he was attempting to curry favor with Northern readers
and was therefore disloyal to his own region. A Macon friend who
was sympathetic with his point of view sent him an address which
he said J. B. Wardlow, Jr., had made in Montgomery County, Virginia, the previous July, and Harris made it the starting point for a
second editorial on "Southern Literature." The address had agreeably
disappointed him, he said, in that he had expected to find in it "a
gushing medley of narrow-minded nonsense . . . a pathetic announcement to the effect that nothing prevented our writers from occupying
a grand and glorious position in the temple of fame but the hampering
conditions of their environment and the jealousy of northern critics."
Instead, he said, the address was marked by breadth and vigor and
by an appeal for Southern writers to build up a literature with su-
ficient merit to arrest the attention of the world. In referring to his
own previous editorial in which he had expressed a similar appeal,
he said: "We remember that Miss Sweetie Wildwood and C. Melnotte
Jonquil were outraged at our blunt methods, and one or two of the
tribe intimated that we were traitors to our section, or something of
that kind." [15]

In another editorial, "As to Southern Literature," Harris declared
that if the South were ever to make any important contribution to the
literature of the world it must get over its self-consciousness and so
control its sensitiveness that it would "be able to regard with indifference—nay, with complacence—the impulse of criticism which
prompts and spurs every literary man and woman whose work is
genuine. We must not forget that real literary art is absolutely im-
partial and invariably just. None other can endure." [16]

The success of Harris' first volume had opened the door of national magazines to him, and they began to solicit his contributions. The
thirty-four folklore stories which he had published in his *Uncle
Remus* volume had by no means exhausted the outlines he had on
hand, and folklorists were sending him additional ones. However,
since he was a novice in the literary field and had no experienced
authors in Atlanta to counsel him, he was uncertain of the course
he should pursue in regard to their publication. Therefore, acting
on his own judgment, he began to accede to the requests from var-

---

[15]Atlanta *Constitution*, January 9, 1881.
[16]*Ibid.*, February 20, 1881.

ious magazines. In the winter and early summer of 1881 he contributed to *The Critic* two legends in a new series which he called "Nights with Uncle Remus" [17] and also an Uncle Remus plantation song, "The Plough Hand's Song." [18] During the same period *Scribner's Monthly* published a plantation song, "A Song of the Mole," [19] and five legends under the heading, "A Rainy Day with Uncle Remus." [20]

Among the American authors who greatly admired Harris' *Uncle Remus* was Mark Twain, who was then enjoying immense popularity as the author of *The Innocents Abroad, Roughing It,* and *Tom Sawyer,* and who was turning that popularity into glorious financial gain, not only through the sale of his books but also through his public readings. In a letter to William Dean Howells dated February 27, 1881, Twain said that he had recently given a reading in Hartford and that the thing that went best of all was Uncle Remus' Tar Baby.[21] Sometime during the summer of that year Twain initiated a correspondence with Harris in which he expressed his warm appreciation of *Uncle Remus: His Songs and His Sayings* as a work of artistic creation, invited Harris to visit him in his Hartford home, and mentioned a ghost story, "The Golden Arm," with which he said he had been familiar since his boyhood.[22] In his reply, Harris, who regarded himself as a mere literary amateur in comparison with Twain, was deferential. He did not know, he wrote, of a higher honor that Uncle Remus could desire than to walk arm in arm with him before the Hartford public, but he modestly disclaimed Twain's generous appraisal of the artistic merit of the Uncle Remus stories by saying that it was the matter of the stories and not the manner of telling them that had attracted public attention and won the consideration of people of taste in the

---

[17]*The Critic,* I (February 26, 1881), 45, 46.

[18]*Ibid.* I (March 26, 1881), 81.

[19]*Scribner's Monthly,* XXI (April, 1881), 968.

[20]*Ibid.,* XXI (June, 1881), 241–48.

[21]Albert Bigelow Paine, *Mark Twain's Letters* (two vols.; New York: Harper and Brothers, 1917), I, 395.

[22]This first letter from Mark Twain to Harris was not among the letters which the Harris family placed in the Joel Chandler Harris Memorial Collection, Emory University, in 1927, nor was it in *Mark Twain's Letters,* edited by Albert Bigelow Paine, 1917. The other letters from Twain to Harris are in the Harris Collection at Emory University. They were published in 1953 by the Emory University library, in its series of *Sources and Reprints* and edited by Thomas H. English.

North. No, he had not heard the ghost story about "The Golden Arm"; would it be too much trouble to send him an outline of it so that he might verify it? Inspired by the evident cordiality of Twain's letter, Harris ventured to ask his advice as to the best procedure he should adopt in publishing other fables he was ready to write up.[23]

In his reply of August 10, Twain assured Harris that in reality the stories themselves were only alligator pears, that one merely ate them for the salad dressing. "Uncle Remus," he said, "is most deftly drawn, and is a lovable and delightful creation; he and the little boy, and their relations with each other, are bright fine literature, and worthy to live for their own sakes; and certainly the stories are not to be credited with them." In answer to Harris' question concerning the method of publishing additional legends, Twain advised him to make his next book a subscription one for in that way he could derive the most profit from its sale. He further advised him that James R. Osgood of Boston would be a most acceptable publisher for his second volume, and that Osgood could also advise him on the frequency of publication in magazines. His idea, however, would be to publish only *one* yarn in a magazine every three months, just often enough, he said, to keep before the public and at the same time keep the public unsatisfied, but, the money-conscious Twain emphasized, "I wouldn't let them have such generous meals as you have been giving them.—For the ficklest people in the world are the public." He enclosed a version of the ghost story.[24]

Twain himself was as full of schemes for reaping a harvest of dollars as was his Beriah Sellers in *The Gilded Age*, and one of them was to persuade Harris to team up with him for a lecture tour in which the two would read from their humorous stories. Both had attained national popularity with the reading public, and Twain reasoned that their admirers would surely come in great numbers to see and hear them—at an admission price, of course. Twain had

[23]Julia Collier Harris, *Harris, Life and Letters*, 168, 169.
[24]Paine, *Mark Twain's Letters*, I, 401–403. Twain's version is in *Mark Twain to Uncle Remus*, Emory University Publications, *Sources and Reprints*, Ser. VII, No. 3, 1953, pp. 12, 13. Harris later verified the story in a Georgia setting and included it in *Nights with Uncle Remus* (1883) as told by 'Tildy, the house girl.

never met Harris and he was totally unaware of his reticence and of his old habit of stuttering under excitement.

Instead of writing to Harris about his proposed joint lecture tour, he communicated it to him through his Hartford friend Jo Twichell on the occasion of his visit to Atlanta in the spring of 1882. On his return to Hartford, Twichell cast doubt on Harris' willingness to appear before an audience. But Twain was persistent. On April 2 he wrote Harris that he had thought out a device whereby he could overcome his lack of confidence in reading some of his stories in public and that he would explain when he saw him. He therefore urged Harris to meet him and Osgood in New Orleans somewhere between the first and sixth of May. As an added incentive, he said that Osgood was the only man in America who could lay out a course for Harris and tell him exactly what to do.[25]

Harris reluctantly but hopefully agreed. He wrote Twain that the ordeal of appearing on a stage would be a terrible one, but expressed his gratitude to Twain for even connecting him in his mind with the project. He was hopeful that, if it worked out successfully, he would be able "to drop this grinding newspaper business and write some books I have in mind." [26]

According to a previous arrangement, Harris arrived in New Orleans early on Sunday morning of the first week in May and went to the hotel where Twain and Osgood were staying. Twain had received a description of Harris, presumably from Twichell, as being short, red-headed, freckled, and very shy, and in his *Life on the Mississippi* (1883) Twain wrote that he had no difficulty in recognizing him among the seven o'clock arrivals at the hotel.[27] Later that morning George W. Cable, whose home was in New Orleans and whose *Old Creole Days* and *The Grandissimes* had made him a highly respected and popular interpreter of life in old Louisiana, met Twain, Osgood, and Harris at their hotel, and, from Harris' account of the day's activities, they accompanied Cable to

---

[25]Paine, *Mark Twain's Letters*, I, 417, 418. The purpose of Twain's visit to New Orleans was to gather material for a new book, *Life on the Mississippi* (1883).

[26]Julia Collier Harris, *Harris, Life and Letters*, 170, 171.

[27]Mark Twain, *Life on the Mississippi*, Author's National Edition, vol. IX (New York and London: Harper and Brothers, 1917), 379.

the Presbyterian church of which he was a devout member.[28] In Cable's pew there sat that Sunday morning representatives of four different cultures in American society after the Civil War. One was Mark Twain, who only a few years before then had come roaring out of the Western frontier as untamed and as uninhibited as the frontier itself. His speech at the dinner in celebration of John Greenleaf Whittier's seventieth birthday in 1877 had confirmed the judgment of effete Easterners that he was not a writer of refined taste nor one who had a sense of reverence for religion, holy places, and culture in general. And there was in contrast James R. Osgood, a proper Bostonian, a polished gentleman, book publisher, and withal a worthy representative of traditional New England culture, but Mark Twain's friend and literary adviser. In even more striking contrast with these two, there was plain Joe Harris, the very embodiment of middle Georgia democracy, newly arrived among America's literary elite and still somewhat bewildered by his inclusion among them, as humble as his Brer Rabbit but without his cunning. However unusual the church experience may have been for Twain and Harris, it was a customary one for Cable, who was a strict believer in Calvinistic doctrines and as strict in his observance of them. Harris later said that it was worth the trip to New Orleans just to hear Cable sing.

On Sunday afternoon Harris, Twain, and Osgood went on a sightseeing tour of New Orleans which included their witnessing what Harris described as a wonderfully lively cockfight, despite its cruelty. Harris noted in reading Twain's *Life on the Mississippi* that he had made no mention of the cockfight, and lest his own account of it should come to the attention of the Reverend Jo Twichell, he explained that the same curiosity which leads tourists to witness Sunday bullfights in Spain had led them to visit the cockpit in New Orleans.[29]

During the course of their stay, Cable entertained the three visitors in his home. Among the other guests there were some children who had come in the expectation of hearing Harris read from some of his Uncle Remus stories, but they were doubly disappointed

[28] Joel Chandler Harris, "At a West End Window," Atlanta *Constitution*, January 20, 1884.
[29] *Ibid.*

in finding that Harris was white and that he refused to read any of his stories. To Twain's surprise, he discovered that Harris had never read aloud to people and that he was too shy to venture the attempt now. "Mr. Cable and I," Twain wrote, "read books of ours to show him what an easy trick it was, but his immortal shyness was proof against this sagacious strategy; so we had to read about Brer Rabbit ourselves." [30] If this strategy perchance happened to be the device which Twain had had in mind to get Harris around his fear of appearing on a stage, it completely failed to work, and Harris went back to Atlanta to continue to grind out daily copy for the *Constitution* for the next eighteen years and to write his books in the evenings as time permitted. One positive result, however, came from his New Orleans trip—he would let Osgood publish his next book of folklore stories.

Twichell's report to Twain about Harris' shyness was confirmed during the days when they were together in New Orleans. "He is a shy man," Twain wrote of him. "Of this there is no doubt. After days of intimacy one wonders to see that it is still in about as strong force as ever. There is a fine and beautiful nature hidden behind it, as all know who have read the "Uncle Remus" book; and a fine genius, too, as all know by the same sign." [31] Harris' rejection of Twain's proposal for a joint lecture tour of readings did not shake the latter's confidence in Harris' ability to read "the Negro dialect better than anyone else, for in the matter of writing it he is the only master the country has produced." [32]

Despite Harris' reluctance to meet strangers, he discovered that he could not escape the spotlight of publicity which his Uncle Remus book had turned on him, nor could he be totally indifferent to the friendly magazine editors and publishers who wished to honor him. He therefore agreed to go to New York in June, 1882, with Evan Howell to attend a dinner at the Tile Club in honor of American authors and artists. During the dinner he overcame his reticence sufficiently to engage in genial conversation with the notable guests, but he resisted all entreaties for him to stand and speak or to read one of his stories. While he was in New York, Richard W. Gilder, editor of

[30]Mark Twain, *Life on the Mississippi*, 380.
[31]*Ibid.*
[32]*Ibid.*

Century Magazine to which Harris had contributed two old plantation songs in its May number, arranged another dinner to which he invited Harris and Howell as honor guests. Harris accepted the invitation, but the thought of having to sit through another dinner with celebrities at which he would be expected to speak filled him with such dread that he hastily left for Atlanta, even though he had originally planned to go on to Boston for a talk with Osgood.[33] Thereafter, nothing short of a virtual command issued by President Theodore Roosevelt ever induced him to attend a public dinner. Harris did not call on D. Appleton and Company, his publisher, while he was in New York, and after his return to Atlanta he received a letter from them in which they expressed their regret that he had not done so. His reply was indicative of his modest and unassuming nature.

> Gentlemen:
>
> I hasten to say, in response to a paragraph in yours of the 3rd June, that my failure to call on you was due simply and solely to the fact that I was afraid my visit to you might be construed as in some sort of an intrusion. I do not conceive that I have any right to bore people simply because of the accident that "Uncle Remus" is a passably successful book. One reason of my leaving New York so hurriedly was the fact that I couldn't escape people that I didn't know, and dinner parties at which my awkwardness and embarrassment would have been the most pronounced features. Armed with your invitation, which you intimate was sent to my hotel, I most certainly would have called on you.
>
> Yours truly,
Joel C. Harris[34]

Harris' uncomfortable experience at the Tile Club dinner and his hasty departure to Atlanta led to another exchange of humorous letters between him and Mark Twain. On September 5, Twain wrote him from Elmira, New York, to say he had learned about his "admirable stupefaction" at the Tile Club and renewed his invitation to Harris to visit him in Hartford.[35] On September 12 Harris replied in

---

[33] Julia Collier Harris, *Harris, Life and Letters,* 190.
[34] Courtesy of D. Appleton and Company.
[35] *Mark Twain to Uncle Remus,* 18.

similar vein: "How can you call my stupefaction at the Tile Club admirable? I suffered the agony of the damned twice over, and when I reflected that probably Mr. Osgood was prepared to put me through a similar experience in Boston, I thought it would be better to come home and commit suicide rather than murder a number of worthy gentlemen by making an ass of myself." [36]

In keeping with Twain's suggestion that he should not publish his Uncle Remus stories too frequently in the magazines, Harris spaced his contributions with sufficient regularity to maintain the interest of the public while he was writing additional legends for his second volume. Those who had read *Uncle Remus: His Songs and His Sayings* were, therefore, well prepared to receive *Nights with Uncle Remus* when it was published the first week in November, 1883, by James R. Osgood and Company, the Boston firm which Twain had so highly recommended to him. All of the illustrations were drawn by Frederick Church. In content the volume differed from the previous one in that it contained no humorous sketches, no plantation proverbs or songs, but consisted entirely of folklore legends and conformed to the plan which Harris had sketched out for it. In addition to Uncle Remus and the little boy, there were to be three other characters, African Jack, Aunt Tempy, and 'Tildy, the house girl. Aunt Tempy was to act as a foil to both Uncle Remus and African Jack and to tell the witch tales except for one by Jack. The house girl was to act as a foil for all three, and he envisioned her as "irreverent, indecorous, pert, careless, and yet capable of believing anything that human lips could tell." African Jack was to tell the coast stories in a dialect which he said had even larger possibilities than the cotton plantation (or Virginia) dialect.[37] Of the seventy legends, fifty-three were told by Uncle Remus in the dialect of the middle Georgia antebellum cotton plantation Negroes, nine by African Jack in the Gullah dialect of the coastal rice plantation Negroes, five witch tales by

[36]Julia Collier Harris, *Harris, Life and Letters*, 191. On his trip the next spring to see his wife's family in Canada, Harris stopped over in Hartford for a visit with Twain in his home. Twain's children, who were familiar with the legends told by Uncle Remus, were amazed to find that Harris was white instead of black, so thoroughly had he become identified in their minds with his famous Negro character.

[37]Harris' outline for *Nights with Uncle Remus* was found among his manuscripts which his family placed at Emory University in 1927.

Aunt Tempy, and three ghost stories by 'Tildy, one of which was "A Ghost Story," a middle Georgia plantation version of the story which Mark Twain had sent Harris about a golden arm.

Artistically, *Nights with Uncle Remus* was an improvement over *Uncle Remus: His Songs and His Sayings*. Uncle Remus gained in stature as a convincing portrait of the antebellum plantation Negro both in his characteristic traits and accuracy of dialect. And Harris gave him a new dimension. Since he was not a field hand, he served his master and mistress as a trusted and dependable family retainer and his relationship toward the house servants was somewhat in the nature of an overseer, much to 'Tildy's dislike. African Jack had the same master as did the others but lived on their common master's plantation on the coast where he had learned to speak the Gullah dialect of that region, and once a year he visited the home place in middle Georgia. Harris' inclusion of African Jack in *Nights with Uncle Remus* enabled him to enlarge the scope of the legends and in some instances to give two variants of the same legend, with Uncle Remus telling the version he had brought from Virginia and African Jack the one he had brought from Africa. Although the stories were told by four different persons, each story fitted its respective narrator, and Harris skillfully wove them together into a hamonious unit.

This unity of effect was heightened by the romance which developed between African Jack and 'Tildy, and in the last chapter Harris brought all of the plantation population together in a celebration of their marriage. With laughter, song, and dance they made the occasion a merry one. Uncle Remus went to the big house for the little boy, and on their arrival at the scene of the festivities the old Negro took charge. Urged on by the other Negroes to lead them in a song, he mounted the platform and began to go through the physical motions which served as a prelude to the song itself. First, he raised his right hand to his ear as if intently listening. Then, in Harris' description of his further procedure, "he began to slap himself gently with his left hand, first upon the leg and then upon the breast. The other Negroes kept time to this by a gentle motion of their feet, and finally, when the thump-thump-thump of this movement had regulated itself to suit the old man's fancy" he began to sing in his powerful voice a plantation song that was appropriate to the occasion, "My Honey, My Love." The other Negroes then followed his lead in melodious song which Harris characterized as having been charged with a mysterious and pathetic tenderness.[38]

Throughout this volume, the timeless legends were recounted to the plantation environment, and they were enlivened by the humor, wisdom, superstitious beliefs, and the myth-making imagination of those who told them. The setting was the same as that in the previous volume, Uncle Remus' cabin after dark with the flickering lights and shadows cast by the burning pine knots in his fireplace adding a mysterious touch to the always wonderful and sometimes awesome stories. Outside the cabin lay the world of reality, but inside only the world of make-believe existed both for the narrators of the legends and the little boy who listened to them. The new stories had the same skillful introductions as those in the first volume which Mark Twain had praised above the legends themselves. With the creation of Aunt Tempy, African Jack, and 'Tildy, Harris began to add to his portrait gallery of plantation Negroes, the originals of whom he had known in Putnam County. Although they were minor characters in comparison with Uncle Remus, he drew them with the same sure hand and with the same understanding of their basic natures.

In writing the stories for *Nights with Uncle Remus* it seems clear that Harris was looking over his shoulder at the scientific folklorists who, much to his surprise, had commended the legends in the first volume for their ethnological and scientific value. If it were true that, besides preserving part of the old way of life in his stories, he had also made a contribution to the knowledge of folklore, he decided he should acquaint himself in some detail with folklore itself. He therefore began to read folklore magazines and books by specialists in that field. As a result, he came up with an introduction to *Nights with Uncle Remus* which was, for him at least, a learned treatise on comparative folklore with a complement of references, sources, footnotes, and a glossary of the Gullah dialect. For once—and only once—he assumed a role that was unnatural for him, yet it must be said that he played it reasonably well. However, he stepped back into character at the conclusion of his discourse by reaffirming the position which he had taken in his introduction to *Uncle Remus: His Songs and His Sayings*, that he was responsible only for the setting of the

[38]Joel Chandler Harris, *Nights with Uncle Remus*, (Boston: James R. Osgood, 1883), 401, "The Night before Christmas." The scene was almost a literal transcription of the Christmas celebrations Harris had witnessed when he lived on Turner's Turnwold plantation in Putnam County.

stories and that it had been his purpose in writing them to give readers a glimpse of plantation life in the South before the Civil War.[39]

The response of the critics to *Nights with Uncle Remus* was no less cordial than it had been toward the first venture. The *Nation* said that the book placed Harris in the front rank of American writers and that "regard being had for the literary skill displayed in setting so large a number of stories, must be thought an extraordinary *tour de force*." [40] The New York *Times* said in its review that Harris had "the double talent of being an admirable raconteur and at the same time a philologist of no small merit." Its reviewer was impressed not only by the exactness of the dialect spoken by the different characters but also by the distinct individuality of Aunt Tempy, African Jack, and 'Tildy.[41] *The Critic* said that it did not need the philological relish and found in the stories themselves the pleasing element of poetry. Harris' setting of the stories appeared to the reviewer to be "marvellously like the work of originality and genius." [42]

In both of these collections, Harris took hitherto familiar but neglected materials which were indigenous to the Old South and wove them into a tapestry of poetry and beauty. Here was unstudied art, characterizations without exaggeration for comic effect, humor without satire, kindness without ulterior motive, and human nature without rancor or distrust. Both books not only established Harris as a Southern writer of permanent literature but they also put the world in his debt for his artistic portrayal of a phase of Southern life that had been an intimate part of its past. In the years ahead he would portray Southern life in its unattractive as well as in its attractive aspects, but always as its honest and faithful literary historian.

---

[39]In retrospect, Harris was greatly amused by his learned discourse on folk-lore. The *New York Times Book Review* in its issue of September 19, 1926, printed the following comment which Harris had written (no date stated) in a copy of *Nights with Uncle Remus* which had been sold at auction: "The introduction is a gem. It should be read with eyes half closed in order to get the full effect of the vast learning it contains. The reader will naturally think it represents some knowledge of comparative folk-lore on the part of the author. He is willing to make an affidavit that he knows no more on the subject than a blind horse knows about Sunday."

[40]*The Nation*, XXXVII (November 15, 1883), 422.

[41]New York *Times*, November 20, 1883.

[42]*The Critic*, New Series, I (February 9, 1883), 64.

8

FROM DISUNION TO RECONCILIATION

Before Harris made Uncle Remus the focal point of interest in the folklore stories, Southern writers had not given the Negro anything like an adequate or a serious treatment in their fiction. Harris' predecessors, Longstreet, Thompson, Johnston, and Charles H. Smith (Bill Arp), had portrayed an evolving middle Georgia culture from the Revolution to the Civil War in which the middle- and lower-class whites had predominated. Because their major purpose had been to amuse their readers in the style of comic journalism, they had not dealt with the planters and their slaves nor their relationship to each other. Joseph Addison Turner had recognized the literary potentials inherent in the character of the Negro of the old plantation regime, and he had advocated that the Negro should be given a prominent place in Southern literature.[1] However, he himself failed to do so, not because of any lack of appreciation on his part of the Negro's role in the cultural pattern of the South but because he was such a stickler for othodox grammar that he could not bring himself to employ the dialect that was essential in a true delineation of the plantation Negro.

It was not until the Negroes of the plantation era were beginning to fade from the scene and the younger generation arose to take their place in an environment of freedom that Southern writers began to recapture their picturesque personalities and character traits and to perpetuate them in dialect poems and short stories. Two brothers, Clifford and Sidney Lanier of Georgia, contributed a Negro dialect poem, "The Power of Prayer," to the June, 1875, number of *Scribner's Monthly*, and "Uncle Jim's Baptist Revival Hymn" to the same magazine's number for May, 1876. In January, 1876, Irwin Russell of Mississippi began to publish in *Scribner's* his Negro dialect poems, the most memorable of which was his "Christmas Night in the

---

[1] *The Countryman*, December 22, 1862.

Quarters." In 1877 Thomas Nelson Page of Virginia contributed his first dialect poems of the old plantation Negro to *Scribner's*.

Harris, who brought the new movement to its finest expression, later gave priority to Russell as the first authentic delineator in characterization and dialect of the Negro character in Southern literature. In his introduction to an edition of Russell's poems in 1888, he stated that "Russell was among the first—if not the first—of Southern writers to appreciate the literary possibilities of the Negro character, and of the unique relations existing between the two races and among the first to develop them." He called "Christmas Night in the Quarters" inimitable but criticized its dialect as having been carelessly written.[2] Early in his career, Sidney Lanier turned from writing Negro dialect poems to the presentation of other phases of Southern life in the belle lettres tradition, and Russell died before he could fulfill the promise which his first poems indicated. In the 1880's Thomas Nelson Page continued to portray the old plantation past with the Negro as the central character in short stories instead of in poems, and his first publication of them in book form was *In Ole Virginia* in 1887. In 1889 Harry Stillwell Edwards of Georgia also recaptured pleasing aspects of plantation lore in his first volume of short stories *Two Runaways and Other Stories*.

No one of these writers, however, equaled Harris in depth of characterization, authenticity of dialect, or sureness of insight into the mind and soul of the plantation Negro. Uncle Remus, whether viewed in his role as the storyteller of folklore legends in a plantation setting or as a representative of the older generation of Negroes in an uncongenial environment of postwar Atlanta, was unmistakably real. Harris projected him so completely as an individual character that he cannot be identified as merely a comic type nor simply as a loyal retainer. In fact, the reader of the folklore stories scarcely thinks of Uncle Remus as a slave, for his master and mistress appear only in the background. He is an independent and realistic figure, revealing his humor and his knowledge of human nature in his relationship with the little boy, expressing approval or disapproval of the little boy's conduct, putting the pert 'Tildy in her place, and exercising his rightful authority over

[2]Joel Chandler Harris, Introduction to Irwin Russell's *Poems* (New York: Century Company, 1888), x, xi.

the household and yard servants. If he had an instinctive desire to be free, he gave no outward indication of it, and his personal difficulties came upon him in freedom, not in slavery.

In the postwar Atlanta sketches, Harris portrayed Uncle Remus at a time when, as John Herbert Nelson said of him in his *The Negro Character in American Literature*, "he emerged into the fierce light of a freedom which confused and troubled him and made him all the more appealing." Nelson differentiated Harris from other Southern writers in his delineation of the Negro character by pointing out that in creating Uncle Remus he went outside himself and "entered into the thoughts and feelings of a human type different from his own in spirit, in psychology and emotional temper, in disposition, in talents, and preferences; and has laid bare the very soul that he found there." [3]

The effect which Harris achieved in his first two collections of legends exceeded his original purpose of preserving a phase of Southern life which the outcome of the Civil War had ended. The stories proved to be of interest not only to folklore scholars but also to Northern readers for the understanding which they gave them of a phase of race relationship in the South during the era of slavery. The two volumes served as an offset to the radical politicians who, in Harris' opinion, were hindering the progress of reunion by agitating the old issues and fomenting sectional strife by their efforts to impose laws upon the South in the nature of a "force bill." The warm and cordial response on the part of the North to the stories was evidence of their reconciling influence.

While Harris was making friends for the South, Henry W. Grady was directing his energy toward making his vision of an industrialized South a practical reality. Although the section had been making steady progress since the war in the reorganization of its economy, agriculture was still the primary source of its wealth, and Grady knew that if his vision was ever to be realized the South must create an image of itself as an inviting field for the investment of outside capital toward its industrial development. With his flair for publicizing any enterprise toward that end, he was the moving spirit

[3] John Herbert Nelson, *The Negro Character in American Literature*, Bulletin of the University of Kansas, Humanistic Studies, IV, No. 1 (Lawrence, Kan., 1926), 107, 108.

behind the organization and promotion of the first International Cotton Exposition in Atlanta in the fall of 1881.

The exposition was a gigantic undertaking for Atlanta, which in 1881 had an estimated metropolitan population of only 45,000. Manufacturers of textile and farm machinery were invited to participate, and when the exposition opened on October 5 the buildings which had been erected in Oglethorpe Park held more than eleven hundred exhibits. Grady's promotion had been on a national scale and it was so successful that on opening day representatives from the nation's leading newspapers were present to report the gala occasion; distinguished visitors, including General William T. Sherman, were attracted from many Northern and Southern states. The exposition, which closed on December 31, proved to be profitable both as a financial venture on the part of its investors and as an impetus to manufacturing in the South.[4] In fact, it may well be that the industrialization of the South actually stemmed from the Atlanta International Cotton Exposition in 1881.

A *Constitution* editorial of October 6, probably written by Harris, extolled Atlanta's enterprise in bringing the exposition to a successful opening as being without precedent in the South. The writer, however, saw beyond its material advantages to the South the possibility that the cordial meeting of people from all sections of the nation at the exposition grounds would result in mutual tolerance, respect, and goodwill. It should have, so the editorial emphasized, "an active influence in obliterating the sectional lines which doubt and misunderstanding played upon by officious partisanship have sought to perpetuate."

On the other side of the editorial desk of the *Constitution*, Harris continued to portray the culture of the old agrarian South. The folklore stories had revived memories of his four years at Turnwold and in his non-folklore stories he ranged the entire plantation and all of its aspects for his material. In the Uncle Remus stories he had presented its pleasant features as he himself had observed them. But he had also observed its darker aspects as well, and in the interest of presenting a truthful picture of the entire plantation structure he incorporated these features in his non-folklore stories. Beginning with Uncle Remus, he reconstructed, as Francis Pendle-

[4]Nixon, *Henry W. Grady*, 188–91.

ton Gaines said in his *The Southern Plantation*, the entire institution. "With a sweeping inclusiveness running from the very structure of society, from the great problematic aspects, down to the single lovable personality, Harris's work is the literary history of the plantation." [5]

Moreover, in his non-folklore stories Harris included the various classes of society which he had known—the planters, the middle class, and the poor. Because he was so thoroughly the product of his middle Georgia democratic heritage and so democratic himself in his associations and manner of living, he never successfully portrayed the planters. He never made them the central characters in any of his stories, and when he did include them they conformed more or less to the conventional type without marked traits of individuality. In fact, in some instances he mildly satirized them for their impractical and reactionary traits.

He was most successful in his delineation of the middle-class Georgians, because he knew them as thoroughly as he did the plantation Negro. He was on sure ground when he set forth their humor and integrity, their independence and common-sense, and the force of their vernacular speech. And with equal sureness, he realistically brought to life the poor whites. In his realistic emphasis upon the middle and lower classes and the Negroes rather than upon the planters, Harris departed from the romantic pattern which the serious writers of Southern antebellum fiction had followed. His own boyhood of poverty and misfortune had given him a sympathetic insight into the mind and heart of the poor, the lowly, and the unfortunate.

The warm response to Harris' folklore stories gave him confidence in his ability to present a composite picture of Southern life, and as time permitted, he began to explore the wealth of native material which remained untouched and undeveloped.

With the exception of the folklore stories, Harris concentrated upon no one specific aspect of this inclusive material in his stories, nor did he follow any chronological order in developing it. He wrote as certain phases of remembered events and situations loomed largest in his mind from time to time and as he had opportunity

[5]Francis Pendleton Gaines, *The Southern Plantation* (New York: Columbia University Press, 1925), 75.

to respond to the requests from national magazines for any story that he would send them. *Mingo and Other Sketches* (1884), the first volume of his stories in which Uncle Remus did not appear, contained one story with a postwar setting of 1876 but with a flashback to the plantation era, one with a setting in the North Georgia mountains during the war, and two with a plantation background. The characters portrayed included planters, poor whites, mountaineers, hard and avaricious landowners, and Negroes both in slavery and in freedom. Having no established critical standards to guide him, Harris exercised his own judgment in plot structure and characterization.

In "Mingo," the principal story in the volume, the plot revolves around the hatred of Mrs. Feratia Bivins, a poor but proud white woman, for Mrs. Emily Wornum, the aristocratic wife of a planter and former slaveowner. The scene is the Crooked Creek Church, which the narrator of the story had attended in his youth and to which he has returned for a visit in 1876. Among those whom he recognizes in the church is Mingo, now free but a former slave of the Wornums. Through Mingo he receives an invitation from Mrs. Bivins to share with her and her granddaughter, Pud Hon, "the cole vittles an' po' far'" which she had brought for the noon meal. During the course of the meal she explains to the visitor the reasons for her hatred of Mrs. Wornum. Her son had married Cordelia, the daughter of the Wornums, and they had disowned the girl for marrying one whom they regarded as socially inferior. They had also forbidden Mingo and their other slaves from ever seeing Cordelia again. After the death of her son and Cordelia, Mrs. Bivins had cared for their daughter, Pud Hon, as if she were her own child. Up to that point in her rambling narrative, Mrs. Bivins has been calm and restrained, but when she begins to relate how the aristocratic Mrs. Wornum finally overcame her pride sufficiently to make a visit to see her granddaughter, her voice rises, her eyes flash, and, with an emotional intensity born of her scorn for the woman whom she suspected had come to take Pud Hon away from her, she angrily repeats to her listener the words she had defiantly hurled at "Ole Emily Wornum."

In commenting on the torrent of wrath which Mrs. Bivins, the proud poor white, has unleashed upon Mrs. Wornum, the proud but suppliant planter aristocrat, the narrator of the story says he will not attempt to describe the rude eloquence of attitude and expression which accompanied her recital, but it seemed to him "to represent the real or fancied wrongs of a class, and to spring from the pent-up rage of a century." The voice of Tragedy, he says, was speaking through her: "Its eyes shone; its fangs glistened and gleamed; its rage would have stormed the barriers of the grave." [6]

After Mrs. Bivins and Pud have gone back into the church for the afternoon service, Mingo quietly explains to the visitor, whom he had known when he had lived in the community during his boyhood, what lay behind Mrs. Bivins' outburst against Mrs. Wornum. She had always been hostile, he says, to anyone who had "Ferginny ways" and "she wouldn't a' stayed in a ten-acre fiel' wid um,—dat she wouldn't." She has also held the same attitude toward Negroes, and she tolerated him, Mingo says, only because he helped her to look after Pud as he had promised his dead mistress, Miss Cordelia, that he would.

"Mingo" is one of Harris' neglected stories of the Old South. In sharp contrast with the humor and warm relationships found in the folklore legends, he pictured in stark realism the tragic aspect of the poor whites and thereby added a new dimension to Southern literature. As he had done in the creation of Uncle Remus, so also in his delineation of Mrs. Bivins he had entered into the mind and soul of those poor but independent whites who held a grievance against the planter aristocracy, and he became their articulate voice of protest. In Mingo he created a Negro character who, by his qualities of loyalty, gentleness, quiet dignity, and good manners, deserves to be placed alongside Uncle Remus as a worthy representative of the old-time Southern Negro.

"At Teague Poteet's" is a story in which Harris delineated still another segment of life in the Old South, the independent traits of character of the North Georgia mountaineers. The scene is the Hog Mountain range near Kennesaw, and the time is 1859–1865. The plot involves the unsuccessful efforts of the federal marshals from Atlanta to arrest Teague Poteet for making illicit whiskey and describes the feud between the mountaineers who are Union sympa-

[6]Joel Chandler Harris, *Mingo and Other Sketches in Black and White* (Boston: James R. Osgood and Company, 1884), 24.

thizers and the "Restocrats" who side with the Confederates and live in the valley town at the foot of Hog Mountain. Teague refuses to engage in the war which he believes is being fought to perpetuate the social and economic system of the Southern aristocrats, and as a confirmed Unionist he resolutely declares his stand when he says: "Them air Restocrats kin go wher' they dang please; I'm a-gwine to stay right slambang in the Nunited States." And stay he does. In the mountains, he lives independently of laws which he does not like and of the presence and pressures of the exclusiveness which he feels in the valley village and against which he is in revolt. The romantic element in the story concerns the progress of the love affair which develops between Sis, the attractive and spirited daughter of Teague, and Marshal Phillip Woodward of Atlanta. In the end, Woodward, whose primary mission to Hog Mountain was to take Teague into custody, is himself taken captive by Sis.

"At Teague Poteet's" was unusually long for a short story and the *Century Magazine* published Part I in its May, 1883, number and Part II in its July number. It had a factual basis in that it grew out of a trial of two deputy marshals in Atlanta for killing a mountaineer who had disregarded the law by making "moonshine" whiskey.[7] The characters and the plot were Harris' inventions, but he knew the mountaineers sufficiently well to visualize their traits by their speech, attitudes, and actions within the narrow range of their somewhat isolated existence. The story had the merit of imparting to outsiders the qualities which were identified with this particular segment of Southern society.

It revealed, however, certain elements of Harris' strength and weakness present in his longer short stories and especially in his novels. When he sent "At Teague Poteet's" to the *Century*, Robert Underwood Johnson immediately accepted it but wrote him that he could improve some features of it. "Enough to say," Johnson informed him, "that it is interesting (9 points); true to life, evidently; rapid and fairly buoyant in narrative, and keen in insight of the female characters as misunderstood by man." He expressed surprise, however, that the humor in the story was less rollicksome than would be expected of the author of the Uncle Remus legends.[8] Not

[7] Julia Collier Harris, *Harris, Life and Letters*, 201, footnote.
[8] Robert Underwood Johnson to Joel Chandler Harris, December 18, 1882, in the Harris Collection, Emory University.

without some protest, Harris made the changes which Johnson had suggested. In his letter finally approving the story for publication, Johnson urged Harris to give some consideration in his stories to the importance of the dramatic side and to plot construction no less than to the delineation of character. "Give wings to your imagination," he wrote Harris, "and don't let 'em be clipped by current fashions in so-called 'realism.' We are bound soon to get something great in imaginative fiction or the signs fail. I fear it won't come out of Mr. Howells' methods, however, Cable is nearer to the thing if he would only curb his missionary spirit." [9]

Johnson's admonition to Harris to give more attention to tighter plot construction and greater dramatic effect pointed up the major weakness in his fiction. In his effort to stay close to human nature as exhibited in the normal routine of day-to-day happenings, Harris worked on the principle that realistic character delineation in a story was more important than the contrived manipulation of events for the sake of a dramatic climax. Consequently, he envisioned his characters clearly, endowed them with life, and rarely ever struck a false note, but he found it difficult to tie together the various strands of a plot in a long story in which there were many characters involved in many incidents. The reader, therefore, remembers Uncle Remus, Sis Tempy, African Jack, Free Joe, Aunt Minervy Ann, Mrs. Bivins, Mingo, Blue Dave, Billy Sanders, and numerous other characters whom Harris' creative imagination brought to life even though he may fail to recall the specific episodes in which they appeared.

The two other stories in the *Mingo* volume have an old plantation setting in Putnam County. In "Blue Dave," Harris illustrated the effect which both a hard and a kind master had upon Blue Dave, a Negro slave. "A Piece of Land" recounts the greed of Bradley Gaither for more land and still more land. No ethical consideration deters him from his avaricious course in acquiring what he wants by whatever means is necessary. Bradley Gaither foreshadowed characters of the same type who were later to appear in the stories by Hamlin Garland and William Faulkner.

Although these stories were realistic in theme and presented the darker side of antebellum plantation life, the volume was favorably

[9] Robert Underwood Johnson to Joel Chandler Harris, March 19, 1883, in the Harris Collection, Emory University.

received. The *Constitution* expressed the opinion that in departing from the line of folklore Harris had sustained himself in a comparatively new field.[10] This local evaluation was confirmed by Northern critics. The New York *Times* noted that, in the poor whites of Georgia, Harris had found material as fresh and picturesque as anything in the delightful Uncle Remus stories and that he had handled it with the ease, mastery, and grace of a natural artist.[11] *The Critic* found the white element in the new stories to be as vivid and entertaining as the black element had been in the folklore stories.[12] The *Nation* was particularly impressed by Harris' appropriate use of dialect in his portrayal of the poor whites and the mountaineers. It said that the stories in the new field did not discredit the fame of Uncle Remus. "He [Harris] used rude or corrupt language," its reviewer emphasized, "to express only primitive thought—fierce hate, unreasoning love, a dog's gratitude for kindness, a savage's impulse toward revenge; he never offends or wearies by palpable incongruities between ideas and form." And the reviewer commented that in this respect Harris' perception was more subtle and sensitive than was Bret Harte's.[13]

Even though the *Mingo* volume without Uncle Remus had been successful, Harris did not let his readers forget the venerable storyteller. He followed Mark Twain's practical counsel and kept him before the public by an occasional plantation story and gave additional items of information about the place which he occupied on the plantation of his master and mistress. In his introduction to a witch tale which he published in the *Constitution* on September 6, 1885, Harris described the peculiar relationship of Uncle Remus to the other Negroes on the plantation and to his "Miss Sally." Since he was not a field hand, he did not come under the supervision of the overseer, but he was looked upon as a kind of major-domo by the house and yard servants, and, as a privileged and trusted family retainer, he considered himself to be a partner with them in seeing that the plantation was well conducted. The other Negroes treated him with great deference, for they were well aware of his influence with their master. Harris said it would be difficult

[10]Atlanta *Constitution*, June 22, 1884.
[11]New York *Times*, July 6, 1884.
[12]*The Critic*, New Series, I (August 2, 1884), 51.
[13]*The Nation*, XXXIX (August 7, 1884), 116.

to describe to the satisfaction of those who were not familiar with some of the developments of slavery in the South the peculiar relationship which existed between Uncle Remus and his "Miss Sally." When she was a child, he had protected and taken care of her, and, although she was now a woman with a family of her own, he had continued to regard her as his personal charge. If, therefore, he sometimes appeared to be dictatorial in his concern for her, there was always a feeling of mutual respect and affection between them.

Harris was one of the first authors in America to discern the real greatness of Mark Twain's *The Adventures of Huckleberry Finn* and to express his appreciation of it at a time when it was being condemned in some quarters as immoral trash unfit to be placed on library shelves. His own youthful association in Eatonton with Free Joe and with old George, Harbert, and other slaves at Turnwold had enabled him to perceive that *Huckleberry Finn* was both a wholesome and a truthful book. In a letter to *The Critic* in commemoration of Mark Twain's fiftieth birthday, he wrote that Twain had earned the right to grow old and mellow, that he had put his youth into his books where it was perennial, and that in his last book he had renewed and revived it. "I know that some of the professional critics will not agree with me," he ventured to assert after his usual attitude of awe toward such critics, "but there is not in our fictive literature a more wholesome book than 'Huckleberry Finn'! It is history, it is romance, it is life. Here we behold human character stripped of its tiresome details; we see people living and growing; we laugh at their humor, share their griefs; and, in the midst of it all, behold we are taught the lesson of honesty, justice and mercy." [14] Since Harris' evaluation in 1885 the book has been analyzed over and over again in detail, but American scholars have simply confirmed in their lengthy essays Harris' brief but true summation of the essential qualities of its greatness soon after its publication in America.

By 1886 the name of Joel Chandler Harris had become known in America and abroad but there was a dearth of information about his personal life history. He had been so averse to talking or writing

[14] *The Critic*, New Series, IV (November 28, 1885), 253

about himself or to doing anything that might possibly be construed as self-advertisement that even in Atlanta there were comparatively few people outside the circle of his intimate friends and newspaper associates who knew him by sight. He received letters each day from the readers of his stories in which they requested his autograph, but he regarded the autograph business as a nuisance and refused to comply with their requests. So great, however, was the interest in his personal life that the public accepted without question any item which they saw about him.

Personal journalism was still in vogue in America in the 1880's, and Eugene Field, poet, humorist, and columnist on the Chicago *Daily News*, saw an opportunity to play a joke on Harris by supplying the public with some "inside" information on the life of the creator of Uncle Remus. Accordingly, Field invented and inserted in his column "Sharps and Flats" two paragraphs of biographical data about Harris which were so fantastic that even the most naive reader should have taken them for the huge joke that Field intended them to be.[15] Field said that Joel Chandler Harris had been born in Booghai on the southern coast of Africa while his parents were stationed there as missionaries. The family had returned to America when Joel was a little boy. He had entered school, and developed a wonderful literary ability. He had served in the Civil War with distinction, but when he returned home after the war had ended, he found that his sweetheart had died and his grief over his loss had caused his hair to turn perfectly white. He was now continuing his literary work at his West End home in Atlanta, where night after night passersby could hear him singing some old Negro ballad in a voice of tender sweetness. These fictitious items were widely copied in American newspapers as factual, and Field so enjoyed his joke that he added still further details. He said that Harris had been born at Joel, Africa, instead of at Booghai, and that he had been named Joel after the place of his birth. The press made the correction.

Among the many letters which Harris received as a result of the widely circulated hoax, there was one from a young woman who

---

[15]My source for Field's invented "facts" is the account which was printed in the *Constitution* on the appropriate date—April 1, 1886—when Field's story was going the rounds of the American press.

Joel Chandler Harris at work

Madison Street, Eatonton, Georgia

Street scene during the cotton season in Eatonton, Georgia

Joseph Addison Turner's home, Turnwold plantation, date unknown

Joseph Addison Turner

Louisa Dennis Turner

Joel Chandler Harris, 1892   Esther LaRose Harris, about 1874

Old Atlanta *Constitution* building, corner of Alabama and Forsyth streets. The *Constitution* moved to a new building in December, 1947.

Harris and his newspaper associates. Seated, left to right, are Clark Howell and Harris. Standing, left to right, are Wallace P. Reed, J. K. Ohl, and Frank L. Stanton.

Joel Chandler Harris and James Whitcomb Riley

The Wren's Nest, with Harris standing at the steps

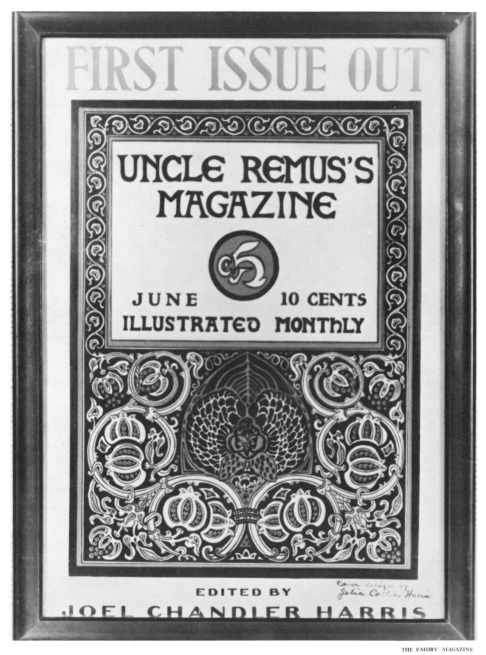

The cover of the first issue of *Uncle Remus's Magazine*, June, 1907

signed her name "Caroline Muggs" and who expressed sympathy that he had been born in faraway Africa. There was also another one from *Lippincott's Magazine* requesting him to prepare a factual statement for publication in order to correct the misinformation which was being circulated as facts. Harris sent the "Caroline Muggs" letter to Fields with the wry comment, "See! O See! what you have done!" The letter was simply more grist for Field's joke mill, and he announced in his column that Joel Chandler Harris was soon to marry a Miss Caroline Muggs of North Carolina, a niece of Stonewall Jackson, whom he had first met at a picnic on Lookout Mountain. Field's announcement was copied by the press as a social item of interest concerning the popular author.

Being a humorist himself, Harris went along with Field's joke. However, since the story was becoming fixed in the public mind as true, he decided to accede to the request of *Lippincott's Magazine* for a correct statement. Reluctantly, he sent the magazine a brief article, "An Accidental Author," the first statement concerning himself which he authorized for publication. His article touched upon the circumstances of his birth only lightly and not at all upon his period of storm and stress, but dealt primarily with his career as an author which he claimed had been accidental. He particularly emphasized that he was not a literary man. "I have no literary training," he asserted, "and know nothing at all of what is termed literary art." [16]

This assertion by Harris of his lack of literary art was not a pose to cover up his artistic deficiencies, nor was it motivated by any desire to forestall just criticism of his work by the literary critics. He was fully aware of his limitations, he frankly admitted them, and, despite the favorable reviews which his books had received, he could never persuade himself that his work entitled him to occupy more than a subordinate and inconspicuous place among the major American men of letters of his day. This is not to say, however, that he was without literary standards of his own, and he always insisted that his books should stand or fall by their literary merit alone. There is ample evidence that he was a conscientious workman. His extant manuscripts in the Harris Collection at Emory University with their false starts, careful revisions, changes

[16]Joel Chandler Harris, "An Accidental Author," 417–20.

in dialect for greater exactness, and his correspondence with his publishers all testify to his constant efforts to improve his technique.

From year to year both Harris and Henry W. Grady enhanced the reputation of the Atlanta *Constitution* as the most progressive newpaper in the South, with Harris leading in the movement through his stories to reconstruct its literature and Grady through his promotional activities to rehabilitate its economy. The success of the International Cotton States Exposition had given Grady an entree with Northern capitalists, and when he received an invitation to address the New England Society in New York on December 22, 1886, he accepted, although he had never before spoken outside the South. He saw in the invitation an opportunity to carry his crusade for industrializing the South directly to those who had capital to invest.

His address on "The New South" was not only the high point of the banquet but also the high point of Grady's brief but brilliant career. Among the guests was General William T. Sherman, who only twenty-two years before had reduced to shambles the city which Grady was zealously trying to rebuild. Also present were J. Pierpont Morgan, Russell Sage, H. M. Flagler, John H. Inman, and many other men of wealth.[17]

If Grady had carried with him to New York any of the old sectional bitterness against the North, he could easily have revived and rekindled it, for, preceding his address, General Sherman spoke and the band played "Marching through Georgia," a song that was still anathema to unreconstructed Georgians. But Grady was skillful in adjusting his feelings and his speech to any exigency that might arise and the occasion inspired him. With light touches of humor he immediately established a rapport between himself and his Northern audience. He praised Lincoln as the embodiment of the spirit of the Cavalier and the Puritan and referred to General Sherman as an able man but one who had been "kinder careless with fire." He graphically pictured the footsore Confederate soldier, "this hero in gray with a heart of gold," as he returned to his home after the war and began his work of restoration without any bitterness or rancor in defeat. He rejoiced that human slavery had been swept

[17]Nixon, *Henry W. Grady*, 242.

from the American soil and spoke feelingly of the "indissoluble union of American States and the imperishable brotherhood of the American people."

In this one eloquent and emotion-charged address, he dramatized the movement toward national reconciliation which Harris had been advancing through his constructive editorials in the *Constitution* and through his revelation of the mind and social structure of the Southern region in his stories. As a result of his moving appeal for the spirit of the victorious North to match the spirit of the defeated but revitalized and forward-looking South, Grady became known overnight as "the great pacificator," and on his return to Atlanta from New York, he received a hero's welcome.

Even so Grady had gone to New York with the primary purpose of interesting Northern capitalists in investing their wealth in Southern factories by assuring them that the South was now free from its old sectional isolation and hostility against the North and that its social and business climate was now favorable for profitable returns on financial investments. In his article on "The Qualities of Greatness in Henry W. Grady," Raymond B. Nixon pointedly states that "the dominant motif of his entire career was devotion to a single cause: the economic upbuilding of the South. His work as 'national pacificator' was a corollary to this." [18] Forty-nine years after Grady had made his historic "New South" speech, the historian, Paul H. Buck, declared that Grady's words no longer seemed important, but that "Grady's faith and Grady's optimism were a living fire peculiar to the New South he served. He became the recognized apostle of the new faith." [19]

In the years that followed Grady's triumph in New York, he spoke here and there in the South on the theme of the development of its natural resources. Harris, tied to his editorial desk, rarely left Atlanta, but he once accompanied Grady to Eatonton where the latter spoke at the Putnam County Fair and sat on the platform with him. After Grady had spoken, there were calls from his boyhood friends in the audience for Harris with the expectation that they would hear from him. Whereupon, he stood up and said, "I'm a-coming; I'm a-

[18]Raymond B. Nixon, "The Qualities of Greatness in Henry W. Grady," *Emory University Quarterly* XXI (Fall, 1965), 153.
[19]Paul H. Buck, *The Road to Reunion* (Boston: Little, Brown and Company, 1937), 194.

coming." However, instead of stopping to make a speech, he walked down among the crowd and explained that he had come to Eatonton to write up Grady's speech, not to make one himself.[20]

So great was the pressure on Harris for writing his daily assignments for the *Constitution* that he had little time to compose additional stories, and it was not until December, 1887, that he published his fourth volume, *Free Joe and Other Georgian Sketches*, a collection of five regional stories which he had previously contributed to *Scribner's Magazine* and *Century Magazine*. All of them dealt with some phase of life in the South, and were full of the spirit of reconciliation and goodwill.

The title story, "Free Joe and the Rest of the World," was based on some recollections of Harris' boyhood in Eatonton. He had known Free Joe, a harmless Negro who had no master when almost all of the other Negroes in Eatonton were slaves, and he had joined with the other boys in playing practical jokes on him. He also knew of slaveowners who lacked the humanitarian qualities of Joseph Addison Turner. In "Free Joe" he combined these factual reminiscences, and by the genius of his creative art lifted them into one of the most memorable of all his non-folklore stories of the old South. This story of the plight of the free Negro in the era of slavery had its moments of humor and kindliness, but these lighter qualities were overshadowed by pathos and by the harsh aspects of a social and economic system that made Free Joe its hapless and helpless victim.

Harris, who had previously shown the gentility and the unassuming nobility of the plantation Negro in Uncle Remus and Mingo, described Free Joe as one who was homeless and shiftless but good-natured and innocent of wrong in thought and conduct, as friendless but friendly, one who found his only pleasure in amusing the children in the village square. Although he was homeless, ragged, and forlorn, he was yet one of "the humblest, the simplest, and the most serious of all God's living creatures." An outcast from the society of his own kind and having no friends among either the white slaveowners or their slaves, he was tossed about as a piece of human driftwood between the two, looked upon with suspicion by

---

[20]L. Sidney Wheeler of Monroe, Georgia, said in a personal interview that he had heard the story from his mother, who was present at the event.

the one and treated with contumely by the other. Harris further described him as "the embodiment of that vague and mysterious danger that seemed to be forever lurking on the outskirts of slavery, ready to sound a shrill and ghastly signal in the impenetrable swamps and steal forth under the midnight stars to murder, rapine and pillage,— a danger always threatening, and yet never assuming shape; intangible, and yet real; impossible, and yet not improbable." [21] Free Joe's lot was rendered even more forlorn by one of the most inhumane features of the slavery regime, for his wife Lucinda was a slave, owned by Spite Calderwood, so called because of his reputation as a hard and insensitive master. When Calderwood discovered that Free Joe was contriving to meet Lucinda, he took her to Macon and sold her to another master.

Harris' stories were usually free from didacticism, but at the close of "Free Joe" he pronounced at least by implication a moral judgment on these dark and callous aspects of the institution which combined to make Free Joe and Lucinda its innocent victims. In his characterization of Free Joe, Harris had once again gone outside himself and entered into the heart and soul of a plantation Negro who was at the opposite end of the social structure of plantation Negroes from Uncle Remus and Mingo. He had portrayed him as a warmly appealing human being caught in a mesh of unhappy circumstances from which he could not free himself.

Three of the other stories in the *Free Joe* volume had a Putnam County and a Civil War setting, but each had a motif of national reconciliation. "Little Compton" was the story of the relationship between Little Compton, a New Jersey Yankee who had settled in Hillsborough (Eatonton) in 1850, and Jack Walthall, a native of the village. The two had become fast friends, but when the war began the local antagonism toward anyone from the North made Little Compton an object of suspicion as an abolitionist and he returned to New Jersey and fought in the Union army while Walthall fought for the Confederacy. Both were wounded in the battle at Gettysburg, taken to the same hospital where they renewed their former friendship, were discharged, and returned to Hillsborough together, each with an empty sleeve. When Sherman's soldiers reached Hills-

[21]Joel Chandler Harris, *Free Joe and Other Georgian Sketches* (New York: Charles Scribner's Sons, 1887), 1, 2.

borough in the fall of 1864, it was Little Compton who persuaded their commander to spare the village from destruction. Little Compton, in his uniform of blue, and Jack Walthall, in his uniform of gray stood side by side and reviewed the Union soldiers as they passed through the village. Harris made the unusual incident which occurred while the war was still in progress "prophetic of the days to come when peace and fraternity would seize upon the land, and bring unity, happiness, and prosperity to the people."

"Aunt Fountain's Prisoner" was another of Harris' major stories in which the focus was upon the theme of reconciliation between the South and the North and one in which he also advanced his own idea as to the method by which the South could re-establish its economy.

After Sherman's soldiers had evacuated the Tomlinson place in Putnam County, Aunt Fountain, one of Judge Tomlinson's slaves, found Ferris Trunion, a disabled Union soldier, lying in a gully. Trunion's injury had kept him from joining the other Yankee soldiers when they departed. Her "prisoner of war" was taken into the home of her master and mistress, who received him coolly at first but kept him with them until he fully recovered. Instead of returning to his northern home, he remained in Putnam County and eventually took over the management of the rundown Tomlinson plantation, filled the eroded gullies, cultivated the Bermuda Grass which Judge Tomlinson had tried to destroy, and established a profitable dairy. By his gentlemanly conduct and energetic business enterprise, he gradually overcame the prejudices of the patrician Tomlinson family.

"Aunt Fountain's Prisoner" illustrated Harris' conviction that the time had come for the South to abandon its old inherited ideas which were identified with a static, aristocratic planter society (which, in fact, no longer actually existed) and to open its mind to new and constructive ideas even though they came from former Northern enemies. He found in Trunion "a practical illustration of the fact that one may be a Yankee and a Southerner too simply by being a large-hearted, whole-souled American." It is also to be noted that in the story Harris advocated a program of diversified farming as a way toward the rehabilitation of the impoverished South in 1887 instead of the building of cotton factories which would tend to draw its people away from the land.

"Azalia" was a long eight-part story which was an example of "Practical Reconstruction" in the year 1873 when, in Harris' words, "the politicians and the editors, both great and small, of every shade of belief, had determined to fight the war over again—instituting a conflict which though bloodless enough as far as the disputants were concerned, was not without its unhappy results." The entire story was an exposition of his oft-repeated belief that if both Northerners and Southerners would pay less attention to the politicians, discard their sectional prejudices which they had formed from reading strongly slanted literature of a propagandist type, discuss their divisive issues in a spirit of tolerance on both sides, and, most of all, talk face to face with each other in their respective environments, they would find a common ground for mutual understanding and goodwill.

"Trouble on Lost Mountain," the second of Harris' stories in which he portrayed the mountain people of North Georgia, was also included in the *Free Joe* volume. It was based on his recollections of his contacts with them during a month's vacation when he was recovering from a nervous condition which had resisted medical treatment. The plot was a conventional one in that a Mr. Chichester, who was an agent of some Boston capitalists who had heard that there was marble in Lost Mountain and had sent Chichester to discover the marble beds so that they could buy up the land, unintentionally caused trouble between Babe Hightower and her lover Tuck Peevy, who mistakenly concluded that Chichester and Babe were in love. The ending was unconventional, however, for Chichester left the mountain but Babe and Tuck Peevy never resolved their blighted romance. There were elements of pathos and tragedy in the story, but more impressive than either the characterization of the mountain people or the plot itself was Harris' love of the mountain scenery which he expressed through Babe Hightower. To her the mountain was far more than a mountain; it was not merely something majestic to admire but a mysterious force and spirit with which she might hold communion but which she never attempted to explain or define. As he never had any affinity for a city environment, the mountain scenery evoked in Harris his innate poetic nature, and he described it in the Wordsworthian manner of an emotional experience recollected in tranquility but without undue sentiment.

In his editorials on the status of literature in the South in the 1880's,

Harris continued to appeal to Southern writers to be artistic and realistic in the presentation of their stories. In his editorial "Literature in the South," which appeared in the *Constitution*, September 2, 1888, he lamented the tendency on the part of contemporary authors, in their haste to supply the popular demand for dialect stories, to sacrifice the essentials of literary art. He insisted that the true purpose of dialect was to portray accurately both life and character. Nor had Southern writers yet overcome the obstacle, he continued, of the romantic tradition in character delineation. "The portrait of the ideal Southerner has been drawn for us by a number of ante-bellum writers, and the figure he cuts is ultra-heroic and romantic. He is drawn after the fashion of that set by Sir Walter Scott and Miss Jane Porter and it is not easy to get away from their influence." As a consequence, Harris went on to say, the Southern novelist who attempted to write the great American novel would have to be bold as well as sympathetic and would have to shatter some of the conventionalities and notions that appeared to be standing the test of time.

The intimate relationship which had existed between Harris and Grady as associate editors of the Atlanta *Constitution* since November, 1876, was brought to an end by Grady's death in Atlanta on December 23, 1889. On December 12 he had addressed the Merchants Association of Boston on "The Race Problem in the South." Since there was a civil rights bill before the Congress, he felt that the time had come for him to deal forthrightly with the issue, for he strongly believed that its passage would rekindle the smoldering fires of sectional hatred, destroy the peaceful progress that was being substantially made toward reunion, and thus curtail the flow of Northern capital to Southern industry. Having stated the problem as he saw it and having cited evidence to show the progress that was being made in an amicable way to solve it, he appealed to his Northern audience for their patience, confidence, sympathy, and loyalty to the republic. "This hour," he said, "little needs the loyalty that is loyal to one section and yet holds the other in enduring suspicion and estrangement." Despite the views which he expressed in regard to the solution of the race problem, those who differed radically with him could not resist the sincerity, the earnestness, and the magnetism of his eloquence, and the speech was another signal triumph for him. So persuasive was its impact that, as Raymond B. Nixon wrote in his *Henry W. Grady*, "Grady's final appeal to the North, reinforced as it was so dramatically by his death, did contribute to the defeat of the federal election law (January, 1891) and thus to the definite acceptance by the North of the attitude that the Negro question should be left to the South to solve." [22]

Before Grady left Atlanta he had become ill with a cold, but he insisted upon fulfilling his engagement in Boston. During his entire New England visit he was under the care of a physician, but he became increasingly ill and on his return to Atlanta on December 17 was too ill to attend a reception in his honor which had previously been planned. He died early on the morning of the twenty-third, and his funeral was held on Christmas Day. The several thousand Atlantans who filed by his casket before the service bore silent testimony to the affection in which they held him.

A memorial volume compiled by the staff of the *Constitution* and edited by Harris was published in 1890 for the benefit of Grady's family. Harris wrote the biographical sketch in which he pointed out the significance of Grady's contribution to Atlanta and the South through his zeal for the upbuilding of the region's material resources and his appeal for national unity. He also emphasized that Grady's vision had included an interest in the new literary revival which had been taking place in the South since the war. He wrote that Grady looked forward to the time when the immense but untouched literary field in the South would be as thoroughly worked and developed as that of New England had been and that this development might be reasonably expected to follow, if it did not accompany, the progress of the South in other directions. [23]

However, Grady's influence was not due to his pen but to the charm of his personality and the persuasive effect which his eloquence had upon his immediate hearers. His name is inseparably linked with the economic upsurge of the New South but his contribution to its literary development in the decades immediately following the Civil War was negligible in comparison with that of George W. Cable, Mary Moailles Murfree, Thomas Nelson Page, Sidney Lanier, Harry Stillwell Edwards, and Joel Chandler Harris.

[22] Nixon, *Henry W. Grady*, 237.
[23] Joel Chandler Harris (ed.), *Life of Henry W. Grady* (New York: Cassell and Company, 1890), 44.

9

PORTRAITS OF THE OLD REGIME

From the day that Harris joined the staff of the Atlanta *Constitution* in November, 1876, he had been grinding out copy for its daily editions and, as time allowed, responding to the requests of magazines for his stories of the Southern region. Even by the end of 1889, the strain was beginning to undermine his health. Periodic illness had confined him to his home, and he had sought recuperation in the mineral waters at Lithia Springs, not far from Atlanta, or else had taken brief vacations in the mountains north of the city. Moreover, life in Atlanta, in Georgia, and in the South became increasingly more complex. And, as the associate editor of one of the South's most progressive newspapers, he felt compelled to write about this growing complexity. But at the same time he tended more and more to seek refuge in the island of quiet which he found in the village of West End and in the privacy of his home.

When the Harrises moved to West End in 1883, its population had consisted of only a few hundred persons, but by 1887 it had become known as a select residential section and among its citizens were Evan P. Howell, T. D. Longino, George W. Adair and his son Forrest, all of whom were prominent in Atlanta's social, cultural, and financial affairs. After the population of West End had sufficiently increased, it was incorporated and had its mayor and councilmen. In spite of his shyness, Harris had served on the council, but resigned his membership in April, 1888, because he disagreed with the majority of its members on the question of tax assessment. In 1887 his property had been assessed at $6,000, but in 1888 it had been increased to $12,000.[1]

Although Harris' income from his magazine articles and the sale of his four published volumes had supplemented his salary from the *Constitution* to the extent that earlier he had been able to en-

[1]Atlanta *Constitution*, April 21, 1888.

large his West End home, he had accumulated no large surplus bank account. Eugene Field, however, in one of his fictitious paragraphs in his "Sharps and Flats" column about the wealth of American humorists had said that Harris led the list with a total wealth of $2,000,000, which included four thousand acres of timberland and a large interest in the Central of Georgia Railroad, and that his greatest delight was in helping the needy. As a result of this widely circulated story, Harris was pestered with appeals for help which at first he did not understand, for Field had published his story during one of Harris' prolonged illnesses. When he had sufficiently recovered to read his accumulated mail, he remarked with his characteristic chuckle to a reporter from the *Constitution* who had come to see him that he was going to Chicago the following week. "What for?" the reporter asked. "To kill Eugene Field," he replied.[2]

By 1890 the Harris home itself had attained a settled appearance. Rose and wisteria vines ran along the lattice work under the overhanging eaves of the front porch, and on both sides of the home there were gardens of Harris' favorite roses. No other residences had as yet been built on his lot, and there was an air of serenity and repose about it in keeping with Harris' love of a pastoral environment. The ties which bound Joel, Esther, and their children together in a congenial home environment became stronger as the children grew older, and the death of Linton in his seventh year was a source of deep grief to the entire family.

Diverted from his literary work by his own illness, his concern for his mother's failing health, grief over the death of Linton, and the pressure of his editorial duties, Harris produced only a few stories between 1887 and 1890, but in 1889, the Century Company brought out his fifth volume, *Daddy Jake the Runaway, and Stories Told After Dark*. In his conviction that the war and reconstruction periods offered inexhaustible material for the Southern writer, he had continued to draw upon this source for these new stories, and in "Daddy Jake the Runaway" the scene was the Gaston plantation in Putnam County during the war. Despite its war background, it was a warm and appealing account of the relationship which existed between Daddy Jake, a trusted household servant of the Gastons,

[2]*Ibid.*, August 28, 1886.

and the two small Gaston children, Lucien and Lillian. Daddy Jake, after the manner of Uncle Remus and the little boy, had endeared himself to Lucien and Lillian by entertaining them with stories, and when they learned that Daddy Jake had run away from the plantation after being struck by the overseer of the field hands they secretly set out in a bateau down the Oconee River in search of him. The entire plantation was thrown into a state of turmoil to find both Daddy Jake and the children. After a series of exciting adventures, all three were eventually found safe and happily returned to the plantation. Except for the little boy in the folklore tales, Harris had not delineated any children in his stories, and his charming portraits of Lucien and Lillian, who were modeled after two of Harris' children with the same name, captivated both young and old readers, and the story proved to be one of Harris' most popular. Eight editions were ordered before its publication in October, 1889,[3] and still others were issued after it was published. As an offset to the cruel treatment which Daddy Jake had received at the hands of the arrogant overseer, the volume also included thirteen new Uncle Remus folklore legends which pictured a pleasant aspect of the old plantation regime.

The years from 1884 to 1891 had witnessed a slump in Harris' literary creativity, but between 1891 and 1899 he published thirteen volumes. He continued to range the entire prewar plantation for his material, delved lightly into the history of Georgia, and wrote a series of stories designed primarily for the entertainment of children. Although his subjects were varied in their theme and their appeal to different levels of readers, he continued to produce most effectively the lights and shadows of the plantation era.

The first of these volumes was *Balaam and His Master, and Other Sketches and Stories* which Houghton Mifflin Company, the successor of J. R. Osgood and Company, published in 1891. The title story, "Balaam and His Master," was an example of Harris' honesty in revealing that not every "Southron" was a chivalric gentleman. Berrien Cozart, the profligate son of a respected pioneer middle Georgian, sold Balaam, his faithful bodyguard, to secure money with which to continue his mania for gambling. "A Conscript's Christmas" was not a glorification of war in that it set forth the unpopularity

---

[3] *Ibid.*, October 13, 1889.

of the Conscript Act in Georgia in 1863. "It won't pan out," said private Chadwick who had been sent along with Captain Mosely to apprehend a deserter from a Confederate camp at Adairsville in order to spend Christmas with his family in the North Georgia mountains. "It has turned more men agin the Confederacy," he asserted, "than it has turned for it."

"Ananias" was a story of the chaos, uncertainty, and despair which befell the South in the years immediately following the defeat of the Confederacy. In his introduction to the story, Harris stated, out of his own knowledge of the period, that the troubles of that unhappy time would never be known to posterity, for, he said, they had never been adequately described. He dealt with them, however, not in a spirit of resentment or as an appeal for sympathy but in the interest of historical truth. Ananias, a former slave of Colonel Benjamin Flewellyn who had owned a large plantation in Putnam County, had been unable to persuade his master that he had not revealed the hiding place to which the stock had been driven for safety during the invasion of the plantation by Federal soldiers in 1864. He had therefore gone off with the army, but after the war had returned to the plantation, and, although now free, had demonstrated his loyalty to his former master by working for him without any contract. Meanwhile, Flewellyn's former overseer, Washington Jones, who was shrewd and calculating in his dealings, opened a general merchandise store, persuaded Flewellyn to buy more farm supplies than he could possibly pay for, and had then foreclosed on the debt and taken over the Flewellyn plantation. Reduced to poverty through Jones's nefarious scheme, Flewellyn moved to Rockville (Eatonton) where Ananias, who had followed him, kept his former master's table abundantly supplied by some mysterious means, Jones accused Ananias of stealing the provisions from him, but since the evidence submitted at his trial was circumstantial the jury refused to convict him.

The similarity between Colonel Benjamin Flewellyn and Joseph Addison Turner was so marked that Harris must have had Turner in mind when he drew the portrait of Flewellyn. Both operated their plantations in an idealistic rather than a practical manner and entrusted the management of their plantations to their overseers.

Both had a fondness for literature, wrote essays in defense of slavery, published essays and poems at their own expense, and edited a weekly newspaper which was devoted to literature, politics, and current news. Both were representatives of literate but impractical Southern planters before the war, both were reduced to poverty by the war, and both were unequal to the task of readjusting themselves to their reversed fortunes after the war. If Harris used Turner as his model for Flewellyn, his primary purpose was not to be unkind, for he never forgot the debt of gratitude which he owed to Turner. However, from the vantage point of his mature years he could see, as he had not been able to do when he was a boy, the eccentricities and impractical idealism of his first literary adviser. In the story, Harris presented a striking contrast between a literate and idealistic planter on the one hand and an illiterate and practical overseer on the other hand, but with the major emphasis on a sympathetic characterization of an ignorant, confused, inarticulate, and misunderstood plantation Negro whose motivations were always good.

Of all the stories in the *Balaam and His Master* collection, the most dramatic was "Where's Duncan?" in which Harris dealt with the tragedy of mixed blood and its terrifying consequences on the persons directly involved. It contained scenes, Harris said, such as had never been described in any of the books that had professed to tell about life in the South before the war. The incidents in the story revolved around a mysterious dark-featured, black-bearded man who in 1826 joined a wagon train that was hauling cotton to Augusta. When the caravan had encamped overnight he revealed his name as Willis Featherstone, stated that he was merely a vagabond but that he had a rich father thereabouts and was on his way to find out how he was getting along. He then propounded a riddle: A father had a son whom he sent to school in Augusta but later came to hate him and sold him to a speculator in slaves. Was he the son? Where was the son's mother? The answers, he said, were a part of the riddle. While the campers were sitting around the campfire not far from the Featherstone mansion, there appeared in the circle of teamsters a tall mulatto woman who said that her master, "Ole Giles Featherstone" had sent her to invite them to his house for supper, but she warned them not to go, for she said he had scrimped her and everyone on his place and that he would scrimp them. When the dark-featured vagabond wanderer noticed the mulatto woman standing in the campfire circle, he suddenly changed from the tune which he had been playing on his fiddle to a plaintive old plantation melody which caught her attention and opened the floodgates of her memory. The implications of the riddle were now apparent, and the scene in which the woman wreaked her revenge upon her master was one of the most powerful and poignant in all of Harris' stories. "Where's Duncan?" was not the kind of story which Harris preferred to write, but he related it in all of its grim and stark reality because he was a truth-teller in his stories of the Old South.

In "The Old Bascom Place," the last story in the *Balaam and His Master* collection, Harris depicted the conflict which arose in the South after the Civil War concerning the road which would lead to the recovery of the region's material prosperity. In old Judge Briscoe he symbolized the point of view of the older generation of Southerners who resisted any change whatever in a rapidly changing era. The judge had lost his elegant home and his extensive cotton plantation as a result of Sherman's destructive march through middle Georgia. Reduced to poverty and forced to live in a modest home in Hillsborough, he became abnormally obsessed in his old age with the dream of regaining his former home and plantation and maintaining them precisely as he had done before the war.

Meanwhile, Francis Underwood, a young man from western New York, bought the old Bascom Place and by the reforms which he instituted developed it into a profitable operation. To the consternation of Judge Bascom, young Underwood brought in Jersey cows, built a barn near the hallowed old mansion for the convenience of the dairymen, reduced the cotton acreage, and grew his needed supplies. He stimulated a renewed interest in farming and turned a decadent and somnolent community into one that was progressive and awake. At first, the people of Hillsborough eyed him with suspicion and treated him coolly because he was a Yankee, but by his breadth of vision and public-spirited endeavors, he broke down their sectional prejudices, and he and the natives worked together for the upbuilding of the community.[4]

Although Harris made the hero of "The Old Bascom Place" the

[4]B. W. Hunt, a native of Connecticut who became a resident of Eatonton after the war, married Louise Prudden, and took an active interest in the town's affairs, was in all probability Harris' model for Francis Underwood. He helped to revolutionize the economy of Putnam County through his encouragement of the dairy industry.

young and enterprising New Yorker instead of the conservative Southerner, he nevertheless portrayed Judge Bascom sympathetically as a type of many of the former Southern planters whose fortunes and manner of life had been completely swept away by the outcome of the war. Never having had to work themselves, they were helpless when misfortune struck, and as bewildered spectators rather than active participants, they watched, in Harris' words, "half-hopefully and half regretfully, the representatives of a new generation trying to build up the waste places." At the same time, however, Harris clearly implied, as he had previously done in "Aunt Fountain's Prisoner," that prosperity for an impoverished South depended upon its willingness to be hospitable to new ideas instead of holding on to the ineffectual dream that it could shape its future in the new era by the traditional pattern of its past.

An era in Harris' personal life came to a close with the death of his mother on March 30, 1891, at the age of seventy-five. With something of the fortitude which had characterized the pioneer settlers of middle Georgia, she had overcome adverse fortune in her own life by the exercise of a patient and resolute will, and she had had a mother's satisfaction in seeing her son rise above the handicaps of his youth and attain a place of eminence among America's most honored and distinguished authors.

Since the publication of *Nights with Uncle Remus* in 1883, Harris had been collecting and verifying additional Negro folklore stories, and the favorable reaction to the thirteen which he had included in *Daddy Jake the Runaway* in 1889 encouraged him to begin a new series in the *Constitution* on July 23, 1892. In its announcement, the *Constitution* stated that they would be the last plantation fables that Harris intended to write, not that he claimed to have covered the entire field but that he had virtually exhausted that part of it which he had been able to reach and with which he was familiar. The new series included twenty-four legends, the last of which appeared in the *Constitution* on November 6. Despite the waning popularity of regional dialect stories in 1892, the public's response to these old plantation legends as told by Uncle Remus was cordial, and in December of that year Houghton Mifflin Company published them, together with sixteen Uncle Remus old plantation songs and thirty-one Uncle Remus sketches with a post-war Atlanta setting, under the title, *Uncle Remus and His Friends*. The volume was similar to *Uncle Remus: His Songs and His Sayings* (1880) in that Uncle Remus was the spokesman in each one of the legends, songs, and sketches.

Harris published *Uncle Remus and His Friends* with some misgivings about its reception by the literary critics. In his rather apologetic introduction to the volume, he took note of the adverse criticism which he said a Boston critic had recently made on the then-current status of literature in America. "What he saw," Harris observed, "was pleasing, perhaps, but not inspiring. . . . Small men were trying to play instruments much too large for them, while others were fiddling away with futile earnestness on one string. . . . There was nothing new, nothing hopeful, and even those who had given signs of promise were returning to barren imitations of their early successes." With an unwarranted propensity for underestimating the value of his stories, Harris feared that he might be singled out as an example of an author who was futilely fiddling away on the same old string or else merely imitating his earlier success. As if to supply such a critic with some positive evidence of the value to be found in *Uncle Remus and His Friends*, Harris pointed out that the new legends should be of some interest to serious students of folklore and that the dialect in which they were necessarily written was as authentic as the stories themselves. Once again he emphasized that he had not written the stories out of his scientific interest in them but for the sake of the stories and for the unadulterated human nature that might be found in them.

Having made his respectful bow to those critics who might fault him for bringing out a third Uncle Remus collection, Harris still further disarmed criticism by announcing that the old man would never again bother the public with any more of his whimsical stories. He did so reluctantly, for he said that Uncle Remus had found friends for him in all parts of the world. Moreover, he reasserted that there was no pretense on his part that the stories were in the nature of literature or that his retelling of them touched literary art at any point. "There is nothing here," he modestly declared near the close of his apologetic introduction, "but an old Negro man, a little boy, and a dull reporter, the matter of discourse being fantasies as uncouth as the original man ever conceived of."

If there was any appreciable difference between the legends in the new series and those in the two previous collections, it appeared in their more direct didactic emphasis. The introductions to the stories were just as skillfully written as heretofore and Uncle Remus told the legends with the same degree of effortless artistry, but the little boy had grown older, more inquisitive, and more insistent upon receiving factual answers to his questions of when, where, how, and why relative to the stories of fantasy. He had also become more conscious of right and wrong, and he was often puzzled at the discrepancy between the morality of the animals and what he had been taught that people should exercise in their relations with each other. Moreover, Uncle Remus, who by nature was a gentleman in his own code of conduct, had noticed that the growing boy was developing some traits of character which he himself regarded as unbecoming in the son of his master and mistress. Because Uncle Remus looked upon the boy as his peculiar charge, he employed an appropriate story to instruct him in the code of good behavior, and therefore he endeavored to make the stories in *Uncle Remus and His Friends* relevant to the lesson which he wished to impart.

One thing in the animal stories that puzzled the boy was that the small and weak rabbit always came out victorious over the larger and stronger animals. One night he said to Uncle Remus that his papa had told him the animals did not have sure enough sense. The old man at first feigned great astonishment and then in terms that the boy could comprehend he explained that, although the creatures did not have the same kind of sense that folks had, they had all they needed to get what they wanted. "De littler de creeturs is," he patiently explained, "de mo' sense dey got, kaze dey bleedz ter have it. You hear folks say dat Brer Rabbit is full er tricks. It's des de name dey give it. What folks call tricks is creetur sense. Ef ole Brer Lion had much sense ez Brer Rabbit, what de name er goodness would de balance er de creeturs do? Dey wouldn't be none un um lef' by dis time." Brer Lion, he said, was "mighty strong; he mighty servigrous; but when it comes ter headwork he ain't nowhar." [5] In order to make his point clear to the little boy Uncle Remus told him

---

[5] Joel Chandler Harris, *Uncle Remus and His Friends: Old Plantation Stories, Songs and Ballads* (Boston and New York: Houghton Mifflin Company, 1892), 136.

the legend, "Brother Rabbit Conquers Brother Lion," in which the rabbit outwitted the lion through his superior animal sense.

Even Miss Sally became disturbed over the demoralizing effect which the stories might have on the little boy's concept of right and wrong in his own conduct, and she advised Uncle Remus not to tell him any more stories in which the morality practiced by the animals differed from that which he had learned in Sunday School. Although Uncle Remus disregarded her counsel, he did impress upon the boy that, even though the animals did not know the difference between right and wrong, folks did know the difference and that they would be punished if they practiced trickery on each other. He reminded the boy that he had once told him that the creatures had almost as much sense as folks. "Well, den," said the old man, "I'm bleedz ter tell you dat sense don't stand fer goodness. De creeturs dunno nothin' 'tall 'about dat dat's good en dat dat ain't good. Dey dunno right fum wrong. Dey see what dey want, en dey git it ef dey kin, by hook er by crook. Dey don't ax who it b'longs ter, ner wharbouts it come fum. Dey dunno de diffurnce 'twix what's dern en what ain't dern." [6] To illustrate his preachment about punishment befalling folks who get what they wanted by imitating the animals, Uncle Remus told the boy a tale about "The Man and His Boots" in which the folks who employed lying and trickery to get what was not theirs would come to a bad end, and so folks, he impressed upon the boy, "ain't got no business mockin' de way de creeturs does."

On one occasion Uncle Remus became greatly displeased with the little boy when he observed that he refused to share with his younger brother some cake he was eating, and he resolved to teach him a lesson about stinginess. The next time the boy went to the carriage house where Uncle Remus was at work, the old man pretended not to see him and began to talk to himself, but for the benefit of the boy whom he knew had come to hear a story. "I done put it down in my min' long time ago," he said as if to himself while he kept on working, "dat stingy folks ain't gwine ter come ter no good en'. I done seen too much un it. . . . Whoo! When it comes ter stingy folks, take 'em 'way fum me. Don't lemme come nigh um! I done see too much un um." [7] The little boy soon realized

[6] *Ibid.*, 160.
[7] *Ibid.*, 12, 13.

that Uncle Remus was talking about stinginess for his benefit, and
when he finally got the old man to notice him, he gave him an
explanation of why he had not divided the cake with his little
brother. Uncle Remus seemed to be convinced that the boy was
penitent, but he insisted on making his reproof emphatic: "En yit
I 'spizes stinginess." He then told him the story of "Brother Bear
and the Honey Orchard" in which the rabbit cured the bear of his
stinginess in not sharing with the other creatures his secret of the
place where the hollow trees were full of honey.

There were times when the boy's insistence upon an explanation
of some incident in a story which the boy had difficulty in believing tested Uncle Remus' ingenuity for a satisfactory answer. In the
course of the legend, "Brother Mud Turtle's Trickery," the boy
interrupted Uncle Remus to ask how Brer Fox could know that
the Mud Turtle was laughing at him when he was so deep down
out of sight in the mud and water. In his answer to the boy's
question, Uncle Remus fell back on the necessity for a "willing
suspension of disbelief for the moment" on the part of a listener
to a tale of fantasy, namely to doubt any part of such a tale was
in effect to doubt it in its entirety. "Well," replied Uncle Remus
to the incredulous boy, "ef you gwine ter 'spute dat, you des ez
well ter stan' up en face me down 'bout de whole tale." The boy
was convinced when Uncle Remus went on to say that when Brother
Fox saw the bubbles rising on the water he was obliged to know
that Brother Mud Turtle was down there laughing "fit ter kill
hisse'f." [8]

The plantation songs and ballads in *Uncle Remus and His Friends*
were inspired by those which Harris had heard when he had lived
at Turnwold. In them he preserved for posterity in authentic dialect
and varieties of mood the old plantation Negro's natural aptitude for
rhythmical expression of their emotions. In "The Plough-Hand's
Song" and "The Corn-Shucking Song" he recaptured the experiences
of the field hands in the seasons of planting and harvesting the
crops. The lilting movement of "My Honey, My Love" and "Christmas Dance Song" expressed their lyric moods of happiness in contrast
with "Come Along, True Believers," "Dem Lam's A-Cryin!," and
"Ring Dem Charmin' Bells," each of which conveyed their sincere

[8]*Ibid.*, 175.

religious feelings. The songs ranged in their tempo from the lusty "Hog-Feeder's Song" to the muted melody of the "Nursery Song." These songs and ballads were an outlet for the interest which Harris had early manifested in poetry when he was at Turnwold but which he had subordinated to the prose story by the success of his folklore legends. It was a literary form, however, which he never completely abandoned and some passages in his stories approached the qualities of poetry.

The human interest sketches again focused interest upon Uncle Remus in his other role as an old-time plantation Negro who was living in Atlanta in the first decades of the post-Civil War era. As was true of his creator, the old man found it increasingly difficult to adjust himself to a city environment. On the plantation he had never lacked for food, clothing, and his own cabin. Through the sale of the foot mats, baskets, axe handles, and other domestic articles which he had made, he had managed to have some money with which to supply his small extra needs. The little boy and even 'Tildy shared food with him from the big house. It was only after freedom that he found it difficult to earn the bare necessities. However, by doing odd jobs as a yard man for his Mars John and Miss Sally, who were also living in Atlanta, he managed to get by from day to day. He also cleverly contrived to obtain small handouts of money from his friends on the staff of the *Constitution* whom he frequently visited for that purpose. Accustomed to the quiet and simple life on the old plantation, he was bewildered by the more complex ways of city life. The new age of the telephone and the electric streetcar amazed and confused him. Despite his economic problems and his frequent physical ailments, he maintained his good humor, retained a certain dignity in his bearing, and commanded respect by his adherence to old-fashioned virtues in a changing society and by his sage comments on the vagaries of human nature.

As it turned out, Harris need not have been apprehensive about the publication of *Uncle Remus and His Friends*, for, despite the decline of interest in regional dialect stories by 1892, the legends themselves were timeless, Uncle Remus was ageless, and the little boy was the embodiment of eternal youth. The reviews were again favorable. The New York *Times* found Uncle Remus' budget as amusing as ever and his experiences in and around Atlanta told as freshly as in the previous volumes. In the estimation of its reviewer, Uncle Remus "never takes on age. He only ripens." [9] *The Critic* chided Harris for applying to himself the criticism of the Boston critic that American writers were merely imitating their earlier successes and said that there had been no justifiable reason for him to bid farewell to Uncle Remus and his fantasies on the grounds that they were outdated and outmoded. For, said the reviewer, the new stories showed that Uncle Remus was as full of ruddy life as ever in both the plantation legends and the Atlanta sketches. "In short," the reviewer continued, "few possess such talent as Mr. Harris in picturing dramatically and pathetically, with humor and vividness, the ins and the outs of the tortuous African soul, full as it is of loyalties and vagaries, of enthusiasms and comicalities, of childlikeness and rare sagacity." [10]

Having bade a reluctant farewell to Uncle Remus, Harris published in 1894 the first of a series of six volumes of old plantation stories which were designed primarily for the entertainment of children. These volumes were *Little Mr. Thimblefinger* (1894), *The Story of Aaron* (1895), *Mr. Rabbit at Home* (1895), *Aaron in the Wildwoods* (1897), *Plantation Pageants* (1899), and *Wally Wanderoon and His Story-Telling Machine* (1903). He was probably inspired to write them by the favorable response to his *Daddy Jake the Runaway*, in which the two children Lucien and Lillian had caught the fancy of numerous readers. Although these volumes appeared at intervals over a period of nine years, the setting in each of them was the old Abercrombie plantation in middle Georgia before the war, and the stories were told by different media to the same children, Buster John, Sweetest Susan, and Drusilla, their Negro playmate and constant companion. In an age which was growing more scientific and sophisticated, Harris portrayed these children in their pastoral environment as ones who had been untouched by cold reality and who therefore responded to stories of fantasy, wonder, and make-believe as the projections of their own imaginative natures. The stories which the children heard from Timoleon, the Black Stallion; from Grisette, the Gray Pony; from

[9]New York *Times*, December 18, 1892.
[10]*The Critic*, New Series, XVIII (December 31, 1892), 372.

Rambler, the Track Dog; and Grunter, the White Pig, were Harris' own inventions and they exhibited his myth-making ability apart from the legendary folklore tales which Uncle Remus retold.

Aaron, the central figure in *The Story of Aaron* and *Aaron in the Wildwoods*, was not a Negro. In Harris' fictional account, he was the son of Ben Ali, an Arabian chieftan who had been captured in his native country, brought to America by slave traders, and sold to a planter in Virginia. There he had married and when Aaron, their son, grew to manhood he had proven to be such an unruly servant on account of his proud and sensitive nature that his master had sold him to a slave speculator who in turn had sold him to a coarse and earthy master in middle Georgia from whom he justifiably ran away. Eventually purchased by the benevolent master of the Abercrombie Place, he exhibited such superior qualities of mind, character, and leadership that he became the efficient manager of the plantation and the trusted friend of the plantation children. According to the historian E. M. Coulter, Harris based his characterization of Aaron on Bu Allah, an intelligent and well-educated Mohammedan who was the overseer of Thomas Spalding's plantation on Sapelo Island off the Georgia coast. "The traditions of Bu Allah," Coulter wrote, "were so persistent and wide-spread that many years after his death they inspired Joel Chandler Harris to write two works of fiction based on them. The one entitled *The Story of Aaron. . . .* The other story was called *Aaron in the Wildwoods*." [11]

The initial appraisal of Harris' stories of the Southern region by an academic critic was made by William Malone Baskervill of Vanderbilt University in July, 1895, in the first of his series of critical essays on the new school of Southern writers after 1870. Although Harris had dealt with the antebellum South and the controversial period of the Reconstruction in his stories, he re-emphasized in his response to a letter from Baskervill requesting information concerning himself and his work that he had not written his stories in an effort to perpetuate the old sectional point of view in Southern fiction, nor, on the other hand, had he imbued them with a spirit of conciliation between the North and the South in order to curry

[11]E. Merton Coulter, *Thomas Spalding of Sapelo* (Baton Rouge: Louisiana State University Press, 1940), 83, 84.

favor with Northern readers. "What does it matter," he wrote Baskervill, "whether I am northern or southern if I am true to truth,
and true to that larger truth, my own true self? My idea is that
truth is more important than sectionalism—and that literature that
can be labeled Northern, Southern, Western, or Eastern, is not worth
labeling at all." [12]

In his evaluations, Baskervill rated Harris' plantation folklore stories
as "the most valuable and the most permanent contribution to American letters in the last quarter of this century." [13]

Having critically surveyed the work of such Southern writers as
Maurice Thompson, Irwin Russell, Sidney Lanier, George Washington Cable, Charles Egbert Craddock, Richard Malcolm Johnston,
Thomas Nelson Page, and James Lane Allen, Baskervill stated that,
while the work of each was valuable, "the most sympathetic, the
most original, the truest delineator of this larger life—its manners,
amusements, dialect, folklore, humor, pathos, and character—is Joel
Chandler Harris." [14] With specific reference to Uncle Remus, he
characterized him as "one of the few original creations of American writers worthy of a place in the gallery of the immortals; he
should be hung in the corner with such gentlemen as Colonel New-
come and Sir Roger de Coverley, and not far from Rip Van Winkle,
my Uncle Toby and Jack Falstaff." [15]

The continuing vitality of Uncle Remus was still further attested
in the same year, 1895, when D. Appleton and Company reissued
Uncle Remus: His Songs and His Sayings on the fifteenth anni-
versary of its publication in 1880. The text was the same as that in
the first edition, but the format was new and the reissue was distinguished from the original one by the one hundred and twelve illustrations of Uncle Remus and the creatures by Arthur Burdett Frost.
In 1886 Frost had visited Harris in Atlanta and he had drawn the
twelve illustrations in *Uncle Remus and His Friends* in 1892. Harris
was so pleased with Frost's insight into the real character of Uncle
Remus as he had existed in his own mind and with the breath of

[12]Hubbell, "Two Letters of Uncle Remus," 221.
[13]William Malone Baskervill, *Southern Writers: Biographical and Critical
Studies* (2 vols.; Nashville: Publishing House Methodist Episcopal Church,
South, 1897), I, 43.
[14]*Ibid.*, 46.
[15]*Ibid.*, 67, 68.

life which he said in his preface to the new edition that Frost had breathed into his "amiable brethren of field and wood" that he dedicated the 1895 edition to him. "The book was mine," he wrote, "but now you have made it yours, both sap and pith."

Even though Harris had before him manifold evidence of the universal appeal which *Uncle Remus: His Songs and His Sayings* still had, he was at a loss to understand why the book deserved to be reissued. Having in mind perhaps the growing tendency for scientific realism in American fiction in 1895, he referred in his preface to the matter in the book as dreams and children of dreams, but, so he wrote Frost, "if you could see the thousands of letters that have come to me from far and near, and all fresh from the hearts and hands of children, and from men and women who have not forgotten how to be children, you would not wonder at the dream," nor would he exchange it, he said, for all the fame which his mightier brethren of the pen had won.[16]

With the publication of *Sister Jane: Her Friends and Acquaintances; A Narration of Certain Events and Episodes Transcribed from the Papers of the Late William Wornum* in 1896, Harris for the second time endeavored to write a novel. As the title indicated, the story consisted of loosely connected events in the daily lives of the people who lived in the small town of Halleyton, easily identified as the Eatonton of Harris' boyhood. The composition of this long story was a frustrating experience for Harris. He himself was under no illusion concerning the artistic deficiency of *Sister Jane*. Through William Wornum, his alter ego in the novel, he confessed his inability to give adhesiveness to its component parts and to convey a sense of dramatic effectiveness to climactic situations. "There are gaps and lapses," he had Wornum say, "the reader must fill out for himself. The knack of narration belongs to the gifted few who need neither art nor practice to fit them for the work. When the impressive moment arrives, the apt and trenchant word eludes me. The sparkling phrase, the vivid grouping, and the illumination that flashes the whole scene upon the mind are wanting." [17] This confes-

[16]Joel Chandler Harris, *Uncle Remus: His Songs and Sayings.* Preface and Dedication to the 1895 edition, iv.

[17]Joel Chandler Harris, *Sister Jane: Her Friends and Acquaintances* (Boston and New York: Houghton Mifflin Company, 1896), 128.

sion of his particular weakness in writing a novel was an honest one, but he seemed powerless to correct it. The slow tempo which characterized the action was in keeping with the pace of life in the small antebellum town in middle Georgia, but even the most casual reader could readily identify the paternity of Mandy Satterlee's child early in the story. Also, the apparent failure of the townspeople to identify the stolen boy when he returned to the village after an absence of only a few years was highly implausible.

It must be said to Harris' credit that he was never even moderately satisfied with *Sister Jane*. When he returned the final proof to Houghton Mifflin Company, he wrote to its Mr. Garrison that when the book was published it would not be a credit to the author or the publisher. "I cannot imagine," he wrote out of his conviction that he had made a miserable failure of the entire story, "how I could ever have made the mistake of sending it to you in the first place. If I had the money to pay you for the trouble and expense it has already cost you, I'd recall the stuff and burn it." [18] It was only at the insistence of Walter Hines Page that he was willing to see the manuscript through to publication.[19] He wrote Harris that he had read the manuscript and that with the exception of Uncle Remus himself no Southern characters had walked from life into a book quite so naturally or unblurred, it seemed to him, as had William Wornum, Sister Jane, and the two odd fellows from the country (Grandsir Johnny Roach and Uncle Jimmy Cosby).

Page's perceptive evaluation of the worth of *Sister Jane* was correct, for the strength of the book lay in Harris' realistic delineation of the various types of people who were to be found in Eatonton or in any other small antebellum Georgia town. There was Jane, the sister of William Wornum, who did tailoring work for the planters and the other wealthy families. A mature woman, she possessed a keen mind, a sharp tongue, a sense of humor, and the unerring ability to discern what was true and what was false in her neighbors. In taking Mandy Satterlee and her unnamed, fatherless child into her home, she acted with womanly sympathy even though she knew the social risk of such an act in the small town. And there were Mrs. Sally Beshears and Mrs. Roby, two old, illiterate women who

---

[18]From Harris' letter in the offices of Houghton Mifflin Company, Boston.
[19]Julia Collier Harris, *Harris, Life and Letters*, 343.

owned a few slaves and whose ears were always attentive to the latest village gossip and whose tongues were equally as ready to spread it. In contrast were Grandsir Johnny Roach and Uncle Jimmy Cosby, two wealthy but uneducated old men, who were respected in the democratic community not so much for their wealth as for their integrity of character, their good humor, their tolerant attitude toward those who were in trouble and for their friendly assistance to them. And there was Uncle Jimmy Danielly, a typical, country Calvinistic preacher who gave the impression that he knew who was the father of Mandy's child and who earnestly proclaimed the inevitable judgment of God upon unrepentant sinners regardless of their wealth or social standing in the village.

Among those on a lower social level there was Jincy Meadows, one of the least known of all the numerous characters whom Harris created but one of his most original. He was a blithe and carefree young man whom the townspeople lightly regarded as a half-wit but who in reality possessed a keen mind. When Jane Wornum once told him that she wished all the people whom she knew had half as much good sense as he did, he replied in his whimsical manner, "Well'm, it's so easy to have what folks call sense that I ease my mind by playing the fool."

All of these characters were true to life because Harris had known their prototypes during his boyhood. It was only in his portrayal of the little town's upper social class represented by the Bullard family that he missed the mark. He gave Mrs. Bullard a James River, Virginia, plantation family background, but she was merely an aristocratic prop in the scenery of the middle Georgia democratic drama of village life which he slowly unfolded. Colonel Bullard was respected in the community on account of the social status which his wealth as a planter assured him and for his reputation as a man of piety and charitable deeds, but he remained throughout the story a conventional character. His manifestation of remorse when it became openly known that he was the father of Mandy's child was accompanied by no great pangs of conscience even though he offered to set up a trust fund for the child. Did Harris purposely intend to make Colonel and Mrs. Bullard weak characters, or was his weakness in portraying them due to his inability to enter into the mind and soul of the Southern aristocratic planter? He himself was a man of the people; he understood them and portrayed them with a sure hand.

Harris skirted tragedy in the two major incidents in *Sister Jane,* but he ended the story happily, not as a concession to the traditional romantic point of view in American fiction but primarily because he had an optimistic philosophy of life and therefore did not possess the temperament to write a pessimistic novel. In fact, he said that one reason why he wrote *Sister Jane* was to take out of the mouth of his mind the bad taste of some pessimistic books which he had been reading.[20] He named no specific novels, but by 1896 naturalism with its pessimistic view of life and human endeavor was beginning to replace romanticism and restrained realism in American fiction. Although his *Sister Jane* dealt with some of the dark aspects of erring humanity, its overall philosophy was that of Christian charity that "suffereth long and is kind." It was a philosophy born of Harris' own discovery of the tangled web that imperfect men and women weave for each other, but he believed that the result need not necessarily be inexpiable. Man's inhumanity to man saddened and perplexed him, but it did not lead him to hold a grudge against life or his fellowman. Out of his innately gentle and compassionate spirit, he spoke no ill of his neighbor for he thought no ill of him.

Although *Sister Jane* had a surprisingly good sale of 3,000 copies shortly after its publication, the reviews were mixed. The New York *Tribune* called it a dull book. "It would seem," its reviewer said, "that the author of some of the most excellent pages of discursive narrative in recent American fiction is not necessarily qualified to write a novel." [21] On the other hand, *The Bookman* said "its simple sincerity and quiet honesty of purpose were sufficient compensation for its lack of 'sparkling phrase' and 'vivid grouping.' . . .[22] The most discerning critic of the book was *The Literary World,* of London. Its reviewer concluded that the story must have been autobiographical, for, he wrote, "Mr. Harris writes too feelingly not to have lived among the scenes and the situations he depicted." [23] When John Henderson Garnsey, a family friend from Joliet, Illi-

[20]*Ibid.,* 341, footnote.
[21]New York *Tribune,* December 20, 1896.
[22]*The Bookman,* V (March, 1897), 77.
[23]*The Literary World,* C (February 26, 1897), 191, 192.

nois, was reading the manuscript at Harris' request during one of his visits in Harris' home, he remarked that he felt as if he knew William Wornum of whose manuscript Harris purported to be merely a transcriber. "That's just the trouble," Harris confessed, "I'm afraid someone will find out who he is and ruin me." [24] Indeed, to those who knew the real qualities of Harris' mind and heart, the similarities between him and Wornum were obvious. Both were sensitive and diffident with respect to women; both were painfully aware of their awkwardness; both were readers of the Bible and their favorite authors were Shakespeare, Montaigne, and Sir Thomas Browne; both derived satisfaction from their contemplation of nature in its order and serenity in contrast with man's inner turmoil and profitless struggles. "I could but compare the feeble and fluttering troubles of humanity, its spites and disputes, its wild struggles, its deepest griefs and its most woeful miseries, with the solemn majesty of nature. I could but feel that the solitude of the great woods and the infinite spaces of the sky, though dumb, were charged with the power and presence of the Ever-Living One." [25] A reflection upon this contrast between nature and man moved him with pity and compassion for all the human atoms "that were surging and struggling, grabbing and grasping, and jostling against each other." As a novel, *Sister Jane* was a failure, but, through William Wornum, Harris revealed more nearly his own mature personality traits than he did in any other one of his books.[26]

During one of Garnsey's visits to the Wren's Nest, he wrote a character sketch of Harris as he appeared in January, 1896, soon after his forty-eighth birthday. Garnsey described him as being under middle height with a rotund body, ruddy complexion, light blue eyes, light, sandy hair and mustache now far from their former fiery red, and with the greatest good nature in his smile. His habits were simple in the extreme and his wants were few. He despised the average curiosity seeker and hero worshipper and avoided by hook or

[24]Julia Collier Harris, *Harris, Life and Letters*, 344.

[25]Joel Chandler Harris, *Sister Jane*, 214.

[26]There were other autobiographical elements in the novel: the time was 1848–53, the years of Harris' childhood in Eatonton; his mother and Jane Wornum operated a tailor shop; both lived in humble cottages separated from the mansions of wealthy planters by only a hedge; the problems which confronted Mary Harris and Mandy Satterlee on account of their half-orphaned sons; the charitable responses on the part of the townspeople in both instances.

crook the ubiquitous interviewer. Conversation came easily and naturally with him when he was among friends in his home, but to the person who gushed at him or gave the impression of being greatly impressed by him he was more reserved than the proverbial oyster. His world was his home and roses were his passion. Garnsey quoted him as saying that if the greatest position on earth were offered him he would not take it, for the responsibility, he said, would kill him in two weeks.[27]

In December of the same year Frank G. Carpenter, also a family friend, visited Harris in his home to secure information for a magazine article and found him to be even more bashful than he had been when he was a boy. He did his writing now at home, Carpenter said, in order to escape curiosity seekers who interrupted him at his work in the *Constitution* office. He told Carpenter that the Uncle Remus of his stories was a composite of three or four old Negroes whom he had known as a boy and that perhaps he had added something to them. He emphasized, however, that Uncle Remus was such a real person to him that he could hear him talk and that his voice rang in his ears while he was writing about him. He said further that after writing some two thousand words of editorials every day he found it restful to do his literary work at night.[28]

After the publication of *Sister Jane*, Harris turned again to short stories, and in 1898 Houghton Mifflin Company brought out in book form *Tales of the Home Folks in Peace and War*. With one exception, the stories in this volume were interesting sidelights on middle Georgia life during and after the Civil War. They had the familiar hallmarks of Harris' humor, his sincere delineation of character, and his wholesomeness of viewpoint, but they lacked the depth of characterization and the spontaneity of style which had distinquished his folklore and the non-folklore collections, *Mingo*, *Free Joe*, and *Balaam and His Master*. The one story in the collection which did not have a middle Georgia setting was "A Belle of St. Valerien." It is considered here not for its literary merit but for the fact that it was the only story which Harris contributed to the *Atlantic Monthly*.

[27]John Henderson Garnsey, "A Character Sketch of Joel Chandler Harris," Atlanta *Constitution*, March 8, 1896.
[28]Frank G. Carpenter, Atlanta *Constitution*, December 20, 1896.

The editors of the *Atlantic* had long urged Harris to send a story, but he had hesitated to do so because of his firm conviction that his writings did not merit a place in the magazine which he regarded as the most distinguished American literary periodical. "I've been trying," he wrote Houghton Mifflin Company as far back as October 2, 1889, "to write something for Mr. Aldrich, but to save my life I can't come up to what I conceive to be the Atlantic's standard." In a postscript to the same letter he added the following self-effacing comment: "It is enough for a Southern tough like me to be in your catalogue." [29] In a subsequent letter to the same publisher, he reiterated his reason for not complying with the *Atlantic's* request for a contribution. "I am glad that Mr. Scudder has charge of the Atlantic. He was there before, but somehow I was afraid of Mr. Aldrich. It seems too absurd that a country cracker should be allowed to flourish forth in the pages that have contained Lowell, Emerson, Holmes, Whittier, and the rest. I had a Florida story started for the Atlantic called 'In the Slues and Winders,' but I gave it up. The atmosphere [of the *Atlantic*] was and is too much for me." [30] On December 1, 1890, Harris wrote that he had in prospect a story which he felt might be suitable for the *Atlantic*. "A number of people," he said, "are capering about in my mind, chief among them is a young girl called *Miss Toxie*. When I get better acquainted with them I shall put them in a story of that name and send them to *The Atlantic*. Just warn Mr. Scudder." [31]

It was not, however, until nine years later that Harris sufficiently overcame his awe of the *Atlantic Monthly* to send its editor a contribution, but the story was not about Miss Toxie. In his evident belief that the readers of the elite *Atlantic* in New England would not be interested in his usual story of democratic middle Georgians, he laid the scene of his story in the Canadian village of St. Valerien and called it, "The Belle of St. Valerien." The plot concerned a romance between Euphrasie Charette and her two suitors, Joe Bilette, her village admirer, and Cy Pettingill, an American whom Euphrasie had met when she was working in a mill just across the Cana-

[29] Joel Chandler Harris to the publisher, in the offices of Houghton Mifflin Company, Boston.
[30] Harris to the publisher, August 26, 1890, in the offices of Houghton Mifflin Company, Boston.
[31] Harris to the publisher, in the offices of Houghton Mifflin Company, Boston.

dian border in the United States. Harris had visited his wife's family in Upton, Province of Quebec, and his descriptions of the scenery in the story were based on actual observations, but his portrayals of the French-Canadians and of their speech were forced. For some unexplained reason, he made of Cy Pettingill, Euphrasie's American suitor, the most unattractive character in all of his stories, for he endowed him with no redeeming quality. In departing from the material with which he was most familiar in an apparent effort to come up to his concept of the standards of the *Atlantic*, he wrote a story that was the least representative of his character delineations and his style. He thereafter sent no other story to the *Atlantic*.

The rather mediocre quality of the stories in *Tales of the Home Folks in Peace and War* clearly indicated that Harris needed some fresh approach to his presentation of life in the South, and he fortunately discovered it in creating the character of Aunt Minervy Ann. He contributed her accounts of her experiences during the early years of Reconstruction to the February, May, June, July, September, and October, 1898, *Scribner's Magazine*, after which Charles Scribner's Sons published them as *The Chronicles of Aunt Minervy Ann* (1899).

For the material of these new stories Harris revived his memories of the three years, 1867—70, which he had spent at Forsyth as an employee of the *Monroe Advertiser*. While there, he had observed the reversed economic and political fortunes of the former prosperous planters. Also, in those years the Ku Klux Klan and the Union League were keeping a wary and suspicious eye on each other, but no outward eruptions had occurred on either side in the community. Those former slaves who had chosen to remain with the families of their old masters were looked upon by the Union Leaguers as being disloyal to their race and they were thus caught between two loyalties. These were the years when both races felt the emotional tensions and the uncertainties of racial relationships in the era of transition. By 1899, however, stability and mutual respect had evolved from the conditions of chaos and fear which had prevailed in the years when Harris had lived in Forsyth, and he felt that the time had come when he could recount the story of those troubled years without reviving old animosities. Even then, there was a risk involved for Harris, but his reputation for fairness in dealing with the South's problems was well established. Through Aunt Minervy Ann's reminiscences he recalled the tension and anxieties which had existed for both races in the South immediately after the war, with a faithful adherence to actual conditions but in a spirit of tolerant understanding of the stresses which prevailed. Serious situations were relieved by Aunt Minervy Ann's good humor and her sound judgment.

In her striking individuality of character, Aunt Minervy Ann was a creation worthy to be placed alongside Uncle Remus. She was a composite of several old-time Negroes whom Harris had known on the Turnwold plantation, in the home of the Harrisons in Forsyth, and in his own home in Atlanta. The older generation in the South recognized in her an authentic representative of her race during the early Reconstruction years, as it had recognized in Uncle Remus a genuine type of the antebellum plantation era. They were different, however, in their temperaments, and in their speech. Uncle Remus possessed a quiet dignity, a gentle humor, a mature wisdom, a dialect influenced by the speech which he had heard on a Virginia plantation before he came to middle Georgia, and by the subtle approach which he made toward interesting the little boy in the plantation fables. While he was on the old plantation, he was not disturbed by any personal problems. On the other hand, Aunt Minervy Ann was black and proud of her color. She described herself as "Affikin fum 'way back fo' de flood an' fum de word go." Her dialect showed little evidence of having been influenced by the language which she had heard her white associates use. When she was provoked to anger, her words could be sharp, and she was fearless in defense of justice without considering the reaction upon herself. At other times, she was the embodiment of gentleness, sympathy, and compassion. Her laughter was loud and infectious, and in telling her stories she suited her words to the mood and to the nature of the incidents which she recalled, whether of sympathy for the misfortunes of others, indignation at wrongdoing, or comical situations.

Noteworthy among the eight chronicles in the collection were "An Evening with the Ku-Klux," "How Aunt Minervy Ran Away and Came Back Again," "How She Joined the Georgia Legislature," and "The Case of Mary Ellen." In each of her stories, she recalled the years of the tragic era in Southern history for both the whites and the blacks and the dilemma which confronted her in her relationship to her former master and his family and to the radical element of her own race. Only an author of Harris' understanding of the issues involved and his good taste and sane method of presenting them could have recalled them without the possibility of opening up the old sectional wounds.

In 1899, at the invitation of George H. Lorimer, editor of the *Saturday Evening Post*, Harris began to contribute a series of stories to that periodical which dealt with blockade running and spy adventures during the Civil War, a phase of that conflict which he had not touched upon before. All of these stories were inventions by Harris for he did no historical research in preparing them, but his ability to give reality to his characters and their actions endowed these fictional stories with a sense of historical truth. They met with such a popular response that in May, 1900, Doubleday, Page and Company published them under the title *On the Wing of Occasions*.

Of all the stories in the collection, the one which was universally admired was "The Kidnapping of President Lincoln." The Federals had captured Mrs. Elise Clopton, a Confederate spy from middle Georgia and sent her directly to President Lincoln who, instead of imposing the death penalty, detained her at the White House until Confederate officials under safe conduct passes could arrange to return her to the South. Lieutenant Francis Bethune was detailed for the mission, and he took along with him a private, Billy Sanders, whom Harris described as a seemingly naive, uneducated middle Georgian of the yeoman class who was noted for his humorous stories. They were also charged with carrying out a bold plot to kidnap the President and deliver him to the Confederate authorities. They went directly to Lincoln's office in the capitol where he and Sanders soon discovered in each other a kindred spirit and swapped humorous anecdotes about hound dogs, horse races, and experiences of pioneer days while weightier matters of state and of the war were put aside. Sanders came to look upon Lincoln as a "patient, kindly man, with the bright smile and sad eyes, with Melancholy at one elbow and Mirth at the other."

The plot was doomed to failure because of Sanders' open admiration for Lincoln. They could no more have kidnapped him, he confessed, than they could have a member of their own families. In turn, Lincoln, in words ascribed to him by Harris, spoke of his grief over the wounds being inflicted on both sides by the war. "If I know my own mind," he said to them, "I know no North and no South. All that I hope for and pray for is the Union—the Union preserved, and the Union at peace, with all factions and all parties working together for the greatness and the glory of the Republic. I would, if I could, take the South in my arms and soothe all her troubles, and wipe out all the old difficulties and differences, and start the Nation on a new course. I have the will, but not the power." [32]

Harris' warm and sympathetic portrait of President Lincoln was another example of the contribution which he made in his maturity to the liberation of literature in the South from its sectional prejudices. In the same story he had also created a new character in Billy Sanders, the embodiment of middle Georgia democracy and as indigenous to the culture of the old South as Uncle Remus and Aunt Minervy Ann. Having portrayed practically every type of the old-time Negro, Harris had created in Billy Sanders a character of the middle-class Georgians who would enliven his future stories and eventually become his spokesman on current events, political issues, and politicians.

Ever since Harris had declined Mark Twain's suggestion in 1882 to join him in a lucrative lecture tour and give up his newspaper work, he had desired to be released from its time-consuming demands in order that he might devote himself entirely to his literary projects. Other tempting offers had come his way. On November 5, 1885, R. W. Gilder of the *Century Magazine* had written him: "Why do you not make an arrangement to do less writing on the daily paper and more permanent literature in the pages of the Century?" [33] On November 24, 1886, the *Century* made him a specific offer of $2,500 for his literary output for a year.[34] Harris declined the offer because he did not feel that it was sufficient to support the needs of his family.

Eventually, however, the time came when he had to decide between his newspaper work and his literary commitments. On September 5, 1900, he submitted his resignation to the *Constitution*, af-

---

[32]Harris, *On the Wing of Occasions*, 241, 242.
[33]R. W. Gilder to Joel Chandler Harris, Harris Collection, Emory University.
[34]Frank H. Scott to Joel Chandler Harris, Harris Collection, Emory University.

ter having been on its staff for twenty-four years. In an interview with him which the Atlanta *Journal* carried the next day, he emphasized he had not resigned because of any differences between him and the *Constitution* but solely because he wished to devote all of his time to work which he said was more congenial and more profitable. He said further that he had literary projects which would cover several busy years and that he could not hope to complete them if he were under the necessity of turning out editorial copy day after day. "Please don't make a splutter about it," he said to the interviewer. "I am too old to relish the brief notoriety that is the result of a newspaper article. Just say, in your kindly way, that an old family hoss, grown tired of stopping before the same doors every day, has kicked out of the harness and proposes to keep the flies off in his own way." In its issue of September 7, the *Constitution* made an official announcement of his retirement, but promised that he would continue to furnish it with contributions whenever a subject struck his fancy.

Harris had been engaged in newspaper work since 1862 with only a few brief interruptions. He had also published eighteen volumes of stories about life in the Old and the New South. Had he waited too long to free himself from the chores of daily newspaper writing to compose additional literature of permanent value? He was only fifty-one, but time and his health were fast running out.

10

UNCLE REMUS IN RETIREMENT

After Harris resigned from the *Constitution* he confined his activities more closely than ever to his home in West End. The spotlight of national publicity into which his fame as an author had thrust him had only served to intensify his unassuming nature, and he persistently refrained from any action that might be interpreted as self-advertisement. Only a year before his retirement he had written his publisher, Houghton Mifflin Company, that his keenest regret was that he had ever allowed his name to appear on his books. "There was no need," he said, "for such a display and it has created for me a world of discomfort." [1] Now that he was no longer before the public as a newspaper editor he looked forward to spending his remaining years in the quiet seclusion of his home, completing some stories on which he was working and writing others which he had in mind.

Always fond of the pastoral aspects of nature, he often referred to himself as "The Farmer" and he found abundant satisfaction in his rose gardens and among the trees on his four-acre tract. The accumulation of wealth had never had any allurement for him, and his wants were few and of the simplest kind. Intimate friends of the family stopped by to talk with him, not as a famous author but as a friendly and companionable neighbor. Julian, his oldest son, helped him with his heavy correspondence, and he had leisure now to concentrate by day as well as night on his literary work.

During his retirement Harris continued the habit which he had first formed when he was on the staff of *The Countryman* of reading the current magazines and books, and through these media he kept abreast of the trends in American fiction. In 1900 he knew that

[1] Joel Chandler Harris to publisher, October 1, 1889, in offices of Houghton Mifflin Company, Boston.

the novel had superseded the local-color story and that it dealt largely with the contemporary American scene, whereas he had continued to write, with one exception, the regional short story in the framework of the South in its periods of peace, war, and reconstruction. He was familiar with William Dean Howells' insistence upon realism in the novel, and he was also aware that Henry James was advocating that the novel should be a work of literary art. Both of these novelists were concerned with segments of American life which set forth its sociological, economic, and psychological problems, all of which were quite different from the culture he knew best in his Southern environment.

He also knew that both Howells and James, the latter in particular, analyzed their characters in meticulous detail in their reactions to contrived situations and in regard to the impact which their environmental conditions made upon them. He himself gave priority to character delineation in his stories, but he stayed close to the broad and basic qualities of human nature which he felt were inherent in a democratic and unurbanized American society.

Mark Twain was also still writing at the turn of the century but no longer in nostalgic vein as in the 1870's and '80's, for the rollicking and uninhibited humor which had characterized his *Innocents Abroad, Roughing It, Tom Sawyer*, and *Huckleberry Finn* had given way to sardonic laughter and unconcealed satire as he contemplated the hypocrisies, cruelties, and injustices of "the damned human race." He and Harris were now worlds apart in their philosophy of human nature, and the bonds of the cordial personal relationship which had drawn them together as humorists no longer existed.

These new emphases in structural technique, method of character delineation, and thematic content which had arisen in American fiction since Harris published his first successful volume in 1880 did not disturb him to the degree that they once did. Accustomed to working in comparative isolation from both Southern and Northern authors, he had evolved his own literary technique, and, despite its deficiences, he had maintained a respected position among his contemporary writers and his books continued to be in demand by both publishers and readers. He was disturbed, however, by the wave of materialism which had swept over America since the end of the Civil War. It seemed to him that progress had come to be identified with the accumulation of wealth. As he looked at his own region he saw evidence that its people were becoming more and more enamored with industrialism to the neglect of those qualities in the old agrarian society which he felt were worth preserving in the new civilization. Both as an editor and author he had advocated those progressive measures in education, agriculture, and race relationship which he believed were in the best interest of its people in a changing order. But he had also advocated that cultural values should keep pace with economic growth and not be bypassed or ignored in an all-out effort to attain economic affluence.

As he contemplated the status of American fiction in 1900, the trend which most disturbed him was its mood of pessimism, futility, and defeat. Such an attitude toward life was at variance with his cultural heritage and with his own hopeful and wholesome philosophy. Out of his own personal experiences he had learned that man could face poverty, obscurity, and adverse fortune and survive them with honor and integrity. He had not as yet subscribed to any one religious creed or covenant, but he was not without convictions of depth and meaning. Mrs. Harris was a devout Roman Catholic, but there is no evidence that she had exerted any influence upon him to identify himself with that church. When he was once asked about his religious beliefs, he said that the question was a difficult one for him to answer. "I can only say," he replied, "I believe in all good men and all good women. I should not want to live if I had no faith in my fellow-men." [2]

Although American fiction had become increasingly pessimistic under the impact of social, economic, and scientific determinism, his own wholesome stories of the Southern region had retained their appeal to American readers. But now that he was free from his editorial burden to concentrate his attention upon further stories, what kind should he write? Should he continue to present the South as he knew it in an effort to counteract the misrepresentation which he repeatedly asserted the antebellum writers had given through their sectional and ultraromantic fiction? Should he reflect in his new stories the current social, economic, political, scientific, and religious problems which confronted the South and the nation as a whole? Should he attempt to change his technique and subordinate realis-

[2]Atlanta *Constitution*, December 20, 1896.

tic character delineation to plot structure and thereby conform
more nearly to the criteria then in vogue? Once before he had
stepped out of character in his treatise on folklore in his introduction to *Nights with Uncle Remus* and once he had gone outside
middle Georgia and the South for the setting of "The Belle of St.
Valerien." In both instances he had written in a vein that was not
characteristic of him either in content or style. He therefore wisely
chose to stay within the bounds of the region with which he was
most familiar and continue to present its culture in his own style.
He would leave it to the critics to judge whether or not he had
conformed to acceptable artistic standards in his presentation.

Among the new stories on which Harris was working during the
year he resigned from the *Constitution* was a novel of colonial Georgia during the time of the Revolutionary War which centered about
the legendary exploits of Qua, a Negro slave. He had become interested in this era of Georgia's history as far back as 1896 when he
wrote his *Stories of Georgia,* and he had mentioned Qua in the first
one of Aunt Minervy Ann's chronicles. In accounting for her African origin and her imperious manner, he had stated that her great-
grandmother was an African princess and that Qua, her brother,
had died in Augusta, Georgia, at the age of one hundred. The two
eagles tattooed on his chest evidenced that he had been either the
ruler of his tribe or the heir apparent before he had been brought
to Georgia as a slave. Since Qua played no part in Aunt Minervy
Ann's stories of Reconstruction, Harris made no further reference to
him in those stories. However, in response to a letter from Bliss Perry concerning a manuscript from him that Walter Hines Page had
suggested he write, Harris wrote Perry on October 2, 1889, that he
hoped to send him before long the first part of a romance of the
Revolution covering the war in Georgia which, he said, had never
been adequately treated in history. "I had intended to call it 'Sal-
ette,'" he said, "but a very queer negro character has taken possession of the affair (in my mind) and I suppose I shall have to call
it 'Qua, a Romance of the Revolution.' " [3]

Word that Harris was writing a novel of the American Revolution with its setting in Georgia became known to publishers, and

[3] Joel Chandler Harris to Bliss Perry, in the offices of Houghton Mifflin
Company, Boston.

he received a letter of February 13, 1900, from Charles Scribner's Sons in which they asked him if they might have first chance at it.[4] Also, when William Dean Howells wrote him for contributions to a publishing enterprise in which he was interested, Harris replied that he had two stories in prospect, one of which he said he had called "One Mile to Shady Dale" and the other "Qua; A Romance of the Revolution." Of the first, he merely said that it was a story of Georgia folk about the beginning of the Civil War, but he was more explicit about the second, saying that Qua was an African prince who had been brought to America about 1760 and had died in Augusta some fifty years later. He also said that both his great-grandmother and his grandmother had known Qua, and that they had entertained him when he was a lad with stories of pioneer days in middle Georgia in which Qua was a leading figure.[5]

The publishing scheme about which Howells had written Harris never materialized, and for some reason known only to Harris he laid the projected story of the Revolutionary War aside and nothing more was heard of it until 1927 when the unfinished manuscript, which consisted of seven completed chapters, was discovered among the Harris papers his family had placed at Emory University.[6]

Why Harris failed to complete the story after having written seven chapters is a matter of speculation. The text was well written, the conflicting loyalties between the Whigs and the Tories in eastern Georgia were graphically presented, and the historical characters, were delineated with realistic accuracy. Had he continued Qua to its conclusion on the same level as the seven completed chapters the finished product would have maintained his reputation as a writer who could recapture and bring to life the events and personalities of the past.

Having given up his story of colonial history, Harris concentrated on the composition of the other novel which he had mentioned in his letter to Howells, "One Mile to Shady Dale," a story with a Civil War setting. Since he had been a part of those years, he had only to recall the tensions of that unhappy era and give them the sem-

[4]Harris Collection, Emory University.
[5]Julia Collier Harris, *Harris, Life and Letters*, 452, 453.
[6]In 1946 Thomas H. English edited these seven chapters and they were published by Emory University in its Series of *Sources and Reprints*, Ser. III, Nos. 2 and 3.

blance of truth in fictional form. On completion of the story, he
made a profitable arrangement with Henry T. Coates and Company
for its serial publication in *The Era*, a Philadelphia literary magazine. Harris and Coates agreed on a change of title from "One Mile
to Shady Dale" to "Gabriel Tolliver, A Story of Reconstruction"
and installments began in the January, 1902, number of *The Era*
and ended with the November number. McClure, Phillips and Company then published it in book form.

The publication of a novel which brought before the American
public even in 1902 the controversial issues which had produced bitter resentment and harsh words during the Reconstruction years
involved once again the possibilities of adverse criticism for both
Harris and his publishers. As if to forestall such a reaction, *The
Era* accompanied its first installment of *Gabriel Tolliver* with a
statement that it was Harris' intention to be fair to both sides. "This
is evident," the publisher emphasized, "in many passages, and the
story must take rank, although in the guise of fiction, as an important contribution to the history of the time." [7]

As it turned out, the fears of *The Era* proved to be groundless,
for Harris once again succeeded in presenting the Southern point
of view without resorting to sensational incidents or racial extrem-
ism, but with no sacrifice of historical truth. The entire story communicated a spirit of goodwill and national unity.

In this respect, Harris' *Gabriel Tolliver* differed from George
W. Cable's *John Marsh, Southerner (1894)*, and Thomas Nelson
Page's *Red Rock, A Chronicle of Reconstruction* (1898). Cable
had alienated the South with his attacks upon Southern conservatism by the publication of his *The Silent South* in 1885 and his *The
Negro Question* in 1890. This alienation was still further augment-
ed by his *John Marsh, Southerner*, a novel in which he presented the
difficulties which a liberal Southerner faced in the South during the
era of Reconstruction. In his advocacy of reforms in education, race
relationships, civil rights, and in government, Cable was far ahead
of his time, and liberals like John Marsh were still in the minority.
In fact, in 1885 Cable had established his residence in Northhamp-
ton, Massachusetts, where he felt the environment was more congenial than it had become in New Orleans because of his evangelistic

[7] "New Books," *The Era*, IX (January, 1902), 53.

crusade for reforms in the South. On the other hand, Thomas Nelson Page, in his *Red Rock, A Chronicle of Reconstruction,* glorified the civilization of the Old South and defended it as a way of life which produced men and women of quality with courtesy and high breeding. He asserted that adversity had only served to bring out the nobility of their character, that they had reconquered their section, and that in doing so they had preserved the Anglo-Saxon civilization. Cable looked forward to a reformed South in which the old sectional and ultraconservative ideas would give way to more liberal views; Page romanticized the Old South and condemned the men of lesser breed who had destroyed it.

In order to show how far the South had progressed along the road to reunion with the other sections of the nation, Harris stated at the beginning of *Gabriel Tolliver,* for the sake of the historical record, the state of mind which characterized the people of the South just after the end of the war. They had been led to believe, as Joseph Addison Turner had repeatedly asserted in *The Countryman,* that in spite of reverses on the battlefields the Confederacy would eventually be victorious, and so Harris wrote, out of his own recollections of his boyhood in Putnam County, "when the curtain suddenly went down and the lights went out, no language can describe the grief, the despair, and the feelings of abject humiliation that fell upon the white population in the small towns and village communities." The older men, he said, soon recovered from their first shock at the turn of events for which they had been unprepared, but "when they opened their eyes to the situation they found themselves confronted by conditions that had no precedent or parallel in the history of the world." It was a time, he went on to say, when there was little ready money, when business was at a standstill, when the courts were demoralized, and when the whole social fabric was threatening to fall to pieces. Moreover, the older white people were uncertain as to how to interpret the motives of the recently freed slaves, many of whom were roaming the highways, restless and silent, and there were those who looked upon the situation with apprehension and forebodings of possible trouble.[8] However, the younger people did not view the situation with undue alarm. Gabriel Tolliver, who was seventeen in 1865, the same age of Harris at that time, thought that in taking to the high-

[8]Joel Chandler Harris, *Gabriel Tolliver,* 110, 111, 112.

ways the former slaves had reacted to their freedom in a normal way, that they were simply testing the nature and the limits of their freedom. He, therefore, saw nothing ominous in their unorganized wanderings.

As Harris reflected on the contrasting points of view concerning the possibility of racial conflicts from the vantage point of his maturity in 1902, he felt that young Gabriel Tolliver's conclusion was the correct one, and said that if Gabriel's elders could have judged the situation as clearly as had the boy, a dreadful tangle and turmoil could have been averted. "Your historians will tell you," he commented, "that the situation was extraordinary and full of peril. Well, extraordinary if you will but not perilous." [9] Harris kept the entire story within the bounds of that concept—extraordinary, but not perilous.

Harris localized the scene of *Gabriel Tolliver* at Shady Dale, the Eatonton of his boyhood, but in it he made the reactions of its people to the extraordinary circumstances of Reconstruction typical of those in other small towns and communities in the South. They were watchful, cautious, restrained but not vindictive against those who would foment trouble between the races.

In retrospect, Harris pronounced tolerant judgment upon the emissaries from the North who infiltrated the South and in secret meetings with the former slaves sought to arouse their fear that they might be re-enslaved. Perhaps, he said, Gilbert Hotchkiss, a character in the novel whom he described as the son of a fanatical Northern abolitionist who had come south to exhort the freed slaves to join the Union League for their own protection, sincerely believed that they were in real danger of losing their freedom. "Who shall judge?" he wrote. "Certainly not those who remember the temper of those times, the revengeful attitude of the radical leaders of the North, and the distorted fears of those who suddenly found themselves surrounded by a horde of ignorant voters, pliant tools of unscrupulous carpetbaggers." [10] Nor did he harshly condemn the Reverend Jeremiah Tomlin, a former slave who was still living on his former master's plantation, for yielding to the persuasive influence of Hotchkiss to join the Union League. Harris explained his defec-

[9]*Ibid.*, 114.
[10]*Ibid.*, 176.

tion by saying that in common with all men of both races he had been eaten up by a desire to become prominent and that both his congregation and Hotchkiss had fed his ego.

Harris concluded his story of Reconstruction on the familiar note of reconciliation. It took the form of an address by Gabriel Tolliver, who had become a lawyer, before a large assemblage of those who had undergone the worst years of Reconstruction. The day before he spoke, Judge Vardeman, under whom he had read law, had asked him, "Why should a parcel of politicians turn us against a Government under which we are compelled to live?" Gabriel elaborated on the question in his speech, and when he asked if there was any Confederate soldier who had feelings of hatred against the soldiers of the Union the shouts of approval which greeted his question left no doubt as to their attitude. Harris blamed the politicians in the Federal Congress of 1867–68 for sowing the seeds of racial dissension in the South during the beginning of the Reconstruction years He noted, however, that matters had changed greatly since those days, and all for the better. "The people of the whole country understand each other, and there is no longer any sectional prejudice for the politicians to feed and grow fat upon." [11]

From an artistic point of view, *Gabriel Tolliver* had the same deficiencies in structure as those which had appeared in *Sister Jane*, but Harris did not agonize over them. He warned the reader at the outset of the story that it did not conform to the exacting standards of literary art in a novel. "Let those who can do so," he wrote, "continue to impart harmony and unity into their fabrications and call it art. Whether it is art or artificiality, the trick is beyond my powers. I can only deal with things as they were; on many occasions they were far from what I would have them be; but as I was powerless to change them, so I am powerless to twist individuals and events to suit the demands of or necessities of what is called art." [12] With all of its artistic faults, *Gabriel Tolliver* holds an important place among Harris' stories of the Southern region in his purpose to go behind the bare statements of history to reveal the spirit of a people in their effort to bring order out of chaos.

The reviews of the book were mixed, but on the whole they were

[11]*Ibid.*, 242.
[12]*Ibid.*, 6.

favorable. No one of them said that he had revived sectional bitterness, but the New York *Times* expressed disappointment in that while there were many Negroes in the story there was no Uncle Remus.[13] The *Outlook* praised the novel for its simple and unaffected style, saying that there was no literary assumption in it, no pretense of style, and that therefore it was full of literary art of a delicate and charming kind.[14] *The Critic*, reviewing it primarily as a novel of Reconstruction, called it one of the sanest books on the South published in a long time.[15]

While *Gabriel Tolliver* was still appearing serially in *The Era*, McClure, Phillips and Company published *The Making of a Statesman*, a collection of four stories which Harris had contributed to the *Saturday Evening Post* in 1900 and 1901. These stories, like so many of his others, savored of old times in middle Georgia, but neither Billy Sanders nor Aunt Minervy Ann lifted the stories above the level of pleasant but mediocre narratives. In fact, the volume, in comparison with his previous one, indicated that he had earlier mined the richest literary ore from the Putnam County and middle Georgia area. Was his creative power now on the wane? Could he yet find some new source of inspiration?

By 1902 Joel Chandler Harris was a familiar name to readers of his books in America and abroad, but to Georgians he was just plain Joe Harris, who was known to wear his fame as an author lightly and about whom they had heard practically nothing since the announcement of his retirement from the *Constitution* in 1900. They must, therefore, have read with interest but with some surprise a news dispatch from Oxford, Georgia, in the June 8, 1902, issue of the *Constitution* that Emory College would confer upon him the honorary degree of Doctor of Literature at its forthcoming commencement. The news story, which was accompanied by a picture of Harris, stated that the degree was one which Emory had never before in its history vouchsafed any man and that he was the first whom the college had regarded as worthy and deserving of the honor by his attainments in literature.

Knowing Harris' reputation as a shy and unassuming man, the

---

[13]New York *Times*, November 12, 1902.
[14]*The Outlook*, LXXII (December 13, 1902), 900.
[15]*The Critic*, XLI (December, 1902), 581.

correspondent ventured the hope that he would be present to receive the degree. But it was as foreign to his modest nature to don academic regalia as it was pleasing to Mark Twain to wear the robe and insignia of his honorary Oxford University degree, and the degree was awarded in his absence.

During the winter and spring of 1902, Harris suffered a prolonged illness from which he was slow in recovering. Someone suggested that he might benefit from a stay at Warm Springs in Meriwether County, Georgia, which was then only a local summer resort. Harris was greatly pleased with the place on his arrival there and he described it as just what he had been looking for. On the wide veranda of the rambling, old-fashioned hotel situated in a grove of pines and oaks he rested and built up his physical strength. Its waters, he wrote, "have strong medicinal properties, having been found to be a sure cure for various forms of rheumatism, and all manner of skin diseases, dyspepsia, kidney and liver trouble." He was glad that he had found Warm Springs and promised to visit it again.[16]

The low state of his health prevented Harris from a sustained concentration of his writing during 1902 and 1903, and it was not until the late fall of 1903 that he produced another volume, *Wally Wanderoon and His Story-Telling Machine.* Since the story was designed to be in harmony with the Christmas season, he told it from the viewpoint of the children who had lived on the Abercombie plantation (Turnwold) in Putnam County before the war and about whom he had previously written in *Little Mr. Thimblefinger, The Story of Aaron,* and *Aaron in the Wildwoods.* As had been true of those volumes, so *Wally Wanderoon and His Story-Telling Machine* had a deeper meaning than appeared in the apparent purpose merely to entertain children in 1903 with stories of the old plantation. Harris had been increasingly concerned with the effect which the growing scientific emphasis upon origins, factual explanations, and the tracing of influences was having upon the art of telling a story for the sake of the story itself. Had he read Keats, he would have agreed with him that all charms fled at the touch of cold philosophy. Through Wally Wanderoon he expressed his protest against this scientific influence upon the old art of storytelling.

On one of their adventures, the Abercombie children had chanced to

[16]Atlanta *Constitution,* June 29, 1902.

meet a strange little man by the name of Wally Wanderoon who told them as he poked here and there among the bushes that he was looking for the Good Old Times which he had known before the war had changed everything. He said that he had discovered a relic of the Good Old Times, an old-fashioned story-telling machine in the form of a tall box with an opening near the top through which an old-fashioned storyteller, the last of his kind, told his stories. But "sad to relate," he told the children, "even he tried to imitate the style of those who think that in telling a story, they have to explain everything and even tell where the story grew." As for himself, Wally Wanderoon declared that he desired stories which required no prefaces of explanation, no footnotes, and no scientific investigations into the origin and development of the story through the ages. Therefore it was only when the man in the machine reverted to the familiar "once upon a time" without any scientific explanations that he would listen to one of his stories or permit the children to hear them. The stories that composed the volume were therefore entirely of times far away and long ago about a world of wonder and the imagination, of good fairies, of princes and princesses, a world in which the worst magically changed to the best.

However, throughout the narration of these stories which were set in opposition to the realities of a materialistic and scientific day, the storyteller in the machine and Wally Wanderoon carried on an argument about the best way to tell a story. The man in the machine attributed their difference in viewpoint to the fact that they had been brought up in opposite schools of thought. "It was one of the principles taught in the university where I graduated," the man in the machine stated, "that a story amounts to nothing and less than nothing, if it is not of scientific value. I would like to tell the story first, and then give you my idea of its relation to oral literature, and its special relation to the unity of the human race." [17] To this procedure Wally Wanderoon strenuously objected. Neither he nor the children should be subjected to his pesky problems of origins and influences, but the man in the machine stubbornly insisted that a popular tale handed down in oral tradition was simply one of the husks of history. "Then give us the husks," was Wan-

[17] Joel Chandler Harris, *Wally Wanderoon and His Story-Telling Machine* (New York: McClure, Phillips and Company, 1903), 180.

deroon's conclusive rejoinder, "and keep the corn, and the cob, too, for that matter." [18] Literature for Harris was an end in itself, not a means to an end.

The best product of Harris' creative imagination during the years of his retirement was *A Little Union Scout*. He called it neither a historical romance nor a historical novel, but a plain recital of some adventures which befell a young fellow named Harry Herndon, his Negro "Whistling Jim," and Carrol Shannon during the Civil War. After its serial publication in the *Saturday Evening Post*, February 6–March 19, 1904, McClure, Phillips and Company brought it out in book form. It was briefer than *Sister Jane* or *Gabriel Tolliver*, had fewer characters, was more unified in structure and more progressive in movement through its various episodes toward a climax. The Civil War served only as the setting for the adventures of Shannon who, after he had joined the Confederate forces under the command of General Nathan B. Forrest in Tennessee, was assigned to capture an elusive Union scout by the name of Captain Frank Leroy. Shannon eventually discovered that Captain Leroy was in fact Jane Ryder, a young, ingenious, and spirited Northern woman who hated the secessionists and conducted her spying against them under various clever disguises, sometimes as a poised and dignified lady of middle age and sometimes as a handsome and courageous young man. Against a background of raiding parties and small skirmishes between the Confederates and the Federals, a romance developed between Shannon and Jane Ryder. Despite their strong sectional loyalties, the romance progressed through one adventure after another.

A Little Union Scout struck a popular response from both general readers and the reviewers. On May 14, 1904, the McClures wrote Harris that it had already had a sale of over 4,000 copies only a few weeks after its publication.[19] The New York *Times*, which had been coolly critical of *Gabriel Tolliver*, gave it an extended and cordial review. "A Little Union Scout," it said, "emphasizes the long established fact that Mr. Joel Chandler Harris easily stands among the very best of the storytellers and is at the same time in full possession of the oldfashioned disposition to exercise his storytelling abilities in making his readers acquainted with one company

[18]*Ibid.*
[19]Harris Collection, Emory University.

after another of the delightful characters of which his imagination seems to have an unlimited supply." The reviewer went on
to say that there was never in any of Harris' stories anything
that was "morbid, questionable, introspective, or preachy . . . but
just a good, straight tale about human, likable people. . . ." He
particularly noted that there was little of the bitterness of civil strife
in the story but much of human kindness, unselfishness, and chivalry.[20]

When Harris published *Uncle Remus and His Friends* in 1892,
the third volume of his folklore legends, he had consigned his venerable
storyteller to a place among "the affable ghosts that throng the ample
corridors of the Temple of Dreams" where he fully intended to leave
him. Meanwhile, Harris had come upon the outlines of additional legends, and when George H. Lorimer, editor of the *Saturday Evening
Post*, wrote him that he wanted some new Uncle Remus stories, he
began to consider the possibility of renewing the series. However,
when he responded to Lorimer's request, he had Uncle Remus to tell
his stories in rhyme instead of prose. The first of the legends in verse,
"Mr. Rabbit Run Fur—Mr. Rabbit Run Fas," appeared in the *Post* of
September 9, 1903, and they continued to appear at intervals during the
remainder of 1903 and during 1904 and 1905. In September, 1904, D.
Appleton and Company published *The Tar-Baby and Other Rhymes of
Uncle Remus*. The collection consisted of fifteen of the rhymed folklore tales which had previously appeared in the *Post* and ten of the old
plantation ballads as sung by Uncle Remus which had been originally
published by D. Appleton and Company in *Uncle Remus: His
Songs and His Sayings* in 1880, probably with the idea of showing
the difference in the two different media of expression. The volume
was illustrated in color by A. B. Frost and E. W. Kemble, and its
large sale indicated that Uncle Remus had an appeal to a new
generation of readers.

The legends in verse, however, did not carry the effectiveness of
those in prose because of the absence of the old plantation setting,
the old man's cabin, the little boy as an eager listener, and the adroit
methods which Uncle Remus employed at the beginning of his stories
to catch the boy's attention. Even so, the response to the tales in verse
encouraged Harris to develop the outlines which he had on hand, but

[20]New York *Times*, May 7, 1904.

after the pattern of those in the three previous volumes. One reason why he had laid them aside was the fact that he had not been able to verify their authenticity as genuine folklore legends. However, in a letter of July 11, 1903, to James Whitcomb Riley he said he had verified every outline which he had practically thrown away from a copy of Heli Chatelaine's book on Angola which some one had sent him. In the same letter he confessed that he was not altogether satisfied with the new stories. "I haven't been doing much this year (1903)," he wrote Riley, "besides the new Remus stuff—and I have a suspicion that it isn't quite up to the old mark." [21]

The writing of these new legends posed a real problem for Harris. It was not due to his lack of genuine folklore material, for he had verified each one of the outlines on hand to his satisfaction. Nor did the old plantation dialect give him any trouble, for he employed it with the same degree of accuracy as he had done in the volumes of 1880, 1883, and 1892. Nor was Uncle Remus himself a part of his problem. It was true that he was older, but time had not affected his good humor, his innate kindness and gentility, nor had it diminished his keen insight into human nature or impaired his superb mastery of the art of telling a story effectively.

Uncle Remus and his plantation legends were timeless, but the times had changed. Except for the memory of the older generation of Southerners, the plantation era was now merely another chapter in their region's history. The old-time Negroes of Uncle Remus' type were themselves becoming legendary, and, although Uncle Remus was ageless, the original little boy to whom Uncle Remus had told his stories had now grown to manhood. But a little boy was essential to give Uncle Remus an appropriate listener. A plantation background was also necessary, for it would have been incongruous for Uncle Remus to tell his ancient stories against a backdrop of the modern industrial city of Atlanta. But there was an even greater problem than these for Harris to consider. After 1900 regional dialect stories had gone out of fashion in America's literature. What possible appeal would tales of fantasy of the time "way back yander" have for readers in a contemporary realistic, materialistic, and scientific society especially when those tales were told in a language now spoken by only the oldest of Southern Negroes?

[21] Julia Collier Harris, *Harris, Life and Letters*, 488.

With some misgivings, therefore, concerning the quality of the new Uncle Remus stories, Harris contributed ten of them to *Collier's* and six to *Metropolitan Magazine* during 1903–1905. McClure, Phillips and Company then published them in book form the latter part of 1905 under the title, *Told by Uncle Remus: New Stories of the Old Plantation*, with illustrations by A. B. Frost, J. M. Condé, and Frank Verbeck. In his introduction, "The Reason Why," Harris set the stage for the new stories. Uncle Remus had never been able to adjust himself to the hurry and the harrassments of life in Atlanta, and one day he told his Miss Sally that he was going back to the old plantation where he could get a breath of fresh air. Much to his surprise and satisfaction, she informed him that soon after the impending marriage of her son (the original little boy in the previous folklore stories) to an Atlanta young woman, the entire family would move back to their old plantation home for their permanent residence. The son who was born of this marriage became the little boy in Uncle Remus' new stories of the old plantation. In the course of the stories, it appeared that Miss Sally's grandson had been born in Atlanta, that his parents still lived there, and that their son was merely visiting his grandmother in the country to improve his health. Harris never reconciled this development with Miss Sally's statement to Uncle Remus that after her son's marriage the entire family would make the old plantation their permanent home. His main objective had been to get Uncle Remus and a new little boy in a plantation environment as the appropriate setting for the new folklore series. However, he merely sketched in this environment. There was the big house and Miss Sally, but there was no mention of Mars John, Sis Tempy, 'Tildy, or the field hands at work or play. There was a mulatto nurse from Atlanta whose duty it was to see that the boy was kept neat and clean, that he never played in the dirt and never sat in the sun lest he might freckle.

This little boy was so different from what his father had been at his age that he troubled and perplexed Uncle Remus. He never laughed and was literal in his thinking and talk far beyond his years, for he once told Uncle Remus that to him A was always A. To Uncle Remus these traits in one so young seemed unnatural, and the problem which confronted him was how to win the boy's confidence, make him laugh with the spontaneity of childhood, and bring him to see that A could sometimes be more than A. By means of the ageless legends Uncle Remus sought to initiate him into a world of wonder and makebelieve which he believed was the natural right of every young boy. Uncle Remus proceeded cautiously with his kindly patience, irresistible good humor, and insight into human nature to show the serious, matter-of-fact boy that there was a world of imagination which lay beyond reason and to reveal to him its wonders and delights.

At first, the literal-minded boy listened quietly and respectfully to the legends, for his mother had taught him that it was impolite to ask questions. But Uncle Remus kept watching him for some evidence of spontaneous interest, and, when he once timidly admitted that the stories did make him laugh, the old man was highly pleased and told him how the stories used to make his papa laugh when he was a boy. "La, honey! You sho' dunno nothin'; you oughter hearn me tell tales when I could tell um. I boun' you'd 'a' busted de buttons off'n yo' whatchermacollums. Yo' pa uster set right wha you er settin' an' laugh twel he can't laugh no mo'." His reference to the old times put Uncle Remus in a nostalgic mood, and he sadly mused: "But dem wuz laughin' times, an' it looks like dey ain't never comin' back. Dat 'uz 'fo' eve'ybody wuz rushin' 'roun' trying ter git money what don't b'long ter um by good rights." [22]

This comparison by Uncle Remus of the difference between the old times and the new was a recurring theme throughout the stories in *Told by Uncle Remus: New Stories of the Old Plantation.* The quest for material wealth which Uncle Remus had observed when he had lived in Atlanta disturbed him, for it seemed to him that people in the old days "wuz in about ez happy ez folks is deze days." In the story of "Little Mister Cricket" he told the boy it was a mighty pity that he had not been brought up on his grandmother's country home "stidder up dar in 'Lantamantarum, whar dey ain't nothin' 'tall but dust, an' mud, an' money. De folks up dar ain't want de mud an' dust, an' de mo' dey has it off de mo' dey gits on um; but dey does want de money, an' de mo' dey scuffles fer it, de mo' dey has ter scuffle." [23] In another story, "How Wiley Fox Rode in the

[22]Joel Chandler Harris, *Told by Uncle Remus: New Stories of the Old Plantation* (New York: McClure, Phillips and Company, 1905), 58, 59.
[23]*Ibid.*, 89, 90.

Bag," he said to the Atlanta-born boy: "You may think dat deze times is de bes'; well, den, you kin have um ef you'll des gi' me de ol' times when de nights wuz long an' de days short, wid plenty er wood on de fire, an' taters an' ashcake in de embers." [24] Both Uncle Remus and Miss Sally, now a grandmother, disapproved the scientific methods by which the boy's mother had repressed the boy's imagination, but Miss Sally, not wishing to create a family misunderstanding by interfering, left it to the ingenuity of Uncle Remus to show him a side of life he had missed.

In the midst of the changing culture, the sage Uncle Remus took a philosophical attitude toward the passing of time; those who preferred to go along with it could do so if they would just let him stay where he was. One day the boy asked Uncle Remus to tell him the story about the time when all of the animals were meateaters, for his grandmother had said it was one which he used to tell his papa when he was a boy. "Yasser!" exclaimed Uncle Remus, enthusiastically. "It seems des like yistiddy I wuz tellin' dat tale ter yo' pappy. . . . It seems jus' like 'twuz yistiddy, but he done grow'd up, and now here you is. . . . Ez Miss Sally say, Time is got a heaper flewjus mixt up wid it. You think it's a-standin' still, but all dat time it's des a-callyhootin', an' a-humpin', an' a-totin' de mail. You can't hear de engine, but dey's one dar, an' a mighty big un at dat, an' it's gwine yander." Since Uncle Remus's metaphor about Time was incomprehensible to the literal-minded boy, he interrupted him to ask where the engine was going. "It's gwine whar it's gwine, dat's whar it's gwine," Uncle Remus replied with an air of absolute finality. "It ain't doin' nothin' but des a-gwine, an' when it gits whar it's gwine, it keeps on a-gwine; an' ef you wanter go wid it, go you kin, ef you'll des let me stay right whar I is." [25]

In an effort to bring Uncle Remus back to the subject of the animals having once been meateaters, the boy told him that his grandmother had said that he was not the only person who had said that the animals ate something else other than vegetables and that she

[24] *Ibid.*, 39.

[25] Joel Chandler Harris, *Uncle Remus Returns* (Boston and New York: the Houghton Mifflin Company, 1918), 83, 84. Harris contributed this legend to the March, 1906, number of *Metropolitan Magazine*. It was a story in the same series as those in *Told by Uncle Remus*, 1905, and published in *Uncle Remus Returns* in 1918 by Houghton Mifflin Company.

had told him how Plutarch had said something about the sheep eating fish. "Plutarch!" the old man exclaimed in wonderment. Did Miss Sally say on what plantation Plutarch had lived? When the boy shook his head, Uncle Remus felt relieved. "Well, he ain't never is live in deze parts, kaze ef he had I'd 'a' know'd 'im." The question of a rival storyteller of animal legends having been settled to Uncle Remus' satisfaction, he proceeded to tell the boy the story for which he had asked, "Brother Rabbit, Brother Fox, and Two Fat Pullets."

Since Uncle Remus was a born storyteller, he derived no pleasure from telling his ancient legends to a doubting listener. He knew that he had succeeded in interesting this fact-demanding boy in his tales, but it baffled him that he could not bring him fully to that "willing suspension of disbelief" without which he felt it was a waste of his time to tell them to him. When Uncle Remus reached the place in the legend, "How Old Craney-Crow Lost His Head," where he said that "de Swamp" went to sleep, the boy was astonished. How could a swamp go to sleep, he asked. Uncle Remus replied: "It's des like I tell you, honey; you kin take my word er you kin leave it. One way er de yuther, you won't be no better off dan what you is right now. All I know is dis, dat you can't tell no tale ter dem what don't b'lieve it." [26] The boy's mother had told him that Uncle Remus' stories were merely fables and he asked him whether or not he himself believed them. "Does you speck I'd tell you a tale dat I don't believe?" he answered. "Why, I dunno how I'd put de words one atter de yuther. Whensomever you ain't b'lievin' what I'm a-tellin', honey, des le' me know, an' I won't take de time and trouble fer ter tell it." [27]

Uncle Remus also resented the implication on the part of the boy that he himself had made up the tales. When he was telling the legend, "Brother Rabbit and Miss Nancy," he pointedly asked him how he knew the tales were true, implying that Uncle Remus himself had made them up. Uncle Remus groaned and shook his head, for he knew that the boy's mother had planted the seed of doubt in his mind. "Maybe you think I done it, honey," he gravely replied, "but ef you does, de sooner you fergit it off'n yo' min', de better fer you, kaze I'd set here an' dry up an' blow way 'fo' I kin tell a tale er my own make-up; an' ef dey's anybody deze

[26] Joel Chandler Harris, *Told by Uncle Remus*, 131.
[27] *Ibid.*

days what kin make um up, I'd like fer ter snuggle up ter 'im, an' ax 'im ter l'arn me how." [28]

Uncle Remus continued in his efforts to break down the boy's resistance; eventually, however, his patience became exhausted. As the boy's health improved at his grandmother's country home and he was not under the direct restraining influence of his mother, he no longer felt repressed but became willful, disobedient, hard-headed, and a nuisance to Uncle Remus in his workshop. One day he picked up the old man's sharp shoe knife and his awl, scattered his shoe pegs over the floor, and then sat down on his shoemaker's wax. Uncle Remus sharply reproved him and told him that he had become known on the plantation as "Mr. Hardhead." He in-sisted, however, that Uncle Remus tell him a story. Uncle Remus agreed to do so, but he told the meddlesome boy that he could "git up an' mosey long ef" he wanted to. The legend, "The Hard-Headed Woman," was one which he felt was applicable to the hard-headed boy if he would be still enough to listen to it. Uncle Remus was later relieved to learn from Miss Sally that this obstinate boy would soon return to his home in Atlanta.

Harris' earlier suspicion that the stories in *Told by Uncle Re-mus: New Stories of the Old Plantation* were not up to the standard of those in the previous three volumes of folklore legends was well founded. Although Uncle Remus maintained his commanding stat-ure as a superb storyteller and as an original and individual char-acter, he appeared in a light somewhat different from that of the previous stories because of his role as the defender of the ancient legends in a culture that had become increasingly realistic. In his nostalgic preference for the simple life, in his protest against the obsession to gain wealth at the expense of inner contentment, and in his conviction that the effect of modern scientific emphasis in the training of children was stifling their natural traits of wonder and imagination, Uncle Remus was voicing, perhaps unconsciously, Harris' own points of view. Nor were the legends by way of com-parison as compact and interest-compelling. The fact that Uncle Remus was under the necessity of telling the stories to a doubting listener made the introductions more argumentative and lengthy than had been true in the earlier stories, in which the rapport

[28] Joel Chandler Harris, *Told by Uncle Remus*, 267.

between the old Negro and the little boy had been one of their most attractive features.

Told by Uncle Remus was the last book which Harris published during the years of his retirement. Some time during 1905, his oldest son Julian and a group of young businessmen in Atlanta conceived the idea of launching a monthly literary magazine in Atlanta if they could persuade Harris to come out of retirement, lend his name and influence to the enterprise, and assume the responsibility of editing it. They knew full well that he had been totally averse to publicizing his name or fame, but they also knew that the success of their venture depended on their securing his agreement to become its editor-in-chief. They were willing to comply with any and all of his demands and to give him time, if necessary, to make a decision.

11

A NEW VENTURE—AND THE LAST

While the idea of establishing a new literary magazine was germinating and taking form in the mind of Julian Harris and his financial backers, Harris received national recognition for the contributions which he had made to America's literature. On May 15, 1905, Robert Underwood Johnson in his official capacity as the preliminary secretary of the American Academy of Arts and Letters, then being formed from the National Institute of Arts and Letters, wrote Harris that at a conference of its first twenty members he had been elected to membership in that body. In the letter Johnson gave the names of the other Americans who had also been elected to membership at the same time. The list included William Dean Howells, Mark Twain, Henry Adams, Theodore Roosevelt, Thomas Bailey Aldrich, Henry James, William James, and Thomas R. Lounsbury.[1]

No geographical consideration had been taken into account in the selection of the new academy's membership since meritorious achievement in their respective fields was the sole qualification for election, but Harris was the only Southern author among his contemporaries who was chosen.

In the fall of the same year, Harris received further recognition of the national stature he had attained. The occasion was the visit of President and Mrs. Theodore Roosevelt to Atlanta when the President made an address at the Georgia State Fair at Piedmont Park on October 20, 1905, and spoke later in the day at a luncheon in his honor at the Piedmont Driving Club. The city had made elaborate preparations to give Roosevelt, a Republican, a warm and friendly welcome to the Democratic South. The *Constitution* stated that his welcome to Atlanta would surpass anything of the kind ever witnessed in that section and

[1]Robert Underwood Johnson to Joel Chandler Harris, May 15, 1905, in Harris Collection, Emory University.

200

that the demonstration of goodwill would show to the world the respect and honor which the South felt for the President of the United
States.[2] Civic pride in the progress which Atlanta had made since 1864
was also involved. By evidences of the city's material prosperity and the
generosity of mind on the part of its people, they would impress upon
the President that a new spirit animated the South. The welcome which
Atlanta accorded Roosevelt was all that the *Constitution* had
promised it would be. A holiday atmosphere prevailed; schools were
dismissed and banks and offices were closed. A parade moved
through the decorated streets along which some 200,000 people
stood and shouted as the presidential procession passed on its way
to the fair grounds at Piedmont Park where he addressed an enthusiastic crowd of 50,000 persons.

Before leaving Washington Mrs. Roosevelt had made only one
specific request—of Clark Howell, editor of the *Constitution*—concerning her stay in Atlanta, and that was that she be given an
opportunity to meet Joel Chandler Harris on account of the fondness of her entire family for his stories. Inasmuch as her schedule
in Atlanta was limited to only three hours, there was not sufficient
time for her to visit him in his home at West End, and Mrs. Terrell,
the wife of Georgia's governor, invited him to attend the reception
for her at the Executive Mansion. On its balcony Harris stood with
Mrs. Roosevelt, Mrs. Terrell, and Mrs. Clark Howell and viewed
the parade as it passed on Peachtree Street. In its report of the
reception the *Constitution* noted that never before had he "consented to be brought forward in conspicious manner as a celebrity." [3]
The invitation, however, was one that he could ill afford to reject
for it was in the nature of a presidential command appearance.
So complete had been his retirement since 1900 that even Atlantans
who saw him on the balcony must have wondered who he was.

When Harris arrived at the fair grounds, Roosevelt had already
concluded his address and was standing on the steps of the New
York building, where he was being introduced to the guests who
had been invited to attend the luncheon. When Harris was presented to him, he insisted that he remain at his side while he greet-

[2]Atlanta *Constitution*, October 20, 1905.
[3]*Ibid.*, October 21, 1905.

ed the other guests and gave as his reason for his request that "he desired to meet no one in Georgia more than the distinguished author, whom he referred to as one of the foremost citizens of the state." [4]

The luncheon at the Piedmont Driving Club was the grand climax of the day's festivities. John Temple Graves, the South's premier orator since the death of Henry W. Grady, presided as master of ceremonies, and after his introduction of the President, interest centered upon the nature of his response. Would he laud Atlanta for its civic enterprise? Would he extol the South for its material progress since the Civil War? Would he emphasize its industrial development? After all, the committee on arrangements had left nothing undone to impress the President of the United States with Atlanta's resurgent spirit and with the South's revitalized economy and its traditional hospitality to a distinguished guest. After expressing his pleasure at being in Atlanta and his appreciation of the courtesies shown him, he surprised his audience by saying that he was going to ill repay the kindness with which he had been greeted by causing some acute discomfort to a man of whom he was very fond—Uncle Remus. He then prefaced his plea for righteousness and character in public officials by the following appraisal of the significance of Harris' contributions to America's literature:

Presidents may come and Presidents may go, but Uncle Remus stays put. Georgia has done a great many things for the Union, but she has never done more than when she gave Joel Chandler Harris to American literature. . . . Gentlemen, I feel too strongly to indulge in any language of mere compliment, or mere flattery. Where Mr. Harris seems to me to have done one of his greatest services is that he has written what exalts the South in the mind of every man who reads it, and yet what has not a flavor of bitterness toward any other part of the Union. There is not another American anywhere who can read Mr. Harris's stories— I am not speaking at the moment of his wonderful folklore tales, but of his stories—who does not rise up with a more earnest desire to do his part in serving America's problems aright. I cannot too strongly express the obligations I am under to Mr. Harris: and one of those obligations is to feel as a principle that it is my duty (which if I have transgressed, I

Ibid.

have not transgressed knowingly) never as an American to say anything that could be construed as an attack upon any portion of our common country.[5]

That afternoon Roosevelt spoke to the five hundred students of the Georgia School of Technology, all of whom were clad in their over-alls. On his way from there to the Terminal Station, he remarked to Clark Howell that the best feature of the day had been getting Joel Chandler Harris to attend the luncheon. "By George," he declared in his usual vigorous speech, "that was great. He is a wonderful man. I regard him as the greatest educator in the South along the lines he writes of. One of the very pleasant memories of my visit to Atlanta will have been my association with him." [6]

Friday, October 20, 1905, had been a great day for Atlanta, for Georgia, and the South, one that gave tangible evidence of the ful-fillment of Henry W. Grady's dream of a South materially prosperous and of a nation reunited. The day had proved to be an even greater one for Harris. Its primary purpose had been to honor the President of the United States, but he himself had turned the occasion into a day of triumph for Harris. In the presence of the most eminent group of men ever previously assembled in Atlanta, plain Joe Har-ris, Atlanta's most inconspicious citizen, had at last been recognized as Joel Chandler Harris, the one man among them who had made the South favorably known to the nation as a whole, whose books had been reprinted in England and translated into many foreign languages. In its edition the next morning, the *Constitution* carried his picture on its front page and featured the honor which President Roosevelt had accorded him in his luncheon address and in private conversations.

Harris had now reached the pinnacle of his reputation as an author. From the poverty and adverse circumstances of his childhood he had risen to international fame through the twenty-five volumes of his stories about the South. His election to membership in the Ameri-can Academy of Arts and Letters and the evaluation by Theodore Roosevelt of the constructive influence of his stories in the restoration

[5]*Ibid.*
[6]*Ibid.*

of national unity had set the seal of approval upon his work. It would have been fortunate for him if he had been permitted to wear his laurels in the quiet seclusion of his home in West End.

The twilight of his successful career, however, was to be far from the kind which he most desired. During the first months of 1906 the group of young Atlanta businessmen under the leadership of Julian Harris went forward with their plans to establish a Southern monthly magazine. They assured Harris that he would be relieved of all financial responsibility in its management if he would accept its editorship. In fact, they secured a cash working capital of $200,000 and organized the Sunny South Publishing Company to print it, with Roby Robinson as president, Robert F. Maddox as vice-president, W. G. Humphrey as treasurer, and Julian Harris as secretary and business manager, no one of whom had ever had any experience in magazine publishing.

Even with all of these assurances, the promoters encountered stubborn resistance by Harris in their efforts to persuade him to become the magazine's editor. It is reasonable to assume that one consideration with him was the state of his health. The only vacations which he had ever taken had been necessitated by illnesses and these had occurred with greater frequency and had been more prolonged since his resignation from the *Constitution* in 1900. He was far more physically exhausted than even the immediate members of his family realized, for he continued to go about the routine of his daily affairs with at least an outward appearance of his old verve and good humor. Had he been left alone to reach a decision, his declining health would have been a sufficient reason for turning thumbs down on the acceptance of the editorship.

But there were other reasons which must have made him hesitant to be drawn into the enterprise. He knew the history of failure which had been the lot of other men endeavoring to establish a literary periodical in the South. Indeed, he had only to recall the sincere but frustrated ambition of Joseph Addison Turner to secure adequate support, financial or otherwise, to make a success of his *Turner's Monthly* and his quarterly, *The Plantation*. He must also have recalled the short-lived *Crescent Monthly* which had promised so much and achieved so little in promoting literature in the South. On the other hand, he did know that since 1870 there had been no dearth of capable Southern writers, but he could not know if the time had yet come when a new magazine in the South could compete with the established ones in the North for their fiction and other articles. If he judged the future of magazine publishing in the South by its past, he could not have escaped the conclusion that the one which was being proposed was at best a hazardous undertaking, no matter how soundly it might be financed at its beginning.

Then, too, he had become a name as a literary person in America, and he must have felt that no standard short of literary excellence would be expected of a periodical which he edited. In his long journalistic career he had never borne the responsibilities of an editor-in-chief, but he was well aware of the stress and strain which were inherent in such a position. To shape and guide the destiny of a periodical for whose public image he would be primarily responsible was a prospect entirely uncongenial with his shy and sensitive nature. After a layoff of five years as an associate newspaper editor, could he effectively shift his point of view to that of a literary magazine editor-in-chief?

Why, then, all things considered, did Harris consent to come out of retirement at the age of fifty-eight, agree to assume the editorship of a hazardous experiment in magazine publishing in the South, and permit it to be called *Uncle Remus's Magazine*? The answer, of course, remains a speculative one. Perhaps he felt that he had exhausted the material about the Old South which he could turn into fiction and that in the role of editor of a Southern magazine which bore the prestige of his name he could interpret the contemporary South to the rest of the nation. Perhaps it would be nearer to a statement of the truth to conclude that he simply grew tired of being pestered by the aggressive and determined promoters and therefore finally yielded to their importunities. He did so, however, on his own terms.

Such an inference may be drawn from a letter which Harris wrote to James Whitcomb Riley in October, 1906. Among other things, he informed Riley that Julian had resigned his position on the *Constitution* and that he had interested a number of Atlanta businessmen with capital to join him in the new publishing enterprise. "He and they," he wrote in a tone which revealed his impatience at their insistence, "have bedeviled me until I have consented to become the editor of the publication; but their consent was not obtained until I made the whole push sign a contract that I was to have absolute control of the contents, including the advertising." [7] His first objective was to secure contributions from such established authors as Riley, Thomas Nelson Page, F. Hopkinson Smith, and Ruth McEnery Stuart, to whom he wrote personal letters. In addition, he wrote hundreds of other letters to editors whom he had formerly known.[8]

The preparation for launching *Uncle Remus's Magazine* was elaborate and pretentious even though it was directed by amateurs rather than professionals in the advertising field. They issued a sixteen-page prospectus in which Harris outlined his editorial policy. It promised that Thomas Nelson Page, John Fox, Jr., Harry Stillwell Edwards, and James Whitcomb Riley would be among the contributors in 1907.[9] It devoted two pages of reprints from newspapers, all of which expressed their good wishes for the success of the proposed magazine under Harris' editorship. The one from the London *Daily News* warned, however, that hardly ever had an author, no matter how popular, succeeded in editing a magazine in which his own writing was the chief feature. The prospectus also featured the familiar picture of Harris with his black broad-brimmed hat pushed back from his forehead.

The first number had been promised for April, but the inexperienced staff encountered so many mechanical problems that the first number did not come off the presses until June. Even then, its faulty printing and botched illustrations greatly perturbed Harris. In fact, they were so bad that thousands of copies had to be thrown away. In recalling his father's dissatisfaction with this important first number, Julian wrote: "His training as a printer and pressman, combined with his artistic sensibilities, caused him to suffer something of an outrage; and he also feared the result on the magazine's future." [10] In subsequent issues these mechanical difficulties were overcome, and the general appearance of the magazine was greatly improved.

The initial number clearly revealed that *Uncle Remus's Magazine* had been appropriately named, for Harris, who was then identified

[7] Julia Collier Harris, *Harris, Life and Letters*, 528.
[8] *Ibid.*, 527–32.
[9] The only author who produced a contribution was Riley. His "The Hired Man's Dog" appeared in the October, 1907, issue, pages 13–15.
[10] Julia Collier Harris, *Harris, Life and Letters*, 534.

in the public mind with his most famous creation, wrote six of the
articles. Of the other major contributions, Don Marquis, a member of
the staff and a rising young author in Atlanta, wrote one and Richard
H. Edmonds of Baltimore wrote another. In imitation of the succinct
mottoes which Joseph Addison Turner had employed in *The Countryman* to designate its purpose, Harris adopted as the motto of *Uncle
Remus's Magazine*, "Typical of the South—National in Scope."

His first editorial, "The Principles and the Scope of the Magazine,"
was an exposition of that motto. He stated that the magazine might
well have been named *The Optimist* since it would preach a cheerful
philosophy and practice tolerance in all matters where opinions and
beliefs were likely to clash. He particularly emphasized that it would
seek to clear up misconceptions about the South but that in doing so
it would be broadly and patriotically American, that it would hold
itself high above sectionalism, partisan politics and prejudices, and
that in all things it would be conservative but that its conservatism
would represent energy instead of rest.

This declaration of his editorial policy for *Uncle Remus's Magazine*
was noble in purpose and was a sincere expression of Harris' deep-
rooted love of the South and of his loyalty as a Southerner to the
Union. It was consistent with the philosophy of reconciliation which
he had illustrated over and over again in his stories. But as the editor
of a magazine in the environment of the new South he was confronted with a dilemma. With his conservative nature and, like his
Uncle Remus, with a preference for old times, could he make *Uncle
Remus's Magazine* a lively medium for conveying to the nation
Southern views on contemporary issues? Because his chief concern as
a writer had been with the cultural aspects of Southern life and with
his desire to bring the North and the South together in a spirit of
mutual understanding, he had never permitted himself to be drawn
into a partisan discussion of these divisive issues. He needed, therefore,
a spokesman through whom as an editor he could express his views
on contemporary affairs and thus create for himself an image apart
from his identification with the Uncle Remus of the plantation lore
of the old South.

This necessity involved no problem for him since he already had in
Mr. William Hart Sanders, the Sage of Shady Dale, a character
admirably suited to his purpose. Readers were familiar with him

through the roles he had played in "The Kidnapping of President Lincoln" and *Gabriel Tolliver*. He had been a commentator on the current scene in the articles which Harris had contributed to the November and December numbers of *World's Work* in 1900 and to its February number, 1901, at the invitation of Walter Hines Page.

In whatever role Harris had cast him, Billy Sanders, who boasted that he was the grandson of the legendary Nancy Hart, had evoked a favorable response from readers in all sections of the country. Roundfaced and of ruddy complexion, plain in his dress and unaffected in his manners, independent, honest and refreshing in his humorous anecdotes and in his incisive comments on men and matters of current import, he was a survival in the modern progressive South of the pioneers who had settled middle Georgia. Billy Sanders judged every man by his inherent worth as a citizen, not by his wealth, social position, education, political affiliation, or the section of the country where he lived. He heartily disliked sham and pretense, and the devious ways of the politicians never fooled him. As a humorist, he was the culmination of the peculiar middle Georgia type first depicted by Longstreet and later by Thompson. Therefore, it was this humorous and democratic middle Georgia countryman whom Harris made his mouthpiece for editorial pronouncements on politics, politicians, economics, and whatever other phase of the passing scene claimed his attention.

When *Uncle Remus's Magazine* began publication in 1907, muckraking was in vogue in American journalism. A sure-fire method for a periodical to increase its circulation was to attack trusts and monopolies, expose fraud and corruption in politics and government, strike hammer blows against the evils of speculation and concentration of great wealth in the hands of a privileged few families or corporations, and to wave the big stick in defense of the common people. Knowing that some publishers played up these sensational aspects of American politics and big business, Billy Sanders made a visit to the editorial office of the new magazine and gave the staff some practical advice on how to make *Uncle Remus's Magazine* a popular success. He was surprised to find the staff relaxed and unhurried, and he expressed his concern over the conservative nature of the magazine's contents. He warned them that unless they featured something more vigorous and exciting than poetry and love-tales they would be "mighty lonesome when the days git longer." He advised them, therefore, to find some weak-kneed monopoly, drag it out into the broad daylight, and tumble and touse it as an enemy of the people.

"You've got to git you some well-hooks an' a drag-net, an' a couple of sticks of dynamite, an' see what you can fetch up from the nasty deep, as the poet remarks. You've got to do somethin' of the kind; you've got to whirl in an' show folks that your feet ain't gone to sleep. Give these young fellows guns an' make 'em fire 'em off from the roof; you've got to let it be known to more than your families an' friends that you're ready for to jump up an' bite a piece out'n a pine wall. You've got to wake up to the fact that ever' magazine with the name has got a company of trained experts a-gwine round the country diggin' in the scrap piles an' huntin' for the bones of bloody murder." [11]

If Harris had been willing to follow Sanders' practical advice, the circulation of *Uncle Remus's Magazine* would probably have zoomed to a spectacular height, but had he done so he would have compromised with his principles for the sake of expediency and this he refused to do. To descend to the low level of a muckraker for financial gain or popularity with a certain type of readers was utterly foreign to his morally sensitive nature. Time would tell whether or not his conservative editorial policy would make the staff "mighty lonesome" in the long run. But regardless of the magazine's success or failure, he was adamant in his purpose to make it one that would appeal to the better nature of everyone in a family circle. He consistently kept it free from even the suggestion of sensationalism and rejected advertisements which did not meet his standards.

"On Knowing Your Neighbors," an essay with mystical overtones, revealed his meditative and tranquil mind undisturbed by "the mania of owning things." In it he discoursed on his love of people and his enjoyment of nature. All men, he said, might see neighbors in nature if they would but achieve the Oriental distinction of unlearning all that was grossly material and clear their minds of all that was binding and fettering to their souls and "thus acquire something of the simple mysteries of the spirit and its infinite emanations." [12] As he had

[11]Joel Chandler Harris, "Mr. Billy Sanders, of Shady Dale, Makes Some Suggestions," *Uncle Remus's Magazine*, I (June, 1907), 7. A file of *Uncle Remus's Magazine* is available in the Atlanta, Georgia, Public Library.
[12]*Ibid.*, 9.

previously done in many of his stories, he voiced in the essay his protest against the materialistic forces which he saw were increasingly becoming more dominant in a highly competitive and acquisitive American society.

The June number also carried the first installment of Harris' new novel, *The Bishop, The Boogerman, and The Right of Way*.[13] Its theme was on the *Silas Marner* tradition in that old Jonas Whipple, a crabbed and crotchety, money-mad bachelor, was transformed into a generous and agreeable individual by his young orphaned niece, Adelaide, who went from Atlanta to Shady Dale to live with him. She was aided in bringing about the transformation through the ingenuity, good humor, and plain talk of Billy Sanders even though Jonas strongly disliked him and said that he should have a tent over 'his head and be rigged up like a clown most of the time. When Adelaide arrived at young womanhood, Sanders, whose round face reminded her of a bishop whom she had known in Atlanta, acted as Cupid's assistant in a romance which developed between her and John Somers, a young man from North Carolina, who had come to Shady Dale to negotiate for the right of way through his property for building a railroad. As was usual in a Harris novel, the complications in the romance between Adelaide and Somers were eventually resolved to the happiness of all concerned. The combination of Adelaide's youthful charm and Billy Sanders' humor and cheerfulness made *The Bishop and The Boogerman* an entertaining story for young readers.

This novel, like Harris' other writings, had a significance beyond its entertaining features, for it carried overtones of a changing South. The time was 1868 but the conflict between old Jonas Whipple and young John Somers over the right of way for a railroad had a relevance to the South in Harris' day. In his stubborn resistance to granting the right of way through his plantation, Whipple was a symbol of many of the older generation of Southerners after the war who resisted change. Young John Somers, also a Southerner, was the symbol of an emerging new South which even in 1868 was beginning to move toward industrialization. The village of Shady Dale had been the home of his ancestors, but he himself had not been born there, had

[13]Part Two of the novel was published in the July number, 25–28; Part Three in the August number, 14–18; Part Four in the September number 26; and Part Five in the October number, 26–30. In 1909, Doubleday, Page and Company published the complete story in book form.

never lived there, and consequently had never formed any sentimental attachment for it. Whatever feeling he may have had for it, so Harris wrote of him, was coldly historical. Nor, Harris commented, was his attitude to be considered a misfortune for him: "Being modern and practical, he was wholly free from the entanglements and misconceptions of prejudice that had outlived the issues that gave rise to them, and he went about his business with a mind at once clear, clean, and cheerful, bearing the signal of hope in his forehead." [14]

In the era of transition in the South, Harris himself refused to be bound by its past, although his interest in that old civilization was warmly historical. He believed, however, that its best hope for the future lay in its forward-looking young men like John Somers, not in its older men like Jonas Whipple who insisted upon maintaining the old order when confronted with new conditions. Having lived during his youth in an environment where the qualities of life which had distinguished the culture of the South from that of any other section of the country, he, as did Uncle Remus, frequently took a backward glance toward that time, but in his maturity he never counselled the South to stand still and muse in regretful reverie over the ways and days that were no more.

Harris included in the first number an Uncle Remus folklore story, "How Brer Rabbit Saved Brer B'ar's Life," in order to give his magazine a flavor of the Old South. In subsequent numbers, however, he held the Uncle Remus articles to a minimum because his major purpose was to identify *Uncle Remus's Magazine* with the South's present and its future, not with its past.

Harris also instituted a book review section and did the reviewing himself under a pseudonym. According to Don Marquis, associate editor of the magazine, Harris could not find a book reviewer who pleased him. One day he announced to the staff that he discovered one who almost suited him, Anne Macfarland, a woman of about sixty years of age whom he said he had known in middle Georgia before and during the war. She was now living in London and through his renewal of an interrupted correspondence with her she had agreed to write book reviews for *Uncle Remus's Magazine* and forward the copy to him. He told the staff that she had a rather sour temper and

[14]Joel Chandler Harris, *The Bishop, the Boogerman, and the Right of Way* (New York: Doubleday, Page and Company, 1909), 173.

for that reason he preferred to edit her copy himself. Her style and critical reviews were so much like those of Harris himself that the staff humored his story, and Marquis wrote that Harris always believed that none of them ever knew her real identity.

Harris' reviews reflected his wholesome outlook on life, his distaste for pessimistic or sordid fiction, and his strong dislike for sophistication in literary art. Like Charles Lamb, he preferred those novels which had stood the test of time. In his first reviews in the June number of his magazine, with the heading "Under the Lamp with the Late Books," he expressed through Anne Macfarland his distaste for some new novels which emphasized naturalism in character delineation. He said that he admired the art of Edith Wharton's *House of Mirth* but deplored the fact that her fine art should have been devoted to such characters. "Neither social agents nor biologists," he wrote, "can deal adequately with the degenerates who figure in this tale." He confessed that he was brought up in a section of the republic where old fashions had always prevailed and he was sure he was none the worse for it. He was even more old fashioned in his condemnation of Robert Chambers' *A Fighting Chance* of which he wrote, "We taste morphine and smell whiskey all through the book." He admitted that the book had been bravely and brightly done but said that he found neither moral nor intellectual gain in it. He hoped that neither Mrs. Wharton nor Mr. Chambers would make the mistake of supposing that books about Buzzards could contain sane and wholsome views of life.[15]

The June number of *Uncle Remus's Magazine* set the pattern for the remaining ones which he edited. In each of them his articles were dominant features, whether in a personal essay, an Uncle Remus poem or legend, a book review by Anne Macfarland, or a lively commentary on some current topic by Billy Sanders. Since his primary interest was in literature, he wrote for the July number his summation of those qualities in a novel which would endow it with permanent value.

What fictive literature needs for its promotion and propagation is genius, let its art be of what strength and flavor it may. . . . There is no secret about it; the novelists who have made themselves immortal do not

---

[15]Joel Chandler Harris, review of Robert Chambers' *A Fighting Chance*, in *Uncle Remus's Magazine*, I (June, 1907), 40–41.

deal in the black arts. Whenever or wherever, you find in a book the apt and happy portrayal of human nature, its contests with its own emotions and temptations, its striving toward the highest ideals, its passions, its platitudes, its meannesses, its native longing for what is true and wholesome, its struggles with circumstance, its surrenders and its victories, and, above all, its humor, there you will find the passport and credentials that will commend it to readers yet unborn.[16]

And he again expressed his concern about the adverse effect which he felt an undue emphasis on materialism was having on American culture in a later essay, "Progress—In the Best and Highest Sense." "One captain of industry," he said, "becomes more famous in a night then twenty authors or painters, and within the course of a few weeks grows richer than all the intellectual workers since Adam." He saw some hope, however, for the cultural progress of the South in that its people were buying and reading more books in spite of its commercialism. "In a small degree," he asserted, "it stands for spiritual progress, and calls for more rejoicing than an increase in the number of cotton spindles in this section." [17]

A relaxing interlude in Harris' arduous editorial responsibilities was his visit to the White House in November, 1907, at the express invitation of President and Mrs. Roosevelt. The mere fact that he was going anywhere outside of Atlanta was in itself a news item, but that he was to be a guest at the White House made his trip even more newsworthy. On November 18 the *Constitution* stated that the dinner would be a notable event since it was one of the few occasions when President Roosevelt had invited a private citizen to come such a distance for a private chat and that it was a unique experience for Harris who was as hard to lure from his fireside as Br'r Rabbit from his burrow. This was another invitation he could hardly decline, particularly in the light of the honor which Roosevelt had shown him at The Driving Club luncheon in Atlanta in October, 1905. He had never dined in Atlanta in the home of any one of his most intimate friends, and he was so awed at the prospect of dining at the White House that he accepted the invitation on the condition that his son

[16]Joel Chandler Harris, *Uncle Remus's Magazine*, I (July, 1907), 80.
[17]Joel Chandler Harris, "Progress—In the Best and Highest Sense," *Uncle Remus's Magazine*, II (January, 1909), 6. Harris wrote this essay for publication in the May, 1908, number of the magazine, but it did not appear until January, 1909.

Julian and Don Marquis go along with him to reinforce, he said, his "faltering courage."

As it turned out, the occasion was far from the ordeal which he had feared that it might be. A Washington dispatch to the *Constitution* described the dinner as a private family affair with only the President and Mrs. Roosevelt, their daughter Alice, and Captain Fitzhugh Lee present. In the friendly warmth of the home atmosphere which prevailed, Harris came out of his shyness, and there was lively conversation about home, children, literature, and other subjects of mutual interest. Roosevelt commended *Uncle Remus's Magazine* for its national rather than sectional spirit and objectives.

The evening proved to be such a pleasant one that Harris, Julian, and Marquis did not leave the White House until midnight. To the Washington newspapers reporters who had waited at his hotel to interview him, he declared that he had had the biggest time of his life. "What other literary gentlemen were present?" one of the reporters asked him. "Now don't put me in that class," he replied. "I don't belong to that tribe. I am just a plain Georgia collard-eater." The hour was too late for an extended interview, and, after telling the newsmen that when he was at home he was usually in bed by nine-thirty, he went to his room.[18] On his return to Atlanta he said to an interviewer concerning his visit with the President: "If Mr. Roosevelt were nominated for a third term, I think I would vote for him. He is a great man—the greatest that there is in the country today."[19]

Harris found it easier to give the readers of *Uncle Remus's Magazine* his impressions of what most impressed him about his visit in the forceful vernacular language of Billy Sanders than in his own orthodox style. Billy was not restrained by reticence, and he said that he had found the White House to be a real home and that his evening there had been more like a family reunion than anything he had "seed since the war." He admired Teddy not only as the President of all the people but also as a man of courageous, upright, and wholesome qualities. "He's clean from head to foot, an' right through his gizzard; he's healthy, an' sane, an' honest, an' what more could you ax a human bein' to be."[20]

[18]Atlanta *Constitution*, November 19, 1907.
[19]*Ibid.*, November 21, 1907.
[20]Joel Chandler Harris, *Uncle Remus's Magazine*, I (February, 1908), 5, 6.

In May, 1908, *Uncle Remus's Magazine* absorbed *The Home Magazine* which was being published in Indianapolis by Bobbs-Merrill Company. The combined periodicals now had a circulation of more than 200,000 a month. In his editorial announcement of the merger, Harris stated that henceforth its name would be *Uncle Remus's—The Home Magazine*. He promised to make the combined publication truly representative of all sections of the country and not as the politicians interpreted them. He re-emphasized that, while he had considerable respect for the old times and the people who made them, he was "just as deeply interested in the tremendous movements of the present, the onward rush of things, the pressure of events, the stimulating energy of modern progress and development; for all of these things have their roots deep in the past, and the impulses that cause their growth are as old as they are new." [21]

Although Harris was genuinely interested in progress in the South and in the nation in the best and highest sense, he represented the conservative position of his region in his religious beliefs. He firmly stated them in his essay, "In the Matter of Belief," which he published in the July, 1908, number of the magazine, the last one which he edited. His pronouncement was prompted by the heated controversy over the attacks which were being made on the validity of the Bible and orthodox Christian beliefs. He said that he laid no claim to being either a theologian or a scientist, but he noted that the new theologians and the scientists were applying logic and reason to the Bible and that they were discarding whatever they found in it to be contrary to reason and logic.

He wrote specifically of a young preacher who had recently said that he could no longer accept the doctrine of the Incarnation since it failed to measure up to the logic of the theology which he had been studying in his seminary. The mystery of the Incarnation, Harris declared, was beyond the understanding through human logic and reason, that in the area of belief not all the learning of the schools could even be measurably helpful, and that each individual must consider the matter for himself apart from considerations of material and physical phenomena. He emphasized, however, that he was not discounting the value of reason but was speaking of that particular type of reason which applied itself to human affairs, the

[21] Joel Chandler Harris, *Uncle Remus's—The Home Magazine*, XXIII (May, 1908), 5, 6.

kind that was polished in the schools and fitted for speculative philosophy and science. But there was, he continued, a form of human reason neither of the schools nor of the academies which found nothing in the Christian religion that could not find an explanation in the mercy of the Creator and in the desperate need of the human race.[22] Harris' statement reflected the impressions which had been made upon him by the circuit riders whom he had heard at the Philadelphia Methodist Church in Turnwold, the evangelical preachers to whom he had listened in Eatonton and Forsyth, and the religious influence of his Catholic wife. It may also be assumed that his point of view was one which was held by readers in the South of *Uncle Remus's—The Home Magazine* in 1908.

At the same time Harris was making Billy Sanders his spokesman on contemporary issues, he also made him the central figure in *The Shadow Between His Shoulder-Blades*, a novel of the Civil War which he contributed serially to the *Saturday Evening Post* in its issues of November 2, 9, and 16, 1907. In the story he pictured Sanders as an old man in his native Shady Dale where on the veranda of a tavern which fronted the courthouse square he recounted his experiences with General Nathan B. Forrest for those who would listen to him. His portrayal of Forrest in this story was one of a far more ruthless and relentless commander than he had given of him in *A Little Union Scout* which had shown the chivalric side of the intrepid Confederate General's nature. During one episode Forrest had executed a disgruntled and disloyal soldier under his command by ordering that he be hanged from a limb of a nearby tree. The sight of his swaying body was one which Sanders never forgot. He told his listeners that "for days an' days—I could feel the shadder of that black, swingin' thing betwixt my shoulder-blades; an' when I'm off my feed I can feel it yit; sometimes it's cold, sometimes it's hot." [23]

Harris' health began to fail appreciably during the spring of 1908.

[22]Joel Chandler Harris, "In the Matter of Beliefs," *Uncle Remus's—The Home Magazine*, XXIII (July, 1908), 5, 6. Harris had also previously written of the impact of the new theology and science on the orthodox beliefs of the Christian faith in his article, "Cheap Criticism of Dear Beliefs," in the *Saturday Evening Post*, July 21, 1900, p. 12.

[23]Harris, *The Shadow Between His Shoulder Blades*, 132. Small, Maynard and Company brought out the story in book form in 1909.

The responsibility of editing the magazine and the task of composing poems, stories, and essays on a variety of subjects proved to be a severe strain on his physical strength. At times he became depressed through fear that he no longer could write creatively. From his outward demeanor, however, not even the members of his family realized how seriously ill he was. Would-be interviewers continued to call at his home, but those without an appointment stood little chance of seeing him. Fannie Lee Leverette, an Eatonton friend since his boyhood, recalled a chance visit which she had made to his home some weeks before his last illness confined him to his bed. He was in the house alone at the time and on hearing a knock at the front door his old aversion toward meeting strangers reasserted itself and he attempted to make a hasty retreat through the back door. "I saw him slipping out the back door," she said, "after hearing me knock. I hollered—'Hey, there! Come on back, I see you.' He recognized my voice, turned, laughed and said, 'Hey, yourself! Come on in, take off your hat, and stay with us. I thought you were one of these red-headed female magazine writers come around to write up my red head again.' " 24

During April and May he continued to give his attention to his editorial work, but he grew more listless and discontinued his walks among his rose gardens. It was not, however, until July 2 that the critical state of his condition became known to the public through a story in the Atlanta *Journal*. He had been seriously ill for a month and had been confined to his bed for the previous ten days. The next morning the *Constitution* reported that his condition was causing deep concern and that the crisis had not yet been passed. In its edition that afternoon the *Journal* announced that he was near death. The sorrowful news, it said, had penetrated to the most remote corners of the city by word of mouth and the telegraph had flicked it to all parts of the civilized world. On Saturday, July 3, the *Constitution* carried the news that Joel Chandler Harris had died at his home in West End at eight o'clock on the preceding evening, and that he had been baptized in the Catholic faith a week before his death. Dr. W. A. Crowe, his family physician, said that the immediate cause of his death was acute nephritis but that he had suffered for some time from cirrhosis of the liver.

Simplicity marked his funeral rites at St. Anthony's Catholic

24Fannie Lee Leverette to Paul M. Cousins, July 2, 1928.

Church in West End, on Sunday afternoon, July 5. Father O. N. Jackson read the 129th Psalm and referred to Harris' recent commitment to the Catholic faith, a step which he said the noted author had contemplated for some time but had held back from out of deep conscientiousness and extreme regard for the seriousness of such an important step. Six of Harris' friends served as pallbearers: Albert Howell, Jr., Forrest Adair, Roby Robinson, Samuel M. Inman, Lucian Lamar Knight, and A. P. Stewart.[25] He was buried in the family plot in Westview Cemetery near the grave of his mother and those of two of his children and not far from the graves of Henry W. Grady and Captain Evan P. Howell.

Although Harris' books had sold well over the entire period of his twenty-eight years as an author, he died a relatively poor man. His entire estate consisted of his modest home, $15,000 in life insurance, an interest in *Uncle Remus's Magazine*, and royalties from his publications.[26]

Soon after his death, the Atlanta *Journal* proposed that a monument be erected in his memory. Harris had anticipated that such a memorial might be proposed, and shortly before his death he made a specific request of Julian that if people tried "to start any monument business, don't let them do it." [27] He was more concerned about the future of the magazine which he had founded and he asked, if it wouldn't be too much trouble, that the printer set the following words on the editorial page, "Founded by Joel Chandler Harris." [28] The *Journal* abandoned its proposal for the erection of a memorial shaft. Nor need such a proposal ever be revived, for his stories of the Southern region are his enduring monument.[29]

[25]Atlanta *Constitution*, July 6, 1908.
[26]*Ibid.*
[27]Julia Collier Harris, *Harris, Life and Letters*, 586.
[28]Harris' name and fame gave *Uncle Remus's Magazine* a sufficient momentum for it to continue publication through the issue of February, 1913, but without his direct influence it simply became another periodical without any distinguishing features.
[29]On January 18, 1913, Harris' home, "The Sign of the Wren's Nest," was deeded to the Uncle Remus Memorial Association through the generosity of Mrs. Harris and her children and through public contributions, the largest of which were made possible by Andrew Carnegie, and a benefit address by President Theodore Roosevelt. The home is open to the public as a memorial to Harris under the supervision of the Uncle Remus Memorial Association, Atlanta. One of Georgia's main highways has been named in his honor, and his birthday continues to be celebrated in Atlanta.

12

HARRIS' ACHIEVEMENT

The death of Joel Chandler Harris at the age of fifty-nine was widely and deeply mourned. Messages of sympathy came to his family from all parts of the country, the first of which was from President Roosevelt. Editorials in the press were also warmly appreciative both of the man himself and of the significance of his work as an author. In its evening edition of the day before his death, the Atlanta *Journal* wrote of the artless skill with which he had taken the folklore of the antebellum Negro and opened up a new vein in the literature of the Southern people. It said that as a man and a citizen, as well as an ornament to the world of letters, he was needed to leaven the crude materialism of the times. Clark Howell, editor of the *Constitution*, who had known Harris more intimately than any other man in Atlanta since the death of his father Evan P. Howell, wrote of him as follows in the *Constitution* in its edition the day after his death:

From all of his studied unobtrusiveness, the man wrought himself a broad and firm place in the spiritual history and traditions of his people; and it is from things spiritual that the things of substance take their color and substance. . . . His reputation is worldwide because he was the articulate voice of that humble race, whose every mood and tense he knew with complete comprehension. His mission was—and is—broader. For his folklore and his novels, his short stories and his poems breathe consistently a distinguished philosophy. It was the creed of optimism, of mutual trust, and of tolerance of all living things, of common sense and of idealism that is worthwhile because it fits the unvarnished duty of every hour.

The editors of newspapers and magazines outside Atlanta who had known Harris only through his literary work also wrote of him with a particular emphasis on the value of his contributions to America's literature. The Philadelphia *Inquirer* declared that no man since

219

Abraham Lincoln had got nearer to the hearts of the whole people than Harris had succeeded in doing.[1] The Boston *Herald* said that it would be hard to say whether the North or the South would mourn more sincerely the death of Joel Chandler Harris or the more keenly feel his loss. His stories were familiar to the South, it said, but to the North they were a revelation of little-known characters and conditions of life, which were all the more delightful because they were foreign to anything of which the North had had personal experience. His stories, the Washington *Star* asserted, had done more to make the life of the Old South familiar and charming to Northern readers than had the work of any other Southern writer, and that they must be counted as one of those potent influences which, during the last two decades, had so greatly influenced and softened Northern opinion of the South.[2]

These and other expressions of regret over the death of Harris merely confirmed a feeling which had long existed that Harris was the most beloved author in America during his lifetime. If, however, he had lived for more years and had continued to write, he would probably have added nothing new or original to what he had already written. This conclusion is justified by the pleasing but mediocre quality of the essays, poems, stories, and book reviews which he wrote for *Uncle Remus's Magazine*. He was physically weary and his genius was no longer inspired or creative. By 1908, the plantation South had already become a remote period in the rapidly evolving history of the South. By then, too, the South which Harris had known during four years of civil war and the even more tragic years of poverty and civic strife that had immediately followed was now well on its way to a new social and economic order. It had resumed its place in a reunion of the states, and its younger generation looked toward the future with glowing faith in their destiny. Since his genius as a writer was primarily nostalgic, it was fitting that Southern authors younger than he should survey the various aspects of an emerging new Southern culture and that hands other than his should reflect them in their work.

Harris had not been a giant among the writers of American fiction. He had never written a short story with the precision of

[1] Reprinted in the Atlanta *Journal*, July 4, 1908.
[2] Boston *Herald*, July 5, 1908.

technique as Poe had done, nor had he composed a novel which compared with the sombre Puritan tragedy of Hawthorne's *The Scarlet Letter*, or with the conflict between the destructive forces of evil in Melville's *Moby Dick*, or with the psychological penetration and meticulous attention to style and structure that had characterized Henry James's novels. He had never become severely critical of the human race and its institutions of government and church as Mark Twain had done after the publication of his *Huckleberry Finn*. He had, however, within the limitations of his own ability as a literary technician done his work well. In Uncle Remus he had created an immortal character in American fiction and his stories of fantasy and fact in a setting of the Old South had brought pleasure to countless readers both young and old over a period of twenty-five years and earned for him a respected place among his contemporary American writers.

It has often been the fate, however, of an author who was greatly beloved, widely read, and highly honored in his own day to be lightly considered by a succeeding generation if changing times produced a new culture. However, Harris' stories of both the Old and the New South had a lasting interest to readers even in the midst of the social and literary changes which were taking place both in the South and in America as a whole between 1880 and 1908. The republication of the folklore tales attests the current interest in them. In 1946 Walt Disney Productions brought out Disney's *Uncle Remus Stories*, with the dialect somewhat modernized, an edition with colored illustrations of fourteen of the legends from *Told by Uncle Remus* and *Uncle Remus and his Friends* upon which was based the successful motion picture, "The Song of the South." A letter from Houghton Mifflin Company, Boston, on February 2, 1966, stated that their edition of *Favorite Uncle Remus* in 1948 had had a total of nine printings with a sale of 43,000 copies, and that their edition of *The Complete Tales of Uncle Remus* in a single volume in 1955 had gone through five printings of 32,000 copies as of that date. No listing of the characters of the most permanent appeal in American fiction would be complete unless it contained Uncle Remus, nor would any anthology of the most representative stories of the Old South be fully authentic that did not include some of the folklore tales told by Uncle Remus.

No complete edition of the works of Harris has yet been issued, and the volumes of his non-folklore stories have been allowed to go out of print. It remains true, however, that the social and the literary historians of the South before 1908, the students of the English language in America, the scientific folklorists, and the general reader who may be interested in a trustworthy presentation in fictional form of the plantation and early industrial South will find in them a dependable source of information and an ample reward for the time spent in reading them.

In these stories Harris created many memorable characters who were as indigenous to the South as was Uncle Remus but who were overshadowed by him. The list is a long and worthy one. It contains, among others, Miss Sally and the first Little Boy, Mingo, Blue Dave, Mink, African Jack, Sis Tempy, Daddy Jake, Free Joe, Ananias, Aunt Minervy Ann, Mrs. Feratia Bivins, Sister Jane, Grandsir Johnny Roach, Uncle Jimmy Cosby, Gabriel Tolliver, Major Tomlin Perdue, and Billy Sanders. Harris endowed each of them with life, and in the stories through which they moved he recaptured and preserved for subsequent generations the various features of the old plantation culture.

Harris loved the South with a genuine devotion. He knew its people with a comprehensive understanding of their faults and virtues as no other Southern author of his day knew them, and he strongly felt that the antebellum writers of Southern fiction had given a distorted picture of their culture by overemphasizing its romantic features and by including its sectional politics. It was his major purpose in his own fiction to correct that misrepresentation, and in his effort to do so he revealed the Southern mores in both their romantic and realistic features in the belief that factual knowledge brings understanding. He asserted that there was little fundamental difference between James Russell Lowell's Hosea Bigelow and William Tappan Thompson's Major Joseph Jones. The end result was that through his stories he became the apostle of reconciliation between the North and the South.

Southern writers of the twentieth century are therefore indebted to Harris for his pioneer leadership in moving Southern literature from ultraromanticism to realism. Howard W. Odum, in his *An American Epoch*, appraised Harris' work as that of a "vigorous realist, in which he never forgot the tragedies of the South, the poor white man, the darker aspects of slavery, the separation of families, and the hypocricies reflected in sentimentality and religiosity." He said that Harris had picked out from a mass of Southern ruins what had been considered to be inchoate materials and that through clear delineation, a new and effective form, admirable proportions, rhythm and sympathy, he had developed an art that was at once harmonious and beautiful. Odum concluded his analysis of Harris' realistic treatment of life in the South by characterizing him as an essentially modern Southerner crying in the wilderness as a forerunner of those who in the first quarter of the twentieth century had turned the searchlight upon the Southern scene.[3]

In his political affiliation, Harris was a Democrat, but he was liberal in his views and he never used his stories for the propagation of sectional politics. He was openminded and held the welfare of the nation as a whole above that of any section of it. Although his genius as an author shone to best advantage in his interpretation of the South's past, his vision for its future extended beyond cultural and political boundaries. He roundly condemned the radical politicians for the emergence of the Negro problem after the war, and he greatly admired the constructive contribution which Booker T. Washington was making toward the improvement of the lot of Negroes in the South as the president of Tuskegee Institute in Alabama. In an editorial in the *Constitution* on September 20, 1895, he praised the address which Washington had given in Atlanta the day before at the Cotton States and International Exposition as the most remarkable address ever delivered by a Negro in Atlanta. The speech stamped him, Harris said, as a wise counsellor and a safe leader. In turn, Washington later commended Harris for his sane discussion of the problem in the articles which he had contributed to the *Saturday Evening Post*, January 2, January 30, and February 2, 1904. The bugaboo of social equality never frightened Harris. He believed that the problem could be solved through the patient and constructive cooperation of both the whites and the Negroes in the South if the radical politicians would not interfere. The responsibility, he said, for a successful solution must be shared by both races with an intelligent leadership.

Although the South has made remarkable advances in every phase

[3]Howard W. Odum, *An American Epoch* (New York: Henry Holt and Company, 1930), 299, 300.

of its culture since Harris' death in 1908, his contribution toward its advancement was a significant and permanent one. He will be remembered by those who, like him, place loyalty to their common country above a blind and emotional loyalty to any one section of it, by those who in private and in public life take their stand for simple justice to all men irrespective of their race or creed, by those who respect the dignity of the individual without regard to his social, economic, political, or color status, and by those, who out of their generosity of mind, spirit, and wholesome humor, help to soften the blows that afflict erring humanity.

The man and his work were one. Painfully shy, extremely sensitive, and perhaps always conscious—who shall say—of the circumstances of his humble origin, he exhibited in both his life and literature a cheerful philosophy of goodwill and reconciliation that was not born of any shallow optimism. Along the road which he traveled from the poverty and obscurity of his childhood to international fame as an author in his mature years, he wrestled at times in the loneliness of his own soul with personal problems which could have defeated him, but he overthrew them without any erosion of his gentle, genial, and compassionate nature.

BIBLIOGRAPHY

I PRIMARY SOURCES

A MANUSCRIPTS

Journals of Joseph Addison Turner, 1839–67, microfilms, Joel Chandler Harris Memorial Collection, Emory University, Atlanta, Georgia.

Joel Chandler Harris Memorial Collection, Emory University, Atlanta, Georgia.

Harris' letters to Houghton Mifflin Company, Boston; in possession of Houghton Mifflin Company.

B PERSONAL INTERVIEWS

C NEWSPAPERS

Atlanta *Constitution*, 1869–1908.
The Countryman, 1862–66.
Macon *Telegraph*, 1866.
Savannah *Morning News*, 1870–76.
Shreveport (Louisiana) *Journal*, 1930.

D PERIODICALS

Crescent Monthly, 1866.
The Plantation, 1860 (March, June, September, December).
Turner's Monthly, 1848 (February).
Uncle Remus's Magazine, 1907–13.

E BOOKS BY JOEL CHANDLER HARRIS

Uncle Remus: His Songs and His Sayings. New York: D. Appleton and Company, 1880. Illustrations by F. S. Church and J. H.

225

Moser. New edition, 1895, with illustrations by A. B. Frost, to whom Harris dedicated the edition. Gift edition, 1920, with an introduction by Thomas Nelson Page and illustrations by A. B. Frost and E. W. Kemble.

Nights with Uncle Remus: Myths and Legends of the Old Plantation. Boston: James R. Osgood and Company, 1883. (Later editions were published by Houghton Mifflin Company, Boston and New York.) Illustrations by F. S. Church.

Mingo and Other Sketches in Black and White. Boston: James R. Osgood and Company, 1884. (Later editions were published by Houghton Mifflin Company, Boston and New York.)

Free Joe and Other Georgian Sketches. New York: Charles Scribner's Sons, 1887.

Daddy Jake, the Runaway, and Short Stories Told After Dark. New York: Century Company, 1889. Illustrations by E. W. Kemble.

Life of Henry W. Grady, Joel Chandler Harris, editor. New York: Cassell and Company, 1890.

Balaam and His Master, and Other Sketches and Stories. Boston and New York: Houghton Mifflin Company, 1891.

On the Plantation: A Story of A Georgia Boy's Adventures During the War. New York: D. Appleton and Company, 1892. Illustrations by E. W. Kemble.

Uncle Remus and His Friends: Old Plantation Stories, Songs and Ballads with Sketches of Negro Character. Boston and New York: Houghton Mifflin Company, 1892. Illustrations by A. B. Frost.

Evening Tales (Translations of the French stories of Frederic Ortoli, largely the work of Mrs. Joel Chandler Harris). New York: Charles Scribner's Sons, 1893.

Little Mr. Thimblefinger and His Queer Country: What the Children Saw and Heard There. Boston and New York: Houghton Mifflin Company, 1894. Illustrations by Oliver Herford.

The Story of Aaron (So Named), the Son of Ben Ali, Told by His Friends and Acquaintances. Boston and New York: Houghton Mifflin Company, 1895. Illustrations by Oliver Herford.

Mr. Rabbit at Home: A Sequel to Little Mr. Thimblefinger and His Queer Country. Boston and New York: Houghton Mifflin Company, 1895.

Stories of Georgia. New York: American Book Company, 1896. Illustrations by A. I. Keller, Guy Rose, B. W. Clinedinst, and others.

Sister Jane: Her Friends and Acquaintances: A Narrative of Certain Events and Episodes Transcribed from the Papers of the Late William Wornum. Boston and New York: Houghton Mifflin Company, 1896.

Aaron in the Wildwoods. Boston and New York: Houghton Mifflin Company, 1897.

Tales of the Home Folks in Peace and War. Boston and New York: Houghton Mifflin Company, 1898.

Plantation Pageants. Boston and New York: Houghton Mifflin Company, 1899. Illustrations by E. Boyd Smith.

The Chronicles of Aunt Minervy Ann. New York: Charles Scribner's Sons, 1899. Illustrations by A. B. Frost.

On the Wing of Occasions; Being the Authorized Version of Certain Curious Episodes of the Late Civil War, Including the Hitherto Suppressed Narrative of the Kidnapping of President Lincoln. New York: Doubleday, Page, and Company, 1900. Illustrated by George Gibbs.

Qua: A Romance of the Revolution, Emory University Publications, Sources and Reprints, Ser. III, Nos. 2–3. Atlanta: Emory University, c. 1900. Only seven chapters of this novel were completed by Harris. The manuscript was discovered among his papers when they were placed in the Emory University library by his family in 1927.

The Making of a Statesman, and Other Stories. New York: McClure, Phillips and Company, 1902.

Gabriel Tolliver: A Story of Reconstruction. New York: McClure, Phillips and Company, 1902.

Wally Wanderoon and His Story-Telling Machine. New York: McClure, Phillips and Company, 1903. Illustrations by Karl Moseley.

A Little Union Scout. New York: McClure, Phillips and Company, 1904. Illustrations by George Gibbs.

The Tar-Baby and Other Rhymes of Uncle Remus. New York: D. Appleton and Company, 1904. Illustrations in color by A. B. Frost and E. W. Kemble.

Told by Uncle Remus: New Stories of the Old Plantation. New York: McClure, Phillips and Company, 1905. Illustrations by A. B. Frost, J. M. Condé, and Frank Verbeck.

Uncle Remus and Brer Rabbit. New York: Frederick A. Stokes, 1906.

The Shadow Between His Shoulder-Blades. Boston: Small, Maynard and Company, 1908.

The Bishop and the Boogerman. New York: Doubleday, Page and Company, 1909. Illustrations by Charlotte Harding.

Uncle Remus and the Little Boy. Boston: Small, Maynard and Company, 1910. Illustrations by A. B. Frost.

Uncle Remus Returns. Boston and New York: Houghton Mifflin Company, 1918. Illustrations by A. B. Frost and J. M. Condé.

Favorite Uncle Remus. Boston: Houghton Mifflin Company, 1948.

Seven Tales of Uncle Remus, edited by Thomas H. English. Emory University Publications, Sources and Reprints, Ser. V. Atlanta: Emory University, 1948.

The Complete Tales of Uncle Remus, compiled by Richard Chase. New York: Houghton Mifflin Company, 1955. Illustrations by A. B. Frost and others.

F   BOOKS WITH INTRODUCTIONS BY HARRIS

Clarke, Jennie T., *Songs of the South.* New York: Doubleday, Page and Company, 1896, 1913.

Eickenmeyer, Rudolph, Jr., *Down South: Pictures.* New York: R. H. Russell, 1900.

Field, Eugene, *The House, an Episode in the Lives of Reuben Baker, Astronomer, and of His Wife Alice.* New York: Charles Scribner's Sons, 1896, 1911.

Frost, A. B., *Drawings,* with verses by Wallace Irwin. New York: P. F. Collier and Son, 1904.

Goulding, F. R., *The Young Marooners.* New York: Dodd, Mead and Company, 1887.

Russell, Irwin, *Poems.* New York: Century Company, 1887, 1919.

Stanton, F. L., *Songs of a Day.* Atlanta: Foote and Davies, 1893.

———, *Songs of the Soil.* New York: D. Appleton and Company, 1894.

Weeden, Howard, *Bandanna Ballads.* New York: Doubleday and McClure Company, 1899.

II SECONDARY SOURCES

A BIOGRAPHICAL AND CRITICAL STUDIES

Brooks, Stella Brewer. *Joel Chandler Harris—Folklorist*. Athens: University of Georgia Press, 1950.

Harlow, Alvin Fay. *Joel Chandler Harris (Uncle Remus)—Plantation Storyteller*. New York: Julian Messner, 1941.

Harris, Julia Collier. *The Life and Letters of Joel Chandler Harris*. Boston and New York: Houghton Mifflin Company, 1918.

————. *Joel Chandler Harris as Editor and Essayist*. Chapel Hill: University of North Carolina Press, 1931.

Wiggins, Robert Lemuel. *The Life of Joel Chandler Harris from Obscurity in Boyhood to Fame in Early Manhood*. Nashville: Publishing House Methodist Episcopal Church, South, 1918.

B MISCELLANEOUS BOOKS

Bardeen, Charles William. *Authors' Birthdays*, Second Series. Syracuse, N.Y.: C. W. Bardeen, 1899.

Baskervill, William Malone. *Southern Writers: Biographical and Critical Studies*. 2 vols. Nashville: Publishing House Methodist Episcopal Church, South, 1897.

Bradley, Henry Stiles. *Library of Southern Literature*, Vol. V. Atlanta: Martin and Hoyt Company, 1907–13.

Buck, Paul H. *The Road to Reunion*. Boston: Little, Brown and Company, 1937.

Cash, Wilbur J. *The Mind of the South*. New York: Alfred Knopf, 1941.

Davidson, James Wood. *The Living Writers of the South*. New York: G. W. Carleton and Company, 1869.

Derby, James Cephas. *Fifty Years Among Authors, Books and Publishers*. New York: G. W. Carleton and Company, 1884.

Fiske, Horace Spencer. *Provincial Types in American Fiction*. New York: Chautauqua Press, 1903.

Gaines, Francis Pendleton. *The Southern Plantation: A Study in the Development and the Accuracy of a Tradition*. New York: Columbia University Press, 1924.

Halsey, Francis Whiting, editor. *Authors of Our Day in Their Homes*. New York: Pott, 1902.

Hubbell, Jay B. *The South in American Literature*. Durham: Duke University Press, 1954.

————. *Southern Life in Fiction.* Athens: University of Georgia Press, 1960.

Knight, Lucian Lamar. *Reminiscences of Famous Georgians.* 2 Vols. Atlanta: Franklin-Turner Company, 1907, 1908.

————. *Georgia's Bi-Centennial Memoirs and Memories.* Published by the author for private distribution, 1932.

Lee, Ivy Ledbetter. *Uncle Remus.* Privately printed, 1908.

Mabie, Hamilton W. *Commemorative Tributes to Richard Watson Gilder, Joel Chandler Harris, Edward Everett Hale, Carl Schurz, Winslow Homer.* New York: American Academy of Arts and Letters, 1922.

Odom, Howard W., ed. *Southern Pioneers in Social Interpretations.* Chapel Hill: University of North Carolina Press, 1925.

————. *An American Epoch.* New York: Henry Holt and Company, 1930.

Pattee, Fred Lewis. *A History of American Literature Since 1870.* New York: Century Company, 1915.

————. *The Development of the American Short Story.* New York and London: Harper and Brothers, 1923.

Quinn, Arthur H. *American Fiction.* New York: D. Appleton-Century Company, 1936.

Reed, Wallace Putnam. *History of Atlanta, Georgia.* Syracuse: D. Macon and Company, 1889.

Riley, James Whitcomb. *The Complete Works of James Whitcomb Riley.* 10 vols. Indianapolis: Bobbs-Merrill Company, 1916.

Rutherford, Mildred Lewis. *American Authors.* Atlanta: Franklin Printing and Publishing Company, 1894.

————. *The South in History and Literature.* Atlanta: Franklin-Turner Company, 1907.

Smith, Charles Alphonso. *Cambridge History of American Literature.* 4 vols. New York: G. P. Putnam's Sons, 1918.

————. *Southern Literary Studies.* Chapel Hill: University of North Carolina Press, 1927.

Spiller, Robert E., et al. *Literary History of the United States.* Vol. III. New York: MacMillan Company, 1948.

Toulmin, Harry Aubrey. *Social Historians.* Boston: R. G. Badger, 1911.

Trent, W. P., ed. *Southern Writers.* New York: MacMillan Company, 1914.

Twain, Mark. *Life on The Mississippi.* New York: Harper and Bros., 1883.

Watterson, Henry. *Oddities in Southern Life and Character.* Boston: Houghton Mifflin Company, 1882.

Woodward, C. Vann. *Origins of the New South.* Baton Rouge: Louisiana State University Press, 1951.

C PERIODICALS

Adair, Forrest, "Joel Chandler Harris," *The American Illustrated Methodist Magazine,* XI (October, 1899), 124–32.

Armes, Ethel, "A New Version of Brer Rabbit and the Tar Baby," *National Magazine,* XXI (February, 1905), 515–17.

Baker, Ray Stannard, "Joel Chandler Harris," *Outlook,* LXXVIII (November 5, 1914), 594–03.

Ball, Sumter Mays, " 'Uncle Remus' in His Career as Joel Chandler Harris, Author and Editor," *Book News Monthly,* XXVII (January, 1909), 311–16.

Baskervill, William Malone, "Joel Chandler Harris," *The Chautauquan,* XXIV (October, 1896), 62–67.

Bowen, Edward W., "Joel Chandler Harris, A Faithful Interpreter of the Negro," *Reformed Church Review,* XXIII (July, 1919), 357–69.

Brainerd, Erastus, "Authors at Home, Joel Chandler Harris (Uncle Remus) at Atlanta," *The Critic,* III, New Series (May 16, 1885), 229–30.

Coleman, Charles W., "The Recent Movement in Southern Literature," *Harper's New Monthly Magazine,* LXXIV (May, 1887), 837–55.

Cousins, Paul M., "The Debt of Joel Chandler Harris to Joseph Addison Turner," *The Chimes,* XLII (March, 1930), 3–10.

Crane, T. F., "Plantation Folk-Lore," *Popular Science Monthly,* XVIII (April, 1881), 824–33.

Dauner, Louise, "Myth and Humor in the Uncle Remus Fables," *American Literature,* XX (May, 1948), 129–43.

English, Thomas H., "In Memory of Uncle Remus," *Southern Literary Messenger,* II (February, 1940), 77–83.

———, "Joel Chandler Harris' Earliest Literary Project," *Emory University Quarterly,* II (October, 1946), 176–85.

———, "Twice-Told Tales and Uncle Remus," *Georgia Review,* II (Winter, 1948), 447–60.

Flanders, B. H., "Two Forgotten Youthful Works of Joel Chandler Harris," *South Atlantic Quarterly*, XXXVIII (July, 1939), 278–83.

Garland, Hamlin, "Roadside Meetings of a Literary Nomad," *The Bookman*, LXXI (April and May, 1930), 201.

Garnsey, John Henderson, "Joel Chandler Harris," *Book Buyer*, XIII (January, 1896), 65–68.

Gayle, Margot, "Georgia's Aesop," *Holland's Magazine*, LXVII (December, 1948), 8, 9.

Harmon, H. E., "Joel Chandler Harris," *The Bookman*, LXI (June, 1925), 433–36.

————, "Joel Chandler Harris: Prose Poet of the South," *South Atlantic Quarterly*, XVII (July, 1918), 243–48.

Harris, Joel Chandler, "An Accidental Author," *Lippincott's Monthly Magazine*, XXXVII (April, 1886), 417–20.

Harris, Julia Collier, " 'Uncle Remus' to His 'Gals,' " *Ladies Home Journal*, XXXVI (April, 1919), 54, 126.

————, "Joel Chandler Harris—Fearless Editor," *Emory Alumnus*, V (March, 1929), 9, 10.

————, "Uncle Remus at Home and Abroad," *Southern Literary Messenger*, II (February, 1940), 84–86.

————, "Joel Chandler Harris: The Poetic Mind," *Emory University Quarterly*, III (March, 1947), 21–29.

Harris, Mrs. Lundy H., "Joel Chandler Harris," *Christian Advocate*, LXVII (November 9, 1906), 7, 8.

Hess, M. W., "The Man Who Knew Uncle Remus," *Catholic World*, CLXVI (December, 1947), 254–58.

Horton, Mrs. Thaddeus, "The Most Modest Author in America," *Ladies Home Journal*, XXIV (May, 1907), 17, 75.

Hubbell, Jay B., "Two Letters of Uncle Remus," *Southwestern Review*, XXIII (January, 1938), 216–23.

Henny, Michael, "Joel Chandler Harris, (Uncle Remus)," *The Messenger*, I (September, 1908), 225–42.

Lee, James W., "Joel Chandler Harris," *Century Magazine*, LXXVII (April, 1909), 891–97.

————, "Joel Chandler Harris, An Intimate Record of a Beautiful Life," *Southern Woman's Magazine*, December, 1917, pp. 18, 33, 34.

McQueen, Anne, "The Teller of Tales, A Memory of Uncle Remus," *Lippincott's Magazine*, LXXXVIII (September, 1911), 543.

Mims, Edwin, "The South's Intellectual Expression," *World's Work*, XIV (June, 1907), 8979–84.

Mims, Edwin, "The Passing of Two Great Americans," *South Atlantic Quarterly*, VII (October, 1908), 320–31.

Morse, James Herbert, "The National Element in American Fiction Since the War," *Century Magazine*, XXXII (October, 1886), 861–962.

Nash, J. V., "Joel Chandler Harris, Interpreter of the Negro Soul," *Open Court*, XLI (February, 1927), 103–10. (The references to Joseph Addison Turner are inaccurate.)

Nelson, John Herbert. "The Negro Character in American Literature." *Humanistic Studies*, IV (September 1, 1926), 107–19.

Page, Thomas Nelson, "Literature in the South Since the War," *Lippincott's Monthly Magazine*, LXX (December, 1891), 740–56.

————, "Immortal Uncle Remus," *The Book Buyer*, XII (December, 1895), 642–45.

Parsons, Elsie C., "Joel Chandler Harris, and Negro Folklore," *Dial*, LXVI, May 17, 1919, pp. 491–93.

"Personality of Uncle Remus," editorial, *Journal of Education*, LXIX, May 20, 1909, p. 546.

Pickett, L. C., "Uncle Remus," *Lippincott's*, LXXXIX (April, 1912), 572–78.

Reed, Wallace Putnam, "Joel Chandler Harris, Humorist and Novelist," *Literature, An Illustrated Weekly Magazine*, October 27, 1888, 428–44.

Rogers, Joseph M., "A Personal Recollection," *Book News Monthly*, XXVII (January, 1909), 324–27.

Stafford, John, "Patterns of Meaning in *Nights with Uncle Remus*," *American Literature*, XVIII (May, 1946), 89–108.

Stanton, Frank L., "At Snap Bean Farm," *The Delineator*, LXXIII (May, 1909), 78, 79, 715–17.

Ticknor, Caroline, "Some Glimpses of the Author of 'Uncle Remus,'" *The Bookman*, XXVII (August, 1908), 551–57.

————, "The Man Harris. A Study in Personality," *Book News Monthly*, XXVII (January, 1909), 317–20.

Wade, John Donald, "Profits and Losses in the Life of Joel Chandler Harris," *The American Review*, I (April, 1933), 17–35.

Wootten, Katherine Hinton, "At the Sign of the Wren's Nest," *Southern Woman's Magazine*, December, 1917, pp. 19, 33.

————, "Tribute to Uncle Remus," *St. Nicholas*, XLV (December, 1917), 130, 131.

INDEX